# COPYWRITING THAT SELLS

# HIGH TECH

THE DEFINITIVE GUIDE TO WRITING

POWERFUL PROMOTIONAL

MATERIALS FOR TECHNOLOGY

PRODUCTS, SERVICES, AND COMPANIES.

WriteSpark
PRESS

# JANICE M. KING

**Copywriting That Sells High Tech:** *The definitive guide to writing powerful promotional materials for technology products, services, and companies.*

Copyright©2006 by Janice M. King.

Published in the United States by WriteSpark Press. Portions of this book were previously published in the book *Writing High-Tech Copy That Sells,* Copyright©1995 by Janice M. King.

ISBN: 0-9766396-0-2

Library of Congress Control Number: 2005903469

Printed in the United States of America

Publisher's Cataloging-in-Publication
(Provided by Quality Books, Inc.)

    King, Janice M.
      Copywriting that sells high tech : the definitive
    guide to writing powerful promotional materials for
    technology products, services, and companies / Janice M.
    King. — 1st ed.
      p. cm.
    Includes bibliographical references and index.
    LCCN 2005903469
    ISBN 0-9766396-0-2

    1. Advertising copy.  2. High technology—Marketing.
    3. Business writing.    I. Title.

    HF5825.K439 2005        659.13'2
                        QBI05-600042

# CONTENTS

# INTRODUCTION

C opywriting That Sells High Tech is for anyone who develops marketing or press materials (printed or online) for a technology product, service, or company. It is a practical guide to the promotional content, materials, and writing techniques that are successful in today's high-tech marketplace.

I wrote this book because it is an everyday resource that I needed—but could not find—for my work as a freelance copywriter for a variety of high-tech companies. While there are many general books on copywriting techniques, advertising, and public relations, I found their information to be of limited value in the context of marketing communication (marcom) for technology. As an example, finding good ways to handle technical jargon is an issue that simply doesn't exist in the marketing of general business or consumer products. In addition, for most high-tech marketing writers, advertisements and press releases are only a small portion of their work; a greater portion is sales brochures, white papers, articles, and Web content.

Unlike the general books, Copywriting That Sells High Tech focuses exclusively on the marcom materials commonly produced by technology companies. This book is a comprehensive reference of ideas and techniques for all high-tech marcom and public relations materials.

Unless stated otherwise, the information presented here applies equally to printed materials and content delivered on the Web or other electronic medium. The examples presented and issues described in this book are drawn from a range of high-tech industries, including computer hardware and software, telecommunications, networking, and electronics. Although some of the referenced products and companies no longer exist, these examples show that the principles of good writing remain the same over time.

## WHO SHOULD READ THIS BOOK

This book will be of interest to several groups of readers, including:
**Corporate Copywriters and Communication Specialists.** Writers, specialists, editors, and managers in marketing communication and public relations groups. Also, technical writers and editors in documentation groups who produce marketing materials. Whether you address the full range of marcom projects or only a certain type of material, this book will give you practical ideas to improve your writing for every project.

**Corporate Marketing Managers.** Product and marketing managers who provide input for, review, and approve marketing plans and materials. This book will help you recognize and obtain effective marketing and public relations materials.

**Advertising Agency Staff, Freelancers, and Consultants.** Copywriters, creative directors, public relations specialists, and account executives in advertising, marketing, and public relations agencies. Also, freelance copywriters and marcom consultants. As an agency-based or independent communicator, you must offer special skills and expertise to your clients for a wide range of materials. Clients also have higher expectations for the quality and creativity of agency or freelance work. This book will give you a useful everyday reference for generating new ideas and maintaining the freshness and high quality of your work. And if you are new to high-tech products, this book will provide a valuable education in the unique issues and challenges of these markets.

**Students.** College-level students in business communication, marketing, advertising, public relations, and technical communication programs. This book will give you information about the specific writing techniques and project types you will be expected to produce on the job.

While this book was written from an American perspective, I hope that communicators in other countries and cultures will find relevant ideas and techniques. Perhaps you will also gain a better understanding of how U.S. technology companies develop their marketing and public relations materials.

## HOW TO GET THE MOST FROM THIS BOOK

You don't need to read the chapters sequentially, or even the entire book. The content is organized so you can quickly find the most relevant section for a current project or information need. However, you should read Chapters 5 through 7 together as they present a complete, integrated approach to the actual craft of marketing writing. As time allows, read the other chapters—they present useful information to add to your framework of marcom knowledge.

As you read, go online to find examples of materials that reflect the principles and guidelines in this book. Look for examples in the materials from your own company, from competitors, even for non-technical products. Keep a file of samples that are especially appealing, and learn from their application of design and writing techniques. You'll also find useful resources at the Web site for this book: **writinghightech.com.**

Use this book every day to gain ideas for specific materials, to expand your knowledge into new areas, and to find resources for detailed exploration of a topic. The information presented here assumes you have a solid knowledge of the rules of grammar and basic writing techniques, such as constructing a coherent sentence and making a logical flow between paragraphs. This book does not cover:

- General writing skills or issues around the practice of writing such as how to conduct research and interviews or how to develop good work habits.
- Materials that are usually classified as general business communication including procedures, employee communication, community relations, and investor relations.

For the purpose of this book, these definitions apply:

**Marketing Communication.** An umbrella term (often abbreviated to "marcom" in this book) that encompasses all sales, advertising, press materials, and other documents intended to promote the sale of a product.

**Advertising.** Paid marketing messages for a product or company that appear in a magazine, newspaper, online, or broadcast medium.

**Press Materials.** Informational documents that are targeted primarily to journalists and analysts, such as press releases, fact sheets, and backgrounders.

**Product.** The ideas and techniques presented in this book apply to the marketing of technical services as well as products. As used here, the term product includes services, except where distinctions are noted.

The following terms are used interchangeably in this book:

- Copywriting and marketing writing
- Text and copy
- Document, collateral, material, and piece. In many cases, these terms cover both printed and electronic media

*Text examples are presented in this type style* wherever they will help you understand a particular idea or technique. In most cases, these examples are drawn from actual marketing materials for high-tech products.

## WHAT'S NEW IN THIS EDITION

Much of the material in this book was originally published under the title *Writing High-Tech Copy That Sells*. In this book, I have expanded and updated the content throughout and included many fresh ideas and examples. The following items are also new in this book:

- Information about copywriting issues and techniques for Web content and email marketing, presented where relevant throughout the book.
- New document types in Chapters 10 through 12 and a description of the marcom development process in Chapter 4.

- Greatly expanded and up-to-date resources, including books and links to useful Web sites. Many of these resources are listed at the end of each chapter. But you'll also want to check for my latest recommendations on the companion Web site: **writinghightech.com.**
- New marketing communication and PR terms defined in the glossary.

## ACKNOWLEDGEMENTS

Thanks to the many people who provided valuable ideas, resources, feedback, and support for the initial development of this book and this second edition. My clients continue to provide challenging projects that expand my knowledge and stretch my skills as a marketing writer. I appreciate the learning opportunities they offer with each new project.

And special thanks to my family and friends. Your continuing, unshakeable belief in my abilities give me the confidence and motivation to undertake all of my ventures.

## HERE'S TO YOUR SUCCESS

*Copywriting That Sells High Tech* is more than just the title of this book. By applying the ideas presented here, it is something you can do—in every one of your marcom projects.

*Janice King*

# PART 1

# THE FOUNDATION OF HIGH-TECH MARKETING COMMUNICATION

The chapters in this part describe several important issues you must consider when developing any type of marketing materials:

- Preparing a marcom plan, creative platform, and project plan.
- Targeting your audiences.
- Identifying the messages, objectives, and purpose of the document.
- Working successfully throughout the creative process.

While these chapters contain many guidelines you will reference regularly, they are intended more to provide a broad perspective for your work. Read them at least once, then refer to these chapters again as you become involved in specific projects.

# 1

# PLANNING FOR HIGH-TECH MARKETING COMMUNICATION

## SUCCESS STARTS HERE

You have a hot new product to introduce, a major upgrade to announce for an existing product, or a new market to reach. Now you need sales and press materials that will help with this marketing activity. While it is tempting to jump in and start creating documents based on a few initial ideas, marcom activity will be more effective if it is carefully planned.

This chapter describes the typical communication cycle for technology products and how to create solid plans for marcom programs, individual documents, and Web content.

### THE COMMUNICATION CYCLE FOR TECHNOLOGY PRODUCTS

Marketing communication for high-tech products is typically organized around three types of activity:
- Introducing a new product to the market.
- Supporting the sales cycle and decision-making by customers.
- Sustaining communication to the market, the customer base, and the sales force.

Each of these activities involve different types of promotional materials and may be covered by a separate marcom plan.

## *Product Launch Communication*

Introducing a new product to the market (typically called a product launch) involves a number of communication activities that are directed to journalists and analysts, salespeople, and prospective customers (prospects). Some activities may be conducted simultaneously, depending on the sales plan for the product and the scale of the introduction effort.

No matter how the product launch is implemented, it is supported by a variety of marcom materials (Figure 1.1). Product launch materials are developed for multiple purposes including education, announcement, and obtaining feedback.

| Product Launch Activity | Materials |
| --- | --- |
| Infrastructure education | Preliminary press materials, brochures, and data sheets; presentation slides; white papers; backgrounders |
| Sales force and dealer education | Sales kit, presentation slides, white papers |
| Product announcement | Final press release and supporting press materials, all sales materials (print and online), quotes from or reprints of test reports and product reviews |

*Figure 1.1 Promotional materials support product introduction, especially for educating key constituencies before the announcement.*

**Educating the infrastructure.** The market infrastructure includes the key analysts, consultants, and journalists who cover the product type, its underlying technology, or its target market. Your infrastructure may also include beta users, key customers, and alliance partners who receive early information about the new product and can champion it among other buyers.[1]

The process of infrastructure education usually begins a few months before the actual product announcement. This process is intended to obtain feedback on product capabilities and positioning, cultivate positive supporting comments for the actual announcement, and facilitate coverage by publications that have long lead times. Infrastructure education involves personal contact with a small number of people, often under a nondisclosure agreement. Preliminary press and sales materials for the product may be given to these contacts as part of the education effort.

**Educating the sales force.** A key goal of any product launch is to prepare salespeople and dealers for selling the product as soon as it is released. Sales kits and other dealer materials, as well as final brochures and other sales documents, are often distributed as part of the sales education effort.

**Announcing the product.** The actual product announcement may be made simply through an announcement document or a press release or more formally in a presentation at a press conference, trade show, or other event. The announcement is made on, or very near, the date when the product is available for customer purchase. Announcement activity may include sending the press release to publications and wire services, distributing sales materials to prospects and customers, and posting product information on the company's Web site.

**Obtaining market feedback.** The marcom materials for a launch may be used to obtain feedback from the infrastructure, the sales force, and early customers about the product's positioning and marketing messages.

### Sales Cycle Communication

> *Sales is a process of communication, not an event.*
> —*Richard Brock*

As the quote above indicates, marketing communication plays a vital role throughout the sales process for technology products and services. This process requires information of various types, in a variety of formats, directed to multiple audiences, at different stages of the sales cycle. Marcom documents provide both impetus and support for a purchase decision, whether it is made by an organizational committee or an individual consumer.

To develop materials that will best support the sales cycle, you must understand both the general selling process and the specific factors that apply to your products. In general, selling high-tech products involves challenges that are quite different from those for selling other business or consumer products. This section presents a brief overview of common factors in the technical sales cycle and how to target materials effectively throughout the selling process.

Traditional advertising texts describe the multiple stages of the sales cycle with the AIDA Model (Attention, Interest, Desire, Action). This model analyzes how your copy creates prospect awareness of the product (attention), prompts exploration of the product (interest), fosters the buy decision (desire), and motivates the prospect to actually make the purchase (action).

However, for many technology products, the stages in the sales cycle can be described somewhat differently: Awareness, Exploration, Decision, Affirmation, and Retention (Figure 1.2). The first three stages are similar to the AIDA model, although the decision stage is often reached directly from the exploration stage. And the final two stages in the high-tech cycle—affirming the selection and retaining a customer's loyalty—exist because of the significant investment and risk involved in deploying many high-tech products.

| Sales Cycle Stage | Materials |
| --- | --- |
| Creating awareness | Advertising (print and Web), direct mail, email, articles, materials for trade shows and seminars |
| Supporting exploration | Product brochure or data sheet, presentation, video or online demo, trial package, article reprints, application guide, in-depth Web content |
| Motivating a decision | White papers, Web FAQ, case studies, proposal, point-of-sale materials |
| Affirming the selection | Welcome kit, product packaging |
| Retaining customer loyalty | Newsletter, email updates, and direct mail to encourage purchase of additional products and upgrades; user group materials |

*Figure 1.2 Marcom materials support each stage in the sales cycle for high-tech products.*

**Stage 1: Creating Awareness.** The sales cycle begins when a prospect discovers a product. Awareness may come from reading a product advertisement or a mention in a magazine article, or from research undertaken by the prospect to find products that will solve a particular problem or need.

**Stage 2: Supporting Exploration.** The prospect has decided she's interested, and now wants to learn detailed information about the product and company. She may also explore several competing products or alternative solutions at this stage. For complex product sales that involve a committee decision, materials may be produced to address the spectrum of committee participants and their specific purchasing concerns.

**Stage 3: Motivating a Decision.** The prospect selects the product, purchases it, or begins the buying process (e.g., starting contract negotiations for a large or complex purchase).

**Stage 4: Affirming the Selection.** In the post-sale stage, a prospect may need additional information to feel comfortable with the purchase decision.

**Stage 5: Retaining Customer Loyalty.** The sales process is never done, even after a customer buys the product. Sustained communications can help to capture a greater share of the customer's future purchases, reinforce your company's image, and help win back customers lost to a competitor.

All communication throughout the sales cycle must work to build the prospect's confidence and trust in your company, product, and service. At each stage, materials should convey credibility and support the buyer's confidence in making a purchase decision.

## *Sustained Marketing Communication*

Marketing communication does not end after a product is announced or a sale is made. To ensure product success and customer loyalty over the long term, view communication as a sustained effort. Ongoing communication can be directed to the overall market (including the press), to customers, and to the sales force and dealers (Figure 1.3).

| Audience | Materials |
| --- | --- |
| Market | Press releases, articles, advertisements, case studies, email, Web content |
| Customer | Newsletters, email, articles, bulletins |
| Sales force and dealer | Email, case studies, new applications, selling tips, information on the company's promotional activities, specialized Web content |

*Figure 1.3 A variety of print and electronic materials support sustained communication activities.*

**Market Communication.** Sustained communication to the overall market involves reaching prospects, industry analysts, and journalists. For prospects, you want to maintain their awareness of the product as a potential solution to their evolving needs. For analysts and journalists, you want to encourage ongoing coverage of the product as it incorporates new capabilities, addresses new technology developments, or serves new applications.

A sustained communication effort is especially important for products in new technologies. A considerable amount of time and communication may be necessary to educate the market about what your product is, as well as the benefits and features it offers. Sustained market communication typically involves press releases to announce new product capabilities and applications, case studies, articles targeted to different industry publications, email newsletters, and "What's New" content for a product-specific section of the company Web site.

**Customer Communication.** Customers are an important marketing target because the strength of customer relationships is vital to the long-term success of your company. It is common marketing wisdom that keeping an existing customer is easier and cheaper than attracting a new one. In addition, to sustain loyalty in the rapidly changing environment of high-tech, Hippeau notes, "Customers need to be assured that you're still alive and working on the future."[2]

You can reach customers through individualized forms of communication such as direct mail and email, or collectively through newsletters, presentations, Web content, or materials distributed at events or in industry publications.

**Sales Force and Dealer Communication.** Continued communication with salespeople and dealers is essential to maintain their enthusiasm for selling a product. Sustained communication is especially important when a dealer carries multiple, competing products and is constantly bombarded by new information and sales incentives from each vendor. Sustained marcom for this audience often involves email and direct mail, ads in publications targeted to dealers, updated sales kits, dealer newsletters and seminars, a special area on your Web site, plant tours, contests, or other events. In addition, you may need to create localized materials to support international dealers.

## THE MARCOM PLAN

*I love writing. It's the paperwork that gets me.*
*—Peter DeVries*

No matter where you are in the communication cycle for a product, your activities should be driven by a marcom plan. This plan describes strategies, activities, materials, and other deliverables for a product, event, or marketing campaign. A marcom plan also is a guide and a starting point for two other documents that are critical in planning any marcom project: the creative platform and the document plan (both are described in detail later in this chapter).

Marcom plans can focus on only the high-level communication issues, or describe detailed directions and tactics. They can cover sales, advertising, and public relations materials, as well as marketing events such as trade shows, Webcasts, and user group meetings. Separate marcom plans are often developed for different types of marketing activities, such as:

- Product introduction or upgrade announcement campaigns
- Trade shows and other events
- Sustained promotion of a product

- Print vs. Web and other electronic media
- Campaigns focused by market, distribution channel, or other customer segment

A discussion of specific marcom strategies and how to develop them is beyond the scope of this book. However, Patti *et al.* suggest these criteria for evaluating the quality of a marcom strategy:[3]

- Based on research about the product, market, and competition
- Presents a clear message to the market
- Unique within your competitive environment
- Adaptable to all relevant media
- Will be effective in the long term

### Components of a Marcom Plan

While a marcom plan may include a wide range of information, it typically contains a mix of the topics listed below.

**Situation analysis.** An assessment of both past and current marcom efforts as well as the current market perception of your product and company. This information can include a description of marketing challenges, competitor activities, and customer issues. A situation analysis can help you evaluate the likely success of plans and strategies for future marcom campaigns.

**Product information.** A brief description of the product and its major features and benefits.

**Market information.** A description of the characteristics of each target audience or market, as well as distribution channels, sales cycle, and pricing.

*Caution:* If you are relying on market research conducted before the product was developed, verify that the conclusions are still accurate and that the product indeed still targets the expected market.

**Competitive positioning and activity.** The marketing and public relations strategies, messages, and efforts produced by direct and indirect competitors. A description of whether and how marcom and public relations materials must address competitive positioning or directly sell against the competition.

**Strategies.** The planned strategies for the entire marcom program, including goals and objectives for the overall campaign and for each specific marcom document or activity. Distinct strategies and tactics may be defined for communicating to internal and external audiences.

**Tactics.** A description of each element in the marcom program, such as materials, Web content, and events. These tactics describe the specific activities or materials to be produced, how they are to be distributed, packaged, or staged, and how they relate to the product's sales process.

**Offers and promotions.** Describe the major offers, sales incentives, and promotional programs for the product.

**Evaluation.** Criteria and methods for determining the success of the program.

**Print and electronic documents.** A description of the major documents to be produced, including a specific objective and purpose for each. These documents typically include collateral, advertising, press materials, investor communications, and in-person sales presentations.

For Web content, defines the types of new content to be developed, location within the site, integration with databases and other applications, and other planning issues. For an email campaign, describes the number and type of messages, and the need for a customer "landing page" when recipients click through the message to the company Web site. For all materials, describes the coordination of materials with other marketing activities, such as using print and email invitations to encourage visits to a trade show booth.

**Schedules and budgets.** A description of deadlines, estimated costs, and other production considerations for each project or activity in the plan. Specify the responsibilities and assignments of internal and external creative resources such as copywriters, designers, and public relations specialists.

**Cooperative programs.** Describe any support your company will provide for the marketing programs of resellers and other partners.

**Key messages or brand guidelines.** A list of common messages or brand elements that will be applicable to all materials and activities in the campaign.

**PR activities.** For many companies, public relations activities are a major portion of the marcom effort because publicity is a relatively inexpensive way to reach a large audience. The trade press often picks up press releases that announce new products or other company achievements, accepts articles written by company experts, or publishes reviews of a new product or upgrade. As a result, strategies and objectives for press materials become an important part of marcom plans or a separate PR plan.

**Media selections.** Information on the specific media where ads will appear. For extensive advertising programs, this information may be presented in a separate media buying plan.

A marcom plan is usually generated well in advance of the campaign, especially for annual budgeting purposes. But the plan should be flexible enough to accommodate changes in business activity or competitor actions. And, a marcom plan should be adaptable to handle two common scenarios in high-tech product development: "Sorry, that function isn't going to be in the next release after all" or "We added this cool feature last night."

### Setting Objectives in a Marcom Plan

The objectives specified in a marcom plan are typically stated in qualitative terms.

**Awareness.** Creating awareness or a desired brand image and positioning for the product or company. *Our product will be perceived as one of the leaders by prospects in our key markets.*

**Information.** Conveying information about a product or company to a new market or distribution channel. *Leveraging our experience in the banking industry, communicate how our product can solve the problems of customers in other financial-services companies.*

**Brand preference.** Developing preference for your brand over competitors. *Emphasize the quality of our brand and corporate reputation for all products.*

**Encouraging a decision.** Setting the agenda for a purchase decision. *Communicate the importance of future product directions as an important purchasing factor.*

**Supporting the press.** Increasing editorial coverage of your company or product or increasing the visibility of company experts and executives. *Obtain greater product and company mentions in articles, reports, and presentations produced by analysts and industry publications.*

## Measuring Results

Many marcom plans specify the quantitative criteria that will be used to determine the success of promotional activities. Results can be evaluated by a variety of measurements such as number of orders or inquiries received, or amount of press coverage generated. A common measurement in advertising is the cost per thousand (CPM) readers exposed to the ad. For ads on a Web site, a similar measurement is cost per click-through (CPC).

The specific factors for measuring the results of a document or program will vary according to the marketing strategies and objectives. Both qualitative and quantitative factors may be appropriate. The marcom plan can list these factors and the process by which results will be tracked and reported.

## Choosing the Right Material for the Task

Many marketing materials can support a variety of promotional purposes and activities (Figure 1.4). However, in most cases time and budget constraints will not allow you to produce a complete collateral set. When choosing which specific documents to produce, consider the following factors:

- Audience needs and expectations
- Communication needs throughout the sales cycle
- Availability of or plans for related materials
- Distribution, use, and desired "shelf life" of the proposed document
- Schedule, budget, production, and online considerations

| Promotional Activity | Primary Documents | Secondary Documents |
| --- | --- | --- |
| Selling a product through a catalog, other print materials, or online | Brochure or data sheet Catalog page Product order form | Selection guide Price/parts list |
| Announcing a new product or service | Brochure or data sheet Press release Email | Product backgrounder White paper |
| Explaining a technology | White paper Application note | Case studies |
| Attracting clients for a service business | Brochure Consultant profile Services list | Case studies |
| Encouraging visits to a dealer or retail store | Locator Coupon | Product inquiry form |
| Recruiting participants for an event, or inviting trade show visitors | Advertisement Newsletter article Event Web page Direct mail & email | Registration form Live Webcast, Video or CD-ROM from previous event |
| Providing general company information | Company profile FAQ Newsletter Annual report & investor information | Press release Executive profile "What's New" Web page |
| Gathering feedback from prospects and customers | Visitor survey (print or online) | |
| Encouraging customer loyalty | Newsletter (print or email) | User group & event materials |

*Figure 1.4 Guidelines for matching documents to promotional activities. Advertisements and direct mail can also be appropriate for all of these activities.*

## Staging Marcom Materials

To understand the staging of marcom materials, consider the following scenario. You see an ad for a high-tech product in a trade magazine. You visit the Web site or call the toll-free number listed in the ad to request more information. Soon, a data sheet appears in your email or postal mail, along with instructions for requesting a more detailed brochure on the product, a white paper about its underlying technology, or a free subscription to the company's newsletter.

You have just participated in a staged communication activity, where the company qualifies prospective customers according to the type and amount of literature they request. Many companies also adopt this technique to control the costs of print materials; after all, you don't want to send an expensive, four-color brochure to someone who turns out not to be a prospect for the product.

On a Web site, the prospect may be instructed to complete a brief registration form in order to access online documents. This form is designed to capture the prospect's information for lead qualification purposes. It often contains the same types of questions that appear on printed reply cards in magazines.

Describe the staging of materials in the marcom plan. Specify how materials will be sequenced and coordinated with each other and with advertising, public relations, trade shows, and other promotional activities. But make sure you don't make prospects jump over too many hurdles before they obtain the information that helps them determine their interest in your product. As one buyer put it, "Too often you are sent another device so you can send another card for what you really wanted at the start."[4]

## Using the Marcom Plan When Writing

A good marcom plan is a valuable guide to the high-tech copywriter. It presents essential background information for planning a specific document, including the marketing objective, an audience profile, market perceptions and issues, product positioning, and a discussion of brand issues.

A carefully crafted marketing communication plan also can serve as a checkpoint to ensure that your projects are on track. Additional uses for the information presented in a marcom plan include:

- Determining how a particular piece fits into the overall set of materials or other communication activities and media. For example, if you know that a separate brochure will be developed for dealers, you won't need to address their concerns in the customer brochure that is your assignment.
- Ensuring the consistency of messages across multiple pieces.
- Identifying "recyclable" blocks of copy or visuals. These are words, paragraphs, even entire pages of text that you write once, then adapt for use in many different pieces.

## PLANNING FOR ELECTRONIC MARCOM

Any electronic media project involves many of the same issues for planning and the development process described here for print materials. Additional issues to consider include the following:

**Integrating print and electronic materials.** The Web and other electronic media offer exciting ways to present and explore information. However, many high-tech companies still find it faster and easier to produce documents in a traditional print format (e.g., a data sheet or white paper), then post them as PDF files for download from the company Web site.

Determine if an electronic format is really the best medium for the information you want to present and the audience you want to reach. Don't choose an electronic medium just because it is "cool;" it must fit with your overall communication strategy and be accessible to the audience you want to reach. For example, you might want to distribute your full-color, loaded-with-photographs product catalog on a DVD. However, this choice won't be effective if many customers and prospects don't have DVD drives in their computers.

When producing any type of Web content or electronic media project, consider how it will fit with any print material the reader may receive. For example, a presentation disk may use multimedia techniques to show a product overview, with a link at the end to a posted PDF file of a brochure or white paper.

**Working with a design and development team.** For an electronic media project, you will likely work with a different team—with more people in more roles—than is the case for print documents. Multimedia projects often require an interaction between film and video producers, musicians, sound engineers, animators, instructional design experts, software engineers, and scriptwriters.

Web content may require coordination with an e-commerce manager, an information architect, a content manager, Web page designers, and media specialists—each with specific ideas and requirements for the length and type of content you will write.

You may also collaborate more frequently with other writers, as differences in writing style, tone, organization of like material, and other creative structures become apparent very quickly when a visitor clicks from page to page on a Web site.

**Communicating without words.** Sometimes words just aren't powerful enough to deliver a compelling message about a product or company. Visuals, audio, video, and animation elements can add rich meaning and information to a Web page or presentation. In conjunction with the designer or producer, your task is to determine when and how these elements can be used effectively, and to achieve a good blend with the accompanying text. You will learn to think in terms of design ("look and feel") of all elements in the project.

**Planning for exploration and information flow.** When developing a print document, you will likely follow a standard structure for presenting information. You can also expect that readers will go through the document sequentially or, if they jump around, the options for doing so are limited and the context remains clear.

None of these principles are necessarily true in an electronic media project, particularly Web content. You'll need to think in terms of information flow, links and branches for content, and guiding a visitor's exploration of a Web site or multimedia disk.

## PLANNING WEB CONTENT

Since the emergence of the Web, a marcom writer's job has expanded to include online content, both on a Web site and in email. The planning activity for online projects encompasses many of the same tasks and considerations described earlier this chapter for print documents. But other factors also apply, with the distinctions described below for Web content and email.

Writing Web content and HTML-formatted email requires a good understanding of effective online design, usability, interactivity, and technologies for e-commerce, Web presentation, and personalization. Those topics are beyond the scope of this book; see the Resources section in Chapter 10 for recommended reading and Web sites.

### What Is Your Goal?

As with any promotional activity, you should have clear and well-considered goals for developing and maintaining a Web site. These goals will not only give you a means to measure results, they also will guide your choices about the amount and type of content and interaction on the site. The most common goals for a promotional Web site include the following:

**Generate revenue.** E-commerce produces revenue directly from the site by selling a product, service, or event registration. In this case, a visitor's activity on the Web site will encompass the complete sales cycle for the product or service. The site plan must consider all information and interaction that will motivate the visitor to complete a purchase.

**Provide detailed product information.** Web sites with extensive content allow research by customers, reduce sales costs, and identify highly interested prospects (leads). Capture the names and contact information of qualified leads for follow-up by a salesperson, dealer, or telemarketer. Plan how the Web will integrate with existing methods and systems for tracking and responding to a prospect's information request.

**Build a relationship.** The information and interaction on a Web site can support advertising and printed collateral, encourage a visit by a salesperson or dealer, or entice the prospect to visit a store or attend an event. Surveys, feedback mechanisms, and visitor activity tracking are among the means to obtain customer input that can create and sustain a relationship.

**Sustain customer loyalty.** Provide easily accessible newsletters and other materials online. Plan how you can use the Web to cross-sell and upsell products, events, services, or programs to these visitors.

**Guide product selection.** One approach is to create a complete information package for a product through links. For example, you could guide visitors from viewing an online brochure to printing a model selection guide, a detailed data sheet, then viewing a customer testimonial and using a locator tool to find the nearest dealer.

### What Will Visitors Want?

Identify the types of information visitors will want to access, and the types of activity they will want to conduct on your site. Examples include the following:

- Retrieving overview or detailed information about a specific product, service, or event.
- Purchasing a product or registering for an activity online.
- Reviewing background information on a consultant, company, or organization.
- Researching information on a specific topic or interest.
- Finding the location of the nearest store or dealer.
- Obtaining Web-only special prices and sales incentives such as free shipping, feature upgrades, and extended warranties.
- Contacting your company via email to discuss a need or ask a question.

Analyzing visitors' needs and expectations will help you choose the best way to implement information and interactivity for the Web site. For example, you can determine whether to offer complete documents, such as brochures or articles, or instead place a "quick-read" summary on the Web.

**Serving diverse audience needs.** Consider the needs and capabilities of your audience when determining what elements or information to place on a Web site. For example, consider the age, cognitive, and visual abilities of the target audience; cultural considerations; and whether their PCs and Internet connection will be adequate to provide an effective display of or interaction with text content, visuals, and multimedia elements.

You may want to organize areas of the site with content targeted specifically to each audience. For example, create separate customer and dealer areas, or areas that are organized according to audience interests, location, or other factors.

**Accommodating international visitors.** The planning activity should consider how to manage content across separate Web sites for multiple countries or markets or multilingual content on the main company site.

**Using technology appropriately.** Understand the capabilities of Web technologies (e.g., scripts, Flash, personalization, database interaction) and how they can be used effectively to present information, enhance the visitor's experience, and guide online activities.

### Consider the Sales Cycle

Part of the planning activity for Web content is to identify how the sales cycle will flow on the site, and how that flow relates to the typical sales cycle for the product. Answer the question: What will be different for the visitor from the experience of visiting a store, talking with a dealer, or hearing a presentation by a company salesperson?

For example, visitors may find your site when they use an online search engine to seek products of interest. These first-time visitors are looking at this site to determine if your product will make their purchasing "short list." The next step in this cycle is typically a request from the visitor for detailed product information, a call to a salesperson, or a visit to a dealer or retail store.

In another case, the prospect may come to a Web site with the expectation of making a purchase online, based on a promotional offer received in an email. Guiding visitors to an online sale will likely result in different decisions regarding the amount and type of information on the site, and the interactivity the site creates with the visitor.

## Site Plan

For any online project, you will need to understand the design principles, content standards, and content management and presentation technologies used by your company. This information is often presented in a site plan document that covers:

- Goals for the site; an overview description of site content and activities (e.g., e-commerce).
- A profile of the target audience(s) or typical visitors.
- A set of development principles for content, presentation, and navigation on the site.
- Policies about acceptable site content and information on the review process.
- Strategies for using key words and other techniques to improve rankings in search engines.

If a content management system is used for the site, the standards and templates defined by that system will often control many decisions about content and visitor interaction on the site. Similar tools and templates may determine the content and presentation of promotional email.

## Storyboards

Storyboarding is a technique used in film and multimedia production to plan the visuals and flow of a presentation or interaction. For a Web site, storyboards can help you plan the content and appearance of each page (or page type) and chart the navigation paths for visitors.

Storyboards also help you identify forms and other pages that require scripts, custom-generated data, or other special programming to load the correct content or interact with visitors.

## Navigation Flowchart

After you have created storyboards for each page or area on the site, create a navigation flowchart to show how individual pages will link to each other. A navigation flowchart helps you verify that visitors can proceed logically through a particular area or activity on the site.

Develop this flowchart as part of the planning process for the site as a whole and any new content. It can help you minimize the number of links a visitor must make to reach any specific destination in the site—especially for interactions that lead to a sale or an inquiry. See Chapter 5 for more information on defining visitor navigation on a Web site.

## PLANNING AN EMAIL CAMPAIGN

Decisions about content and techniques for an email project will be determined by the campaign strategy, the features of email technology, legal constraints, and market-specific issues. For example, the choice of a text-only or HTML message (which allows embedded graphics) may be determined by reader preferences, compatibility issues with browsers and email programs, and need for graphics. Embedded multimedia elements may become more popular in the future, providing a video or audio clip within the message itself instead of through a link to a Web site.

Several useful books and Web sites are available to help in planning an email campaign; see the Resources section for Chapter 10.

## THE CREATIVE PLATFORM

Some companies and agencies maintain a document that describes the overall creative strategies and guidelines for marcom materials. Called a creative platform, this document describes messages, style, tone, and creative constraints for copy and visuals that apply across all materials (print or online) for a product or campaign. The creative platform defines the range of flexibility allowed for copy and visuals, without specifying particular execution ideas.

The creative platform also is a useful document for refereeing the review process when selecting specific execution ideas. Marcom concepts and draft materials typically are reviewed by many people, such as the product manager, vice president of marketing, sales director, corporate communications manager, and others. Each has an understandably subjective view about what makes a good design or good copy. In the ideal world, these views would be reasonably similar and it would be easy to resolve disagreements about the copy or design. But the more likely case is that the parties will have widely divergent views on creative proposals. This divergence can lead to seemingly endless debates that are based on no stronger rationale than "the VP of sales thinks it's ugly."

To avoid these disagreements, or at least to make them easier to resolve, the creative platform can include criteria for judging design and copy concepts as well as specific executions. It's important that all parties agree in advance to these criteria. By establishing them at the campaign planning stage, you can avoid reviewing and redefining creative criteria with each project.[5]

A creative platform can address any combination of the items that follow.

**Audience profile.** A description of the primary and secondary audiences for the materials including demographics, issues, existing knowledge or perceptions, buying habits, decision process, and preferences for the amount, type, and presentation style of information.

**Brand messages and product positioning.** A description of the product's key messages and desired positioning as well as available supporting evidence such as facts, examples, or case studies. This discussion also can describe the product's brand personality.

**Campaign themes.** The visual and copy concepts that must be included in each marcom project for this campaign. In some cases, themes from a previous campaign must be incorporated into the planned materials or a transition must be made between the old and new themes.

**Style and tone.** The general style and tone that will apply to both visuals and copy in all documents in the campaign, such as formal and businesslike, or informal and energetic.

**Constraints.** Creative or production limitations on the visuals or copy. For example, visuals must be appropriate for both color and black-and-white reproduction or the copy must be structured to accommodate frequent changes in product specifications. Corporate style guidelines for print and Web presentation may also apply.

**Evaluation criteria.** A description of the review process, factors for determining the appropriateness of specific execution ideas, and a list of the people who will review the draft copy and proposed visuals.

## *A Creative Platform for Web Content and Email*

For a Web site or email campaign, define guidelines for consistently structuring and presenting all content. These guidelines will make the content more understandable for visitors as they navigate, and easier for you to expand and maintain. Consider developing guidelines for the following:

- The way content is organized across the site and within similar pages or email messages
- The writing and presentation style
- Use and style of headlines, subheads, bullet lists, and other elements that structure the text for easier reading
- Color, size, font, and other formatting standards applied to the text

Many of these guidelines may already be identified by the site plan, in a style guide, or in a management system for Web content or email campaigns.

## *Using the Creative Platform When Writing*

The creative platform can be a valuable resource when choosing the approach to a particular project, and for staying "on course" as you write. It can help you focus ideas to make them targeted and effective. For example, the audience profile can help you select language and examples that will be most relevant to a document's readers. The information on messages, style, and tone can help you craft the text to meet the document's objectives. And the guidelines provided by the creative platform can help with the sometimes difficult task of choosing what *not* to include in a document.

## THE PROJECT PLAN

A project plan (sometimes called a creative brief or copy strategy) is a writing guide that is specific to each piece or set of Web content. This plan may be part of the overall creative platform or developed separately as you begin each project. It may be in the form of short notes, a detailed outline, or a page-by-page description of content, writing techniques, document elements, and visuals. A project plan helps you reach advance agreement with reviewers on content and organization, and verify the appropriateness of ideas that come up as you work on the project.

As described earlier, a good creative platform provides a long-term guide for content and style that can be used over many different pieces and over time. A project plan applies the principles of the creative platform to the unique aspects of each document or set of Web content.

**Document type.** You can package any given content into many different types of marcom documents. Identify which document type is most suited to the purpose, audience, and intended use. Also identify constraints of budget and production factors for both print documents and online content.

For Web content, think outside of the "document" box. Ask yourself, "What is really the best way to present this information to site visitors?" One of the great advantages of the Web is that because you are not constrained by the physical limitations of print media, you can draw on the wider base of content for a single or set of related Web pages, and give visitors richer information as a result.

**Publication type.** When writing an article or technical paper, describe the target publication. Is it a technical journal, a trade magazine for a specific technology or vertical market, or a general business publication? How does the publication differentiate itself from others that serve the target audience? What are the publication's requirements for submitted articles or papers?

**Audience**. A description of the specific audience(s) for this document. What types of background information will readers have about the technology? What types of new information do they need? Which product or customer names will they recognize? Which examples will be relevant? Do different audience groups have different levels of involvement with the technology or product? How does this piece fit with other information that readers may see? Should this document incorporate personalized marketing in the text and images? If they are separate groups, what are the interests of the decision-makers as compared to the ultimate users of the product? (See Chapter 2 for a complete discussion of analyzing an audience.)

**Brand**. In what ways must the project convey brand or use brand elements? Which branding standards apply to the project?

**Objective and purpose.** Why are you writing this piece? What do you want it to accomplish? Does your purpose match the document's intended use? How well does the purpose for this piece mesh with that of other materials in the collateral set? (See Chapter 3 for more information on the relationship between objective and purpose.) Specify the marcom problem the document must solve or the opportunity the document must capture. A clearly stated objective and purpose will help you evaluate the appropriateness of the copy as you write. Once the document has been published, you can also measure response and other factors against the objective.

**The offer and call to action.** Describe the offer and call to action that will be presented to the reader and the response vehicle (e.g., reply card, toll-free phone number, URL for an online order or response form).

**Personalization**. Specify the document elements that must allow insertion of variable text, as in the case of direct mail letters to customers. Personalization can range from a simple merge of names and addresses to inclusion of multiple text variables that may affect the length or layout of the finished document.

**Schedule and shelf life.** List the due dates for each planned draft and step in the review process. Development of the copy and design may proceed on separate but parallel schedules until they are combined in a final draft/layout. Describe the intended "shelf life" for this document, as either a time period (e.g., at least six months) or a milestone (e.g., until the release of the next version).

**Key messages.** A list of key messages or topics to be covered in the piece. This information may be presented in the form of an outline of the document's content.

**Source material.** A list of interview sources, research reports, and other information available as background for developing content.

**Copywriting guidelines.** Describe the style, tone, format, and length of the text. How will the copy integrate with the images and design planned for the piece? Do you need to consider special formatting requirements when writing the copy? What is the maximum number of words or characters, on each page (print or Web) or for the entire document?

**Document Elements.** The specific elements that will appear in the piece such as headlines, body copy, and sidebars. You may also want to describe planned visuals. For Web content and email, list multimedia elements and links.

**Content Types**. What information does the document need to include? Technical details? A discussion of strategies or issues? How does this content compare with other information the reader will likely see?

**Legal considerations.** List sensitive information, regulatory requirements, copyright and trademark notices, or other legal constraints that must be reflected in the copy.

**International considerations.** Describe the plans for international distribution or localization that may affect the structure or content of the copy (see Chapter 9).

**Assignments**. State the tasks, responsibilities, and schedules for all writers and designers involved in the project.

**Review Process.** Who will review the document drafts, both internally and externally? At what state? For what type of input? How will you verify facts, statistics, equations, names, and descriptive information? How will you resolve conflicting comments?

## RESOURCES

The recommended books and other resources listed below provide additional information on the topics discussed in this chapter. For an updated list and other materials related to this book, visit **writinghightech.com.**

### Books

Sandra W. Harner and Tom G. Zimmerman: *Technical Marketing Communication.* Longman Publishers, 2002. Primarily a college-level text for technical writing students, Chapter 11 presents a useful discussion of marcom planning, strategies, and tactics.

Catherine Kitcho: *High-Tech Product Launch.* Pele Publications, 1999. Provides an in-depth discussion of product launch activities and strategies.

Michael E. McGrath: *Product Strategy for High Technology Companies.* McGraw-Hill, 2000. A good general book on marketing for high-tech products.

Ann Rockley: *Managing Enterprise Content: A Unified Content Strategy.* New Riders, 2002. A good overview guide to content management systems and implementations; also includes guidelines for writers working these systems.

Jim Sterne: *World Wide Web Marketing: Integrating the Web into Your Marketing Strategy, 3rd Edition.* Wiley, 2001. A bit dated, but a good reference to support planning for a Web site.

### Web Sites

Nielsen Norman Group (**nngroup.com**). The site for Jakob Nielsen and Don Norman, well known and highly respected consultants on Web design and usability analysis. Offers numerous reports and white papers with site evaluations and design guidelines.

The following sites provide articles, reports, and news relating to marketing strategies and techniques, both offline and online:

Advertising Age Magazine (**advertisingage.com**)

Ad Week Magazine (**adweek.com**)

MarketingProfs.com (**marketingprofs.com**)

ClickZ (**clickz.com**)

Marketing Sherpa (**marketingsherpa.com**)

Web Digest for Marketers (**wdfm.com**)

BtoB Online Magazine (**btobonline.com**)

Technology Marketing Magazine (**technologymarketing.com**)

## REFERENCES

[1] Regis McKenna: *The Regis Touch.* Reading, MA: Addison Wesley, 1986

[2] "The New Marketing," *Marketing Computers* Magazine, November 1993

[3] Charles H. Patti, Steven W. Hartley, and Susan L. Kennedy: *Business to Business Advertising: A Marketing Management Approach.* Lincolnwood, IL: NTC Business Books, 1991

[4] Vicki James: "Changing Channels of Reader Response," *Business Marketing* Magazine, April 1992

[5] Philip Ward Burton: *Advertising Copywriting, 6th Edition.* Lincolnwood, IL: NTC Business Books, 1990

# 2

## THE HIGH-TECH AUDIENCE

### TARGETING PROMOTIONAL MATERIALS

When beginning a marcom project, ask yourself a simple question: "Who is the audience for this document?" The answer may not be as simple and forthcoming as you might think. For example, consider everyone who might be interested in the data sheet for a product: prospects, certainly; salespeople, yes. But a data sheet also might include information that is useful to current customers, technical support staff, and journalists. Of course, each of these people will have different needs and expectations for the information in the data sheet. But consider all of these potential audiences as you plan and write the document.

This chapter will help you identify and understand the audiences for a high-tech marcom document. It also presents guidelines for developing materials that are targeted effectively to their audiences.

### AUDIENCES FOR HIGH-TECH MARCOM

Most marketing materials have a combination of audiences, but usually one group is the primary audience, while the others are secondary in importance (Figure 2.1). These audience segmentations are usually the same whether the material is published in print or electronic media, including Web content.

| Material Type | Primary Audience | Secondary Audience |
|---|---|---|
| Sales Materials | Prospects, sales reps, dealers, customers | Journalists and analysts, investors, alliance partners, employees |
| Press Materials | Journalists and analysts | Salespeople, dealers, alliance partners |
| Alliance Materials | Alliance partners | Salespeople |
| Presentation Materials | Varies according to document and forum | |

*Figure 2.1  Example segmentation of primary and secondary audiences.*

**Prospects.** Businesses or consumers who are potential buyers of your products. For complex and expensive products sold to businesses, you may need to develop materials for multiple audiences within a prospect's company. Business audiences are often distinguished by level of authority, such as an executive-level decision-maker (the person who approves the purchase), decision-influencers (the people who must support the purchase decision), and other employees (who may be the ultimate product users). For consumer products sold to families, you may need to address the interests of the kids and the concerns of their parents. You may also categorize prospects and customers by factors such as industry, geographic location, demographic profile, application, system environment, and previous purchases.

**Customers.** Companies or individuals who have already bought one or more of your products.

**Journalists and opinion leaders.** Reporters and editors at magazines and newspapers, independent analysts, and researchers at market-research or investment firms. This group also includes industry "luminaries," the influential users and consultants who are frequently asked by journalists to comment on new products or technology developments.

**Salespeople and dealers.** The people who sell your product will often be a secondary audience for sales and press materials.

For materials such as a brochure that promotes a dealer program, dealers and resellers may actually be your prospects and thus, the primary audience.

**Alliance partners.** All companies with which your company has a business relationship for the development, sale, or support of products.

**Investors.** Shareholders, venture capitalists, bankers, and others who have a financial interest in your company, as well as financial analysts and brokers who monitor the company stock.

**Employees.** Sales and marketing staff, technical support personnel, and other employees within your company may be an audience group for certain materials.

Develop profiles of typical audience members to help you better understand a reader's motivations and information needs (Figure 2.2). An audience profile can be developed informally through conversations with customers and sales staff, or formally through surveys and focus groups.

| Audience Profile Factors | |
| --- | --- |
| Demographic | Age, gender, location, estimated income, years of experience, etc. |
| Psychographic | Motivators, interests, values |
| Influence | Job title, role in purchase decision, relationships within their sphere of influence |
| Current situation | Current products and needs |
| Desired situation | Goals, results, outcomes |

*Figure 2.2  Factors to consider when developing an audience profile.*

## AUDIENCES FOR AN ISSUE

If you are trying to persuade readers about an issue, the audience groups are defined somewhat differently: as potential converts, supporters, or opponents.[1]

While the potential converts group will likely be the primary audience, opponents and even supporters can be secondary audiences for a document that covers an issue. For example, a white paper that advocates adoption of one proposed technology standard over another may be targeted primarily to readers who have yet to make a choice. But readers who are inclined to support the other standard (your opponents) may read the white paper for information to confirm or disprove their choice. And supporters of your opinion may read the document to strengthen their understanding of the proposed standard and related issues.

## CONCERNS OF PROSPECTS AND CUSTOMERS

For prospects and customers, three types of concerns can impact the reader's interest in promotional material: buying, emotional, and external concerns. While this section describes the most common concerns in these categories, research the specific concerns of prospects and customers before you develop a marcom document.

### *Buying Concerns*

Buying concerns relate to the purchase decision itself and can involve many varied factors.

**Perception of a problem or need.** The reader must perceive a need or problem to be interested in a product in the first place. However, a reader may not have this perception or not think the problem is important enough to require an immediate solution.

**Perception of a solution.** Some technology products are marketed on the improvements they can offer rather than the problems they can solve. Yet the reader must perceive the value of the promised solution. This factor, which often arises with products in a completely new area of technology, is expressed as "You have a very interesting product, but I don't see how I would use it." The reader's level of experience, skill, and comfort with a particular technology can influence this perception, as well as cultural and social factors.

**Price and value.** Most consumers will choose technology very carefully because they don't have the disposable income to buy anything but the most essential products. These budget constraints also mean consumers don't necessarily see the value in keeping up with the latest product or upgrade.[2]

In addition to budget constraints, business customers will be concerned about value factors such as total cost of ownership, payback period, breakeven point, and potential return on investment (ROI).

**Purchase factors.** Beyond the availability of budgets, other required resources (e.g., staff, system hardware, network links) are critical factors for a business customer in making a purchase decision. Purchase factors also include cost justification, implementation requirements, an assessment of capabilities to be gained, internal decision procedures, and implementation schedules. These factors may vary substantially in each market and among different types of business prospects. Consumers may also be concerned about implementation requirements and the need for add-on products when making a purchase decision.

**A broad view of potential solutions.** Prospects tend to look at products as being part of a continuum of possible solutions to a problem. This continuum also includes competitors' products, other technology solutions, and nontechnical ways of obtaining the same result.[3]

**Company reputation.** Previous experience with your company, its market position, and what others say about the company reputation are also factors that influence a prospect's purchase decision.

Once a prospect is actively considering a product, buying concerns become much more specific.

**Product**. What does it do? How easy is it to learn and use? Will it work with my other products? Is it reliable? How does it compare to competitive products?

**Purchasing**. Where can I buy it? How soon can I get it? Can I get a better price from another source? Are quantity discounts or site licenses available?

**Implementation issues.** What are the system requirements? Will I need to buy additional hardware or software? Who will install it? What type of training is available? What happens with my previous product or version?

**Support and maintenance.** What service or technical support programs are offered? What are the hours and areas of telephone or on-site coverage? What is the cost of the maintenance program? What kind of support resources can I access on the Web?

## Upgrade Concerns

Selling an upgrade can be more difficult than selling the original product because of several common customer concerns.

**Upgrade fatigue.** How many times have you received a notice that urges you to buy the latest upgrade to a product, but you haven't had time to even consider the previous upgrade? Technology often changes too quickly for users to be aware of upgrades, much less make the decision to buy and assimilate them. Another challenge for this type of communication is user distrust that an upgrade will really deliver improvements: "Why is something that slows down my work called an upgrade?"[4]

**Implementation difficulties.** Buyers will be concerned about whether the upgrade offers features and benefits that will make the purchase and implementation worthwhile in terms of time, effort, user disruption, and retraining. Purchasing logistics can also be difficult, such as licensing issues, eligibility requirements, and whether the upgrade is covered under a warranty or maintenance program.

**Total costs.** Even if upgrades are covered by an annual maintenance fee, customers may be concerned about "hidden" costs, such as new hardware or additional software that may be necessary to support the upgrade. Hidden costs are a particular concern of business buyers, who may need to implement the upgrade for large numbers of users, or consider downtime of key systems.

## Emotional Concerns

Emotional concerns play a role in any purchase decision. As Kadanoff points out, "Think of your prospect first as a person, second as a technocrat."[5]

**Self-interest.** A reader may be concerned about protecting his "turf" or job, achieving status or prestige, or making a positive contribution to a team effort. For a business sale, consider the factors by which prospects are measured in their jobs, and the organizational goals they are trying to achieve. For a consumer sale, consider how a prospect might answer these questions: What will the product do for my image? How will I feel when I use it? What positive associations will I gain by using this product?[6]

**Confusion**. A buyer may have inaccurate preconceptions or confusion about a technology in general or about your company and product in particular. You must relate product information to what already may be in the reader's mind, helping to clarify misunderstandings.

**Distrust**. Key decision-makers involved in the purchase of high-tech products are over-marketed, and as a result, are highly skeptical about vendor claims of technological wonders. In general, a reader may not trust your company, profession, or industry, or may not believe claims about the product's functionality, benefits, or performance. Presenting evidence that supports product claims in your materials can help to address a prospect's skepticism and distrust.

**Resistance to the new.** Reluctance to accept change can be one of the strongest factors that hinders marketing of high-tech products. Users are especially resistant to innovation when it involves a discontinuous change instead of a more gradual, continuous change.[7] In addition, a reader may have concerns about existing investments in hardware, software, training, procedures, and other operational resources that may be impacted by adopting a new product. White papers, case studies, and planning guides can address these concerns directly and reassure the reader about the value of making a change.

**Risk aversion.** A buyer may be reluctant to bet on a technology that may not deliver completely or at all. Risk aversion significantly impacts the marketing of expensive, complex products. It also may be a factor in situations that involve usurping an entrenched vendor, even if your company offers a better product. The information in your material should address this issue of risk by showing how it can be eliminated or minimized.

## External Concerns

External concerns encompass the factors in the reader's environment that influence how she will read and respond to your material. These factors can vary by individual reader but typically fall into general categories.

**Business and competitive issues.** Prospects may be more interested in the economic and competitive issues facing their businesses than in learning about the product. Promotional materials may need to address current issues that are general to all prospects (e.g., the state of the economy) or are specific to a target industry or market.

**Limited time and attention span.** Many readers rapidly skim marketing materials—and perhaps miss important messages or details in the process. Keep in mind that readers ask three questions of any promotional material: "What is this all about?", "Why should I pay attention to this?", and "What's in it for me?"

**Disregard for advertising.** American audiences in particular are wary about any form of promotional material. As Ott notes, "All too often, a marketer assumes the receiver of its message is (a) paying attention, (b) cares about receiving the advertising message, (c) cares about the product advertised, and (d) has some prior knowledge of who the advertiser is and what the product is all about. Nothing could be further from the truth."[8] A reader must perceive that she will get value from the information in a piece before she will take the time to read it completely.

**Attention given to competitors.** If you are trying hard to reach prospects with promotional materials, it is safe to assume that competitors are making similar efforts. An undecided prospect will look to all promotional materials for help in making a product choice.

### Prospect Concerns in Different Markets

Concerns of prospects and customers may vary substantially among different markets. When planning and writing marcom materials, consider the specific markets targeted by your company. Many technology companies broadly define their markets as business-to-business or business-to-consumer. Some companies sell only to large corporate and government customers, some sell only to small businesses and consumers, some sell only to selected industries, while others sell products across all of these markets. In addition, your company may segment markets by country to target its efforts appropriately for international sales.

A business-to-business company also may define its markets by either a horizontal or vertical segmentation. A horizontal market is comprised of prospects with similar characteristics, but drawn from a broad range of industries or other market category. For example, a software company may target a word-processing product to all office workers. A vertical market is comprised of prospects within a single industry or category with similar product needs, but substantial differences in company size, operational modes, or other characteristics. An example of this type of market segmentation is a hardware product developed for specialty manufacturers.

A company may segment consumer markets by system type, level of technology expertise, target user, or preferred distribution channel.

Each of these markets has different characteristics, sales cycles, and buying factors. Your materials must address these differences in order to support the sales cycle effectively.

### *When the Audience is a Committee*

Technology purchases by a business often involve a decision made by a committee of representatives from different areas of the company. Technical, marketing, operations, and customer service staff are typical committee members.

The committee evaluates competing products and makes a decision about product purchase or vendor selection. In some cases, the committee is empowered only to make a recommendation, with the final decision made by one or more company executives. These executives are called the "C-levels" and include titles such as chief executive officer (CEO), chief information officer (CIO), chief financial officer (CFO), and chief marketing officer (CMO).

Different members of the committee, and the different C-level executives, will have varied concerns and interests when evaluating a product and company, for example:

- The technical staff and CIO will largely be concerned with technology and implementation factors.
- A CFO will be concerned about purchase and ongoing costs, payback period, and long-term return on investment (ROI).

- The CEO will need to understand how the product will impact the company's ability to increase revenues, reduce costs, reach new markets, or address other strategic issues.

Remember, the ultimate decision-maker may not have the expertise to make sound judgments about a product based on technical or operational factors. Instead, she will rely on the opinions of the evaluation committee or other subordinates, and make a decision if the strategic fit is right.

Identify the typical committee members and executives who will evaluate the product, then research their interests and concerns. This research will help you choose messages, document types, and content that will reach and inform these prospects effectively. You may decide to produce separate brochures to address the information needs and buying concerns of technical and C-level audiences.

## CONCERNS OF SALESPEOPLE AND DEALERS

If your sales force isn't both knowledgeable and excited about a product, how motivated will they be to sell it? This motivation is especially important for dealers or retail outlets that sell many, even hundreds of diverse products. Of course the product itself must be good, with attractive pricing and sales incentives. But marketing materials must motivate a salesperson to promote the product and be helpful to sales reps when they talk to potential customers.

The concerns of salespeople and dealers can vary depending on their involvement with the product, its markets, and the sales cycle. When reading materials targeted to customers and prospects, dealers and salespeople will share many of the concerns described in the previous section. When reading alliance materials such as sales kits, salespeople and dealers will have other concerns.

**Selling factors.** What are the size, location, purchasing power, and other characteristics of the target market? How much time and effort is required to make each sale? What is the potential for profit from the product itself and any follow-on revenue such as service contracts? What is the competition within the dealer's sales territory and from other sales channels?

**Customer relationships.** How easy is it to maintain and support the product? What service resources are available to dealers? What will your company do to help the salesperson maintain positive customer relationships?

**Dealer program factors.** What are the requirements for participating in the dealer program, such as minimum purchases, staff training, and other resource investments? What programs does your company offer for marketing, cooperative (coop) advertising, and generating leads? What incentives, training materials, and other resources will your company offer to help the dealer be successful in selling the product?

These concerns may vary for the different sales channels: wholesale distributors, specialty dealers, retail and catalog outlets, consultants, and system integrators. The dealer's decision-making process for carrying a product may involve a number of people and an evaluation period to assess the potential value of adding the product to their offerings. Local dealers in each international market are likely to have different concerns, based on variations in market characteristics, commerce laws, and business practices.

## CONCERNS OF JOURNALISTS AND ANALYSTS

Marketing materials can help journalists and analysts gain a better understanding of your products, markets, and company. Testing labs and product reviewers will often verify a product's performance against the claims made in a brochure or data sheet. But don't expect a glossy brochure to dazzle these readers. Journalists, analysts, and investors will always read marketing materials in light of additional information they garner from other sources, both internal and external to your company.

Reporters, editors, researchers, and analysts are primarily concerned with obtaining factual, timely, and complete information about a company and its products. They want materials that will support their research efforts and help them write accurate and useful articles or reports.

**Product information.** Which functions does the product support? How is the product packaged? What types of add-on or optional products and services are available?

**Market position.** How does the product relate to the competition, to compatible products, and to industry trends? What is new and different about the product compared to previous versions and competitive products?

**User perception.** Which user applications does the product support? What has been the experience of product users? How is the product perceived by analysts and industry commentators?

**Sales details.** What are the availability date, sales channels, pricing, and upgrade policies for the product?

Journalists for general, business, or consumer publications as well as financial analysts are usually less interested in the technical details for a product. Instead, they want to understand the importance of the product in terms of your company's position or a target customer's revenue growth, competitive positioning, and business needs.

## RESEARCHING YOUR AUDIENCE

You can conduct a number of activities to determine the specific concerns and knowledge of audience groups.

**Talk to customers directly.** Sponsor a focus group or a session at a user-group meeting or industry conference.[9] Conduct a telephone survey of randomly selected prospects (drawn from inquiries or a prospect database). Go on sales calls with salespeople or work in your company's trade-show booth. For a time, take on the responsibility for reading and responding to email inquiries from customers and prospects.

**Talk to salespeople.** Talk to your direct sales staff, dealers, product managers, customer service staff, and anyone else who has regular contact with a broad range of customers. However, remember that some salespeople will define as a "trend" the concerns of the last customer they contacted.

**Research external information.** Read market information that is published in trade magazines or by research firms. Read the magazines and journals your prospects read. What are these publications saying about the state of the industry or problems and needs? Analyze the audiences that competitors seem to be addressing in their materials. How are they describing the prospect's concerns?

**Talk to current and prospective dealers.** Contact the dealer's sales staff or visit a retail store. Read the trade publications that are targeted to this market.

**Use the Internet.** A visitor registration or survey page can collect data on the interests, needs, and demographics of visitors to your Web site. In addition to a "check-box" form of survey questions, include a place where visitors can enter general comments.

When researching the audience for an existing product, identify the type of customer that is buying the product now.[10] Is this customer type different from what your company perceives as the target prospect? In addition, when responding to a Request for Proposals (RFP), Bowman and Branchaw suggest that you look at the orientation and value words it contains for clues about the audience's interests.[11]

## DEVELOPING AN AUDIENCE-FOCUSED DOCUMENT

*I have found that sometimes it helps to pick out one person,*
*a real person you know or an imagined person,*
*and write to that one.*
—John Steinbeck

Imagine that you are a member of your target audience. What preconceptions would you have? What questions would you want answered? What information would you want to receive? What expectations would you have about the manner in which it is delivered? What would motivate you to take the desired action? Now look at your materials; are they addressing these concerns adequately? (Figure 2.3)

| Audience | Interests | Information Need |
|---|---|---|
| Prospects | Learning about the product to determine interest in purchasing | Features and benefits, specifications, applications, pricing, options, and availability |
| Salespeople and Dealers | Learning about the product in order to sell it successfully | Features and benefits, applications, and pricing; needs and concerns of prospects |
| Journalists and Analysts | Learning about the product in order to write an article or prepare an evaluation or recommendation | Features and applications, market needs and fit, comparison to competitive products, compatibility with other products |
| Investors and Alliance Partners | Evaluating the company's capabilities and strengths | Product positioning, place in the market, comparison to competitive products |
| Employees | Learning about the company's products | Features and benefits, applications, needs and concerns of prospects, comparison to competitive products |

*Figure 2.3 Example audience analysis for a product brochure.*

You can use a variety of techniques to develop an audience-focused document.

**Check the content.** Compare the document with the concerns you have identified for each audience group. Does the document address those concerns effectively?

**Address the audience directly.** Does the text talk mostly to the reader ("you") or about your company ("we")? An audience-focused document emphasizes "you" statements over "we" statements. For example, compare the focus of these statements: *Here's how [product] can improve your productivity* ("you" statement), or *We're very proud of our innovative features* ("we" statement).

**Picture the reader.** As you write, keep in mind a representative prospect. Think of someone you have met or interviewed. How would that person respond to your material? Does the information demonstrate an accurate understanding of that person and her needs, concerns, and problems?

**Watch for assumptions.** Make sure your perceptions of audience interests and needs are not skewed by your own perspective. Verify your assumptions with market research, prospect and customer interviews, articles in trade publications, or other sources of reliable audience profiles and information. For example, it is easy to assume—incorrectly—that a target audience accepts the idea that applying technology is the best solution to a particular problem.

**Develop customized materials for each market segment.** In most cases, you can produce one brochure or backgrounder that will be suitable for all target audiences. However, very technical products or those that address multiple markets may require multiple variants of a particular document. For example, a separate product brochure may be appropriate for each decision level, vertical market, or country. If cost is a concern, you may be able to address the different audiences in separate sections of the document. As an alternative, Web content may be an inexpensive way to reach multiple markets or audiences.

**Name the audience in the document.** An example of this technique: *[This brochure] concerns the CIO, the MIS manager, the data communications manager, the LAN manager, and the telecommunications manager.*[12]

**Check for balance.** If the document has multiple audiences, verify that their different concerns are addressed adequately and appropriately.

**Test the document concept.** When a document is in the draft stage, ask a few customers or prospects to review it and respond to questions such as: Do they understand the copy? Does it address their interests? Would it encourage them to take the next step? Ask a salesperson: Can you sell from this document?

**Conduct a post-publication survey.** For existing documents, ask a few readers questions such as: What did the document do well? What information was missing? Was any part of the document confusing or misleading? These answers will help you improve the audience focus of all materials.

## RESOURCES

The recommended books and other resources listed below provide additional information on the topics discussed in this chapter. For an updated list and other materials related to this book, visit **writinghightech.com**.

### Books

You may find useful information about audience analysis in books from a variety of categories including general and technical marketing, media planning, market analysis, and demographics.

### Web Sites

American Demographics Magazine (**demographics.com**)

## REFERENCES

[1] Article in *Public Relations Journal,* February 1994

[2] Mark Lantz, McCann Erickson, speaking at PRSA Annual Conference, 2003

[3] Dee Kiamy, editor: *The High-Tech Marketing Companion.* Reading, MA: Addison-Wesley, 1993

[4] Company advertisement, US West

[5] Marcia Kadanoff: "High-tech marketing should give up technical approach," *San Jose Business Journal,* October 12, 1992

[6] Leslie Grandy, Real Networks, speaking at PRSA Technology Section Conference, 2002

[7] Geoffrey A. Moore: *Crossing the Chasm: Marketing and Selling Technology Products to Mainstream Customers.* New York: HarperBusiness, 1991

[8] Richard Ott: *Creating Demand: Powerful Tips and Tactics for Marketing Your Product or Service.* Homewood, IL: Business One-Irwin, 1992

[9] Article in *Marketing Computers* Magazine, July 1993

[10] Erica Levy Klein: *Write Great Ads: A Step-by-Step Approach.* New York: John Wiley & Sons, 1990

[11] Joel P. Bowman and Bernadine P. Branchaw: *How to Write Proposals That Produce.* Phoenix, AZ: Oryx Press, 1992

[12] Product brochure, Racal-Datacom, Inc.

# 3

# WHY COMMUNICATE?

## ESSENTIAL ANSWERS FOR ON-TARGET MATERIALS

Before you begin writing, know why you want to communicate and what you want to say. To this end, it helps to answer five essential questions for any marcom document:

1. The *promotional activity or context* targeted by the document: What sales or publicity efforts must the document support?
2. The *objective* you want to achieve with the document: What do you want the reader to think or do?
3. The *purpose* of the document's content: What do you want the document to accomplish? To motivate, inform, or persuade the reader?
4. The *messages* to convey through the document's text and images about the product, service, or company. What do you want the document to say?
5. How the document will communicate the *brand.* Will the reader make the right associations for the product and company?

Together, all of these answers should also address the fundamental question of "Why communicate?"

One step in the marcom planning process is to identify the

promotional context—the planned activities which the materials must support. See Chapter 1 for more details on choosing the right materials for the most common promotional tasks.

The combination of objective, purpose, and message can help you select the best document type to meet a communication need. Figure 3.1 shows how objective, purpose, and message could be defined for the marcom documents related to a fictional software product.

Communicating brand means correctly presenting both direct brand elements (e.g., logo and design) and indirect brand qualities (e.g., value, leadership) throughout each document.

| Objective | Purpose | Key Message | Document |
|---|---|---|---|
| Action: Request a visit to a customer site | Motivate the purchase decision by providing highly credible customer references | Proven reliability in high-demand environments. Prominent customers are already using the product | Customer case studies |
| Impression: Integration is easy | Inform by showing all current integrations | Integration verified with key products and technologies | Product interfaces data sheet |
| Action: Purchase a presale consulting project for` application development | Inform by showing the range and depth of potential applications | Adaptable for many different applications | Online application guide |
| Impression: Give technical experts confidence in the product design | Persuade by showing the underlying architecture | The product offers an open platform for adopting new technologies | Technology white paper |

*Figure 3.1 Along with the promotional context, consider objective, purpose, and message together when choosing a document type.*

## OBJECTIVE

*If you don't know where you're going,*
*you might end up somewhere else.*
—Casey Stengal

An **objective** specifies what you want the reader to think (impression) or do (action) after reading the document. It is based on the marketing problem you want to solve or the marketing opportunity you want to address with the document. An objective also considers the messages you want to convey to audiences and the role the piece should play in the sales cycle.

There are two primary types of objectives: impression and action. An example of an impression objective is: *Give technical experts confidence in the product's design.* An example of an action objective is: *Five percent of recipients will request a product demonstration.*

Of course, the overriding objective for any marcom document is to sell the product or prompt another action by the reader. However, you will usually specify one or more focused objectives for each marcom document, based on its target audience and its role in the sales cycle.

An objective can be expressed in qualitative or quantitative terms. Examples of qualitative objectives include:

- Prompting the reader to take a direct or indirect action such as requesting more information or buying the product (direct action); or to support a purchase decision or develop a positive impression (indirect action).
- "Setting the agenda" for a purchase decision by convincing the reader that the areas where your product is better than its competition are the most important to consider.
- Creating an awareness of a product in the market or correcting a market misperception about the value of a technology.
- Providing information that supports salesperson or dealer activities.

Quantitative objectives are expressed in terms of measurable results such as response rates or number of inquiries generated by the document, purchase rates or revenue amounts, attendance levels at events, market share gains, or number of new dealers recruited.

Different objectives may apply at different stages of the product life span, as shown in Figure 3.2.

| Product Stage | Example Communications Objectives |
| --- | --- |
| New product | Fostering awareness of the product or technology among opinion leaders and leading-edge users |
| | Increasing product sales in the next quarter through an advertising campaign or online promotional activity |
| Mature product | Establishing the product as the perceived standard for its category through communication of significant customer contracts, product awards, and other achievements |
| | Creating a solid brand image for a product or company through consistent and sustained communication to the market |
| Different target markets or audiences. | Account for differences in: |
| | Levels of involvement in the purchase decision |
| | Problems, requirements, and environments of prospects |
| | Cultural and business conditions in different countries |
| | Interests and motivations of dealers and the direct sales force |

*Figure 3.2 The maturity of a product can mean different objectives for communications.*

## PURPOSE

The underlying *purpose* of the document helps you select and organize the information it presents. An example of a purpose statement is: ***The purpose of the Application Guide is to inform by***

*showing the range and depth of potential applications, reinforc-*
*ing our message about the high level of product configurability.*

Purpose answers "Why this document, in this form?" Most marcom documents have one of three purposes:

- *Motivate* readers to take an action related to buying a product or service, registering for an event, etc.
- *Inform* readers about a product, service, company, event, or trend.
- *Persuade* readers to make a change in their situation or adopt your views on an issue.

You may have more than one purpose in a document, but one will usually be dominant. For example, a product description brochure has information as its primary purpose, but may include a call to action that has a motivational purpose.

The matrix in Figure 3.3 can help you select a document type based on the purpose for communication.

Several questions can also help you choose the purpose for a particular document.

**Who and Why?** Identify who belongs to the target audience and what they would want to gain from reading the document.

**What need or problem are you trying to address through communication?** For example, is it a lack of compelling reasons to make a purchase (motivate), a lack of information from other sources (inform), or the need to present a viewpoint (persuade)?

**How will the document be used?** For example, a direct-mail piece that must stand on its own (motivate), as part of an online presentation (inform), or as a contribution to an ongoing debate (persuade).

**Where does the piece fit in the sales cycle?** At the very beginning when the reader has minimal information (inform), in the middle when the reader needs additional detail (persuade), or near the end when the reader needs one last incentive to buy (motivate).

## *Motivation*

In a document with a motivation purpose, the copy must give readers a strong incentive or desire to take an action, whether it is contacting a salesperson, browsing deeper into a Web site, or buying the product. Motivation is typically the primary purpose in sales brochures, catalogs, direct mail pieces, and some Web content (see Figure 3.3).

To write copy that serves a motivation purpose, you need a good understanding of what factors will prompt readers to act. For most people, motivation arises out of a sense of need, real or perceived. With some products, you must help the reader recognize she actually has a need. In all cases, show your product as the only or best solution and give the reader a sense of urgency about addressing that need *now*.

| Document (print or electronic media) | Motivate | Inform | Persuade |
|---|---|---|---|
| Advertisement | P | P, S | |
| Brochure or Data Sheet | P, S | P | |
| Direct Mail, Catalog, or Packaging | P | P, S | |
| Proposal | S | P | |
| White Paper | | P | P, S |
| Case Study | | P | S |
| Newsletter | | P | |
| Presentation or Sales Letter | P | P | P |
| Press Release or Q&A Document | | P | |
| Article | | P | P, S |
| Backgrounder | | P | P, S |
| Sales Kit | S | P | |
| Specialized Web Content | S | P | S |

P= Primary, S= Secondary. In cases where symbols appear in more than one column, any of these purposes may apply to that document type.

*Figure 3.3  Guidelines for selecting a document type based on purpose.*

A new opportunity is another factor that can create a sense of motivation for readers. Some people can't resist having the latest technological wonder, while others will be interested because they see value in new capabilities, even if they're happy with their current product or situation.

Several techniques can help you write effective motivational copy.

**Decide whether to use fear or incentive as the basis for motivation.** This choice will be determined in large part by the tone and content of marketing messages: Are they based on positive or negative factors? (See the section "Negative Messages" later in this chapter.)

**Convey a sense that taking the action involves minimal risk.** This technique is especially effective when asking for an order. Describe any refund guarantees, trial units, or service programs offered by your company.

**Adopt the "assumed close" technique used by salespeople.** This means your copy will reflect a sense that the reader has already decided to buy and now just needs information on how to complete the transaction.

**Use terms in the product offer to create a sense of urgency or exclusivity.** Examples include time limitations, special pricing, "select customers," or free add-ons (see the section on "Offers" in Chapter 6).

**Make it easy for the reader to take the action.** Provide all relevant contact information or an order form (see the section on "Call to Action" in Chapter 5).

See the section "Power Words" in Chapter 7 for additional ideas on specific text techniques that are effective for motivational copy.

## Information

A document with an information purpose presents its content clearly and simply, as in a statement of facts, a description of features, or an explanation of a technology concept. Information is often the primary purpose of data sheets, white papers, articles, backgrounders, and comparable Web content. The reader does not need to be convinced of anything, he just needs complete, accurate information.

These techniques can help you write information copy:

- Use text that is specific, concrete, and easy for readers to grasp its exact meaning.

- Make precise word choices—especially for verbs, adverbs, and adjectives—where subtleties of meaning can make a difference.
- Use standard writing techniques such as description, definition, comparison, classification, narration, and showing relationships or cause and effect.[1]
- Ask these questions of your language: Are you judging or describing? Telling or showing?[2] When information is the purpose, use language that will describe and show.

## *Persuasion*

In a document with a persuasion purpose, messages must convince the reader to believe or do something new. These documents are effective when you want a reader to switch brand preferences, try an unproven technology, or adopt a certain viewpoint on an issue. Persuasion can be the purpose for white papers, articles, and presentations.

Writing to meet a persuasion purpose is a difficult task because you must convince readers to adopt a new and unfamiliar belief or to change their views—and all while establishing or maintaining your own credibility. Persuasion also means showing why your assertions are right and proving why other beliefs are wrong.

These factors determine in part whether an attempt at persuasion is successful:

- The source must be credible, whether it is a customer, analyst, or employee communicating on your company's behalf, or indeed the company itself. Readers must believe that the source has the necessary expertise; it cannot appear to be too self-serving.[3] In addition, the source must appear to understand the needs, desires, and motivations of the audience.[2]
- The message must be clear, timely, relevant, and appeal to the self-interest of the audience; it must correspond to the audience's values and attitudes.[3]
- Any proposed action must be clear, feasible,[3] and one that the audience will be willing to accept and act upon.

Specific writing techniques to use when persuasion is the objective are presented below. You can mix these techniques within a document, for example, by appealing first to the reader's emotion, then supporting it with a statement of logic. However, make sure the document's tone and style can accommodate a mix of appeals and techniques.

**Establish credibility.** Create a sense of trust and confidence for the reader. State assertions positively and avoid the use of qualifiers. Assume that readers are already inclined to agree with you.

**Use reason-why copy.** Present the logic behind your arguments by showing the rationale and supporting evidence.[1] Describe logical outcomes or conclusions. Cite verifiable proof, statistics, external people or references that will be accepted by readers as authoritative. Use reason-why copy to present supporting evidence (see Chapter 6).

**Use emotional appeals.** Make sure they are appropriate for the audience, are not overly dramatic, and reflect a genuine concern or situation.[1]

**Consider opposing viewpoints.** Decide whether and how to present different perspectives. You can ignore the opposing view if the audience is friendly; tell both sides if the audience is neutral or hostile.[3] You don't need to include every possible argument for or refutation against your position; instead address only the strongest or most relevant.

**Define terms.** Give new definitions to key words or messages—a limited or special meaning that supports your viewpoint.[1]

**Personalize the argument.** Encourage the reader to identify with an idea that is presented in the text.[4]

**Highlight commonalties.** State areas of agreement or common ground with the audience or link your proposition with something the reader already believes. When readers know that you understand their viewpoints and needs, they will be more inclined to accept your messages.

Choose among these techniques based on how well they fit the audience and the nature of your arguments. Are those arguments aggressive or low-key? How do the arguments support your existing credibility or the credibility you are trying to establish? And remember, no matter what the focus of your persuasive efforts, apply these techniques responsibly and ethically (see Chapter 8).

## MESSAGE

> *To catch a mouse, make a noise like a cheese.*
> —*Lewis Kornfield.*

Does your key marketing message sound like cheese? A good marketing message entices the reader by presenting a product's selling points and key differences from its competition. Successful messages make the materials, product, and company memorable to all members of the target audience and help achieve the desired product or company positioning.

Messages present the critical information or impressions you want to leave in the reader's mind. Messages also support the product or service brand and can be adapted for all marketing materials. Messages may be based on product features, benefits, or differentiation; customer needs or problems; market trends or opportunities; or competitive factors. Consider this example of a product message: **Unlike proprietary products, our product is an open platform for adopting new technologies and interfaces.**

The key messages typically are defined by product managers or other marketing staff as part of the product marketing plan. As a copywriter, your job is to adapt these messages into specific text for use in one or more marketing documents.

Most technology companies use one primary message (sometimes called the "value proposition" or "consumer promise") and a small number of secondary messages across all materials for the company and each of its products. Whatever the number, these messages must be something easy for readers to grasp, and for salespeople and dealers to remember. And these messages must stand the test of different applications in different media, in different environments, with different audiences, and over time.

## Message Types

For high-tech companies, many diverse types of information can be conveyed in marketing messages.

**Technology leadership.** Example messages include: proven, sophisticated, feature-rich, quality, advanced, new, leading-edge, powerful, high-performance, innovative.[5] *Cisco Introduces Industry's First Remote Testing Capability for Monitoring Integrity of Optical Network Core.*[6]

**Market leadership.** Example messages include: first in a market, largest market share, high acceptance level. *With more than 1,000,000 ports shipped worldwide, Dialogic is the world's leading supplier of PC-based computer telephony hardware and software platforms.*[7]

**Application and use.** Example messages include: simplicity, ease-of-use, intuitive interface, customizable, flexible, open, independent, configurable. *This new series is perfect for field-service tasks that require precise measurement.*[8]

**Value and price.** Example messages include: low price, high value, complete solution, available now. *The tools you need to manage your business in one convenient package at one great price.*[9]

**Features and benefits.** Example messages include: unique capabilities, integration, quality, compatibility, interoperability, architecture, platform. *[This product] gives you visual tools to manage time, money, and people across multiple projects.*[9]

**Service and support.** Example messages include: 24/7 telephone support, consulting and customization services, Web-based technical library, service level guarantees, billing options. *Single-source support for both hardware and software makes technology easy to own.*[10]

**Company strengths.** Example messages include: longevity, stability, specialized expertise, strategies, directions, distribution channels. *[We] provide the widest range of connectivity solutions and customer support for the IBM midrange family.*[11]

## Developing Messages

Writing the specific text that conveys broadly stated marketing messages is challenging. Yet, no matter how they are stated, messages should be adaptable to all marcom documents such as advertising, sales collateral, and press materials. A specific statement of a message may also be used on product packaging, trade show banners, and promotional items such as t-shirts for employees and dealers. In addition, the message statements should be easy for salespeople to remember during sales calls, presentations, seminars, or other personal selling situations.

Consider the questions in this section when writing specific messages.

**Audience interests.** What do the members of the target audiences need to know? What are their concerns? What are their needs or wants that the product or service fulfills? What ideas or language will reach them most effectively? Do you need to create different (but related) messages for each target audience? What is the current mindset of prospects in each target market? Will readers be receptive to your messages, or must you overcome misperception, apathy, or a lack of credibility?

**Target media.** In which materials will the messages appear? Will the messages work equally well in all of them? In particular, consider whether each message will retain its distinctiveness and credibility when it appears in press materials and is subjected to a journalist's scrutiny and skepticism.

**Presentation.** Which visual or copy techniques are appropriate for presenting the messages? In ads and other sales materials, a message may be presented through an integration of image and copy. For Web content, consider how the message will be sustained in different areas of the site.

**Uniqueness.** Which characteristics make the product unique and differentiate it from the competition? At least one statement of any marketing message should focus on these unique qualities. In advertising, this statement is called the Unique Selling Proposition (USP), which must be credible and clear to the target market. The primary message should present the one selling point that will clearly distinguish the product. It can be based on a number of factors, such as your company's market position; a unique technology; product choice, packaging, or delivery; pricing; supporting products and services.

**Clarity.** Is it better to state the message explicitly or implicitly? An example of an implicit statement is posing a question and letting the reader draw the desired conclusion for himself. If you are stating the message implicitly, will the reader understand the message in the same way as you do? For clarity of communication, most messages are stated explicitly.

**Longevity.** Will the message remain the same over time? While product brand and positioning may remain consistent over a long period, messages may change to reflect the business climate, market conditions, and actions taken by competitors. For example, Apple Computer has used a variety of messages that describe simplicity—the company's positioning for the Macintosh computer since its introduction. Initially, these messages contrasted the simplicity of the Macintosh user interface against IBM personal computers running DOS. Later, when Microsoft introduced its Windows operating system to compete with the Macintosh, Apple targeted its messages specifically against Windows.

**Congruency.** Are the messages for an individual product or service congruent with all of your company's other messages and with the company image? Can you maintain the consistency of the messages across all marcom materials and marketing activities?

Consider these additional guidelines when writing text that presents product and company messages.

**A good marketing message is not a proclamation, pronouncement, or other lofty statement.** And, while it is tempting to create a message that is very clever or uses highly sophisticated language, you run the risk of creating empty hype that will confuse or alienate the audience. A message will be more effective if it is written in words that are concrete, specific, and easy for the reader to understand.

**Keep the focus on the reader.** In most cases, a marketing message will be centered on the reader ("you"), not on the company ("we").

**Each message must be believable and honest.** A message is made stronger when you support it with verifiable evidence such as test results or market research data, customer testimonials, or endorsements from other credible parties. Stretching the truth not only lessens the believability of a message, but competitors will make sure that any dishonesty will come back to haunt you.

**Use terminology that is familiar to the audience.** As 1960s activist Abbie Hoffman observed, "Never impose your language on people you want to reach." Watch for overuse of acronyms and jargon in messages, unless these terms are widely known in the industry and are critical for presenting information completely and accurately.

**Avoid offensive connotations in your choice of words and images.** Ask several people who have different social and cultural backgrounds to review the message text and point out any areas that might be offensive. Consider the differences in messages that may be needed to address international markets. Each market will have its own cultural considerations and business climate that should be reflected in marketing messages (see Chapter 9).

## Presenting Messages on a Web Site

Presenting messages is a little different in the context of the Web. For example, marketing messages can easily become lost in the visitor's free-form interaction with a Web site. Look carefully at how you weave marketing messages throughout a Web page and the site as a whole. Don't hesitate to use a lot of repetition and reinforcement for each message. You will get tired of them long before a visitor even recognizes the sameness.

## Multiple Messages

As discussed earlier in this chapter, most technology products have one primary message plus a small number of secondary or supporting messages. A primary message clearly states the most important benefit or selling point for the product. For example, an illustration software product might have this primary message: *The most comprehensive design and illustration tool for creative professionals.* The key selling point for this product is conveyed with the words "most comprehensive."

Secondary messages cover additional benefits, dimensions, or brand attributes that strengthen the overall selling proposition for the product. In the following example, an ad for a computer monitor presented a benefit statement for the primary message, while the secondary messages described product features:

Primary: *Bigger Windows* (to emphasize the larger screen area for displaying Windows-based software).

Secondary: *Two-Year Warranty, 16" Fine Dot Pitch CRT, Very High Resolution, Color Calibration System, Low Emission Design.*[12]

*Caution*: Be careful about the number of messages you create for a product. More than three or four messages can overwhelm and confuse both readers and salespeople. You don't need to create a message for every benefit or selling point of a product. Instead, choose the strongest features or benefits that are critical to the product's brand or competitive positioning. Then, distill these items into the fewest messages possible without losing clarity or impact.

When working with multiple secondary messages, present them in order of importance to the reader. This order may be different than what you might perceive as important, so consider market research or the feedback you receive when testing the messages (see the section "Testing Messages" later in this chapter).

Also watch carefully where and how multiple messages appear in a document. Given the short attention span of many readers, present the messages early and often in each marketing piece. Reinforcement of the primary message in particular is critical for helping readers understand and remember the product or company. When this reinforcement of messages is carried through all related marcom documents, it strengthens the buyer's understanding through all stages of the sales cycle.

You can weave messages throughout a document's text without becoming boringly repetitive. For starters, present the primary message in a headline or opening line of the body copy to grab interest and establish brand. In the body copy itself, restate the primary message and present any secondary messages. At the end of the piece, reinforce the primary message in a closing statement, tag line, or call to action. Subheads, captions, and callouts are additional elements to use for weaving messages throughout a document.

This excerpt from a product brochure shows an effective weaving of the primary message (emphasis added):

**Headline**: Open Technology for *Efficient, Effective,* and *Flexible* Solutions

**First paragraph:**...Software solutions to business problems can make people and processes *efficient, effective,* and *flexible*.

**Second paragraph:** *Efficient* software solutions do things right... *Effective* software solutions do the right thing... And *flexible* solutions adapt to new circumstances.

**Closing tag line:** NAS: The *Efficient, Effective,* and *Flexible* Software Solution.[13]

Marketing materials may contain different messages for different audiences such as prospects in different markets or in different decision-making roles; another message set for dealers, third-party developers, and strategic partners; and an additional set targeted at investors and the financial community. Journalists and industry analysts usually receive the messages targeted to prospects but with additional supporting information. For example, consider these variations in the primary message:

**Prospects**. *PrimeWidget makes it easier to manage your daily tasks.*

**Dealers**. *PrimeWidget meets a critical user need that has not been addressed by any other product.*

**Third-Party Developers.** *PrimeWidget offers an open, flexible platform for creating customized applications.*

**Financial Community.** *PrimeWidget addresses a large, untapped market.*

When creating different sets of messages, make sure they don't contradict each other and they reflect a common theme.

### Confused Messages

A danger of using multiple messages is that you will confuse readers. This confusion can lead to several undesirable outcomes as readers may reject the message, misunderstand the product, or not recognize the product's applicability to their needs. For example:

*Windows opened new vistas on the world of personal computing. Now, Windows users can reach new levels of productivity with The Norton Desktop for Windows. This landmark software package makes Windows far more accessible and easier to use. Version 1.0 got rave reviews, and comments like "For every Windows user...shopping for the best Windows utilities bargain around, this is the answer. Every Windows user should have it." PC Computing, December, 1991. Now we're pleased to introduce Version 2.0—for even better Windows.*[14]

This passage, which appears as the first paragraph in a data sheet, has several problems in the way it presents the product's marketing message. First, it is not clear which product the document is promoting (is it Microsoft Windows or Norton Desktop for Windows?). Second, readers may not realize that Version 2.0 is the subject of the data sheet, as much of this opening paragraph focuses on proclaiming the greatness of an earlier version.

These guidelines will help you avoid the trap of confusing messages:

- Are you stating the message in too many different ways? Will the reader perceive that the message means one thing the first time it appears, but something else the next?
- Are you sticking to a short list of primary and secondary messages? Are you introducing irrelevant or contradictory messages later in the piece?
- Are you overloading the piece with messages? Creating multiple messages doesn't mean you need to include all of them in each and every marketing document. Identify the few messages that will have the most impact on the specific audience for each document.
- Are you trying to address too many diverse audiences with a single piece? If different messages are relevant to each audience, it may be better to create separate documents or clearly identify the information that's specific to each audience (document elements such as sidebars or subheads are useful for this segmentation; see Chapter 5).

## Negative Messages

High-tech companies sometimes use negative messages when products are competing head-to-head with little differentiation in price or features. Negative messages can create a sense in the prospect's mind called FUD (fear, uncertainty, and doubt) about your competition. The most common intent of FUD is to cause the prospect to delay a purchase decision until you have the opportunity to present your product.

One technique for creating FUD is to present negative messages about a competitive product. For example, Banyan Corp. used this title for a sales brochure intended to create FUD about its major competitor, Novell Corp.: *Things they don't tell you at Novell presentations.*[15] Reading this, a prospect who was ready to buy a Novell product might hesitate and say, "I'd better check this out."

While it is an extremely powerful approach when done well, FUD and the use of negative messages can easily backfire. Negative messages are tricky for a number of reasons.

**More difficult for the reader to understand.** This difficulty is especially true when the reader skims an ad or brochure.

**Confusion about the object of the message.** A reader may think someone else is saying all those nasty things about *your* product.

**May alienate readers.** Think of how often people complain about negative advertising in political campaigns. Now consider how a negative message could reflect on the image or reputation of your company.

**May describe a problem the reader never knew she had.** This reminder doesn't help her draw a positive conclusion about the product, even if you are positioning it as the solution to this "problem."

**Ammunition for competitors.** After all, negative messages put competitors in an underdog position, which they may be able to leverage to draw a reader's sympathy.

**Ethical and legal problems.** While it is very tempting to exaggerate the flaws of a competitive product in a negative message, the information it presents must be factually accurate and defensible (see Chapter 8).

Some marketers question whether negative messages really work. In a survey of 50 business marketing executives from both high-tech and nontechnology companies, 80 percent said that negative ads were not very effective or not at all effective in boosting sales. And 58 percent said that negative ads were either not very effective or not at all effective in damaging a competitor's reputation.[16]

If you still want to use negative messages, consider the following guidelines:

- Read the section on "Comparisons" in Chapter 6 and "Mistake #6: Negativism" in Chapter 7.
- Always describe how the reader can avoid or get out of a FUD situation; of course, this is usually by purchasing your product.
- Test the negative message with members of the potential audience for the document.
- Check and double-check the facts and assumptions behind negative messages with reputable sources both internal and external to your company.
- Ensure that a corporate attorney reviews the text to deter legal problems (see Chapter 8).

## Testing Messages

No matter how brilliantly phrased a message might be, it is not doing a good job if it doesn't produce the results you want. Testing messages in advance of their use is a way to avoid this problem.

A testing process can address the clarity and effectiveness of different messages. Will the message catch the reader's eye? Is the message relevant to the reader's interests and circumstances? Does the reader come away with the correct information and impression from the message? Will the message motivate the response and action you want?

One way to conduct these tests is with focus groups. You can hire a market research firm to conduct a session or pull together a session at a user's group conference or a trade show. A focus group critique can be a highly useful way to test the messages and concepts of proposed materials before launching a major, expensive marcom campaign.

Sometimes a quick telephone survey of a few customers and salespeople is all you need to determine whether marketing messages will be effective. Ask these contacts for feedback on the message text: Do they understand what the message is trying to convey? Would the message catch their attention and prompt them to act? Is an important buying factor or concern missing from the messages?

Another common test is to evaluate how well a completed document achieved its objectives. These objectives could include the number and quality of sales generated or inquiries received; feedback from sales reps, dealers, customers, and prospects; or market share measurements from independent research firms. While results can reflect a variety of influences, the effectiveness of messages is an important contributing factor to a document's success.

## BRAND

> *If you can differentiate a dead chicken,*
> *you can differentiate anything.*
> —*Frank Perdue*

As a copywriter, brand presents concerns for style and tone, word usage, and coherence of text and image when developing documents. Brand is of vital concern for marketing because of its significant impact on purchasing decisions, customer loyalty, and company or product position in the market. Gain a solid understanding of brand principles by reading the books recommended at the end of this chapter.

Conveying the brand correctly and powerfully will be an underlying goal of all marcom projects. To do so, you need to understand several essential concepts of brand.

**Brand.** In a narrow sense, a brand is a name, logo, or other identifying "mark" that represents a product or company. However, most brand experts use a broader definition that encompasses how a product or company is represented through all communications, customer service, and business activity. Brand usually applies to the company as a whole, but can also apply to a product line (often called a sub-brand), and to individual products. Different brand considerations—even different brands—may apply in various international markets.

**Branding.** The processes that present brand through written materials, customer transactions, public relations, and other promotional efforts.

**Brand promise.** The unique value and quality a customer will receive from the company or product. The brand and brand promise is especially important when marketing services, because in many cases there are no "tangible" factors for differentiation.

**Brand attributes.** Specific values, benefits, or characteristics that deliver the brand promise. These are often expressed through the key messages for a product.

**Brand personality.** The distinctive expression of the brand. Personality is the most immediate way a customer can distinguish your brand from that of a competitor. As an example, consider the contrasting brand personalities of PC makers Gateway (the folksy cow spots) and Dell (very corporate).

In print materials, brand is conveyed through visual techniques such as logos, color and design, style, paper type and size, as well as the tone, style, and content of the text. Similarly on a Web site, brand is conveyed through the types of content presented and its tone, style, and visual design.

### Conveying Brand with Words

A brand can seem very esoteric, amorphous—something that is difficult to express in words. In actuality, you can use several techniques to convey brand correctly when writing a marcom document.

**Develop and use branding standards.** Many companies have branding guidelines that cover only the use of logos, tag lines, and other visual and design elements. Defining brand standards that cover text will help to assure consistency across documents and the correct presentation of brand at each customer touchpoint, in each communication. These brands standards may be different in each international market.

**Define writing style and tone.** Because branding is often about subtleties in impression and meaning, the style and tone of materials can do a great deal to support—or confuse—brand image.

**Use word lists.** Develop a list of acceptable phrases and words (nouns, verbs, adjectives, and adverbs) that you can use in describing the product, service, or company.

**Words and visuals.** Check for congruency with each other and with brand personality and attributes.

**Consider document elements.** Convey the brand through what you emphasize in the content as a whole and in headlines, subheads, and other document elements.

**Use brand names correctly.** Most companies use the brand name as one element of a product name. For example, the product name *Microsoft Windows NT* contains the following brand components:

| *Microsoft* | *Windows* | *NT* |
|---|---|---|
| *(company brand)* | *(product line brand)* | *(individual product name)* |

Your company may have rules for how brand names appear in print and whether any abbreviated forms are acceptable. A logo or image may also be considered part of the brand and also have specific guidelines for use and appearance. Although trademark symbols are not really a part of the brand name, you will need to use them when appropriate (see the section "Trademarks" in Chapter 8).

## RESOURCES

The recommended books and other resources listed below provide additional information on the topics discussed in this chapter. For an updated list, visit **writinghightech.com**.

### Books

Chuck Pettis: *TechnoBrands: How to Create & Use "Brand Identity" to Market, Advertise & Sell Technology Products.* Amacom, 1995. The examples are a bit dated, but the principles are still sound. Unlike many branding books, this is specifically focused on technology brands.

F. Joseph LePla and Lynn M. Parker: *Integrated Branding: Becoming Brand-Driven Through Companywide Action.* Quorum Books, 1999. Describes how all of a company's activities support brand; includes a chapter on expressing brand through marcom and PR efforts.

## Web Sites

The following sites provide articles, reports, and other resources related to marketing messages, positioning, and brand:

Advertising Age Magazine (**advertisingage.com**)
Ad Week Magazine (**adweek.com**)
Brand Week Magazine (**brandweek.com**)
MarketingProfs.com (**marketingprofs.com**)
ClickZ (**clickz.com**)
BtoB Online Magazine (**btobonline.com**)
Technology Marketing Magazine (**technologymarketing.com**)

## REFERENCES

[1] John B. Karls and Ronald Szymanski: *The Writer's Handbook: A Guide to the Essentials of Good Writing,* 2nd Edition, Lincolnwood IL: NTC Books, 1990

[2] Lauren Kessler and Duncan McDonald: *Mastering the Message: Media Writing with Substance and Style.* Belmont, CA: Wadsworth, 1989

[3] Dennis L. Wilcox and Lawrence W. Nolte: *Public Relations Writing and Media Techniques.* New York: HarperCollins, 1990

[4] Burton Kaplan: *Strategic Communication.* New York: Harper Business, 1991

[5] Regis McKenna: *The Regis Touch.* Reading, MA: Addison-Wesley, 1986

[6] Press release, Cisco Systems

[7] Corporate backgrounder, Dialogic Corp.

[8] Product brochure, John Fluke Manufacturing Co., Inc.

[9] Product brochure, Microsoft Corp.

[10] Web content, Hewlett-Packard

[11] Press release, Andrew Corp.

[12] Product ad, Mitsubishi Electronics America, Inc.

[13] Product brochure, Digital Equipment Corp.

[14] Product data sheet, Symantec Corp.

[15] Product brochure, Banyan Corp.

[16] "Copy Chasers," *Business Marketing Magazine,* June 1992

# 4

## THE WRITING PROCESS

## DEVELOPING THE BEST IDEAS, STYLES, AND METHODS

"The enhanced PrimeWidget product will be ready to launch next month. We'll need a brochure." These words set into motion a flurry of activities as a marketing communicator tries to take the project from idea to printed piece and posted Web content. While each marcom project has its own activities and schedules, most projects reflect the typical development and review processes described in this chapter.

In addition, high-tech copy demands special consideration of three creative issues:

1. Identifying the best concept for a document's content.
2. Defining an appropriate writing style and tone for each project.
3. Working effectively with graphic and Web designers.

This chapter also covers these creative issues and presents suggestions for addressing them successfully.

### THE DEVELOPMENT PROCESS FOR A MARCOM PROJECT

Developing any type of marketing material typically follows a five-stage process: planning and concept, research and interviews, writing and review (a stage often repeated multiple times), publication, and evaluation.

The development process described here can apply to projects that are handled completely by in-house staff as well as to those that involve freelance or agency-based writers. However, when external resources are involved, additional write-review-revise cycles may be necessary. This is particularly true for agency-developed projects, where drafts may undergo extensive review within the agency before they are given to the client company.

### Planning and Concept

As described in Chapter 1, each marcom project begins with some form of planning. It may be as casual as a few notes about the outline and schedule or it may be a formal document plan that details all aspects of the project's development. An informal plan may be appropriate for small projects that involve only one or two people, while a formal plan will help large projects that involve many people in the development and review cycles.

A document plan and creative platform help the writers and designers in developing the document, and can facilitate the review process. By getting agreement in advance from key reviewers about the scope, objective, and outline for the document, you are less likely to face questions about these issues when the draft is going through review. Of course, conditions may change at any point in the project, forcing you to reconsider all or parts of the document plan.

The project plan will also influence the creative concept for the document. Strategies and techniques for developing a good concept are discussed later in this chapter.

### Research and Interviews

Spending the time and effort on research and interviews before you begin writing can significantly improve a document's focus, content, and impact. You may conduct research and interview activities several times during a document's development, as you find new sources or need new types of input.

## Research

It always seems there's never enough time for the research stage, but finding good input can save time during the writing and review stages. Depending on the subject matter, you may find useful insights, background information, and reusable text in a variety of research resources (Figure 4.1).

---

**Research Sources**

---

Existing white papers, product plans, market studies, and engineering documents published by your company

Studies and reviews published by the trade press, market research firms, or industry analysts

Magazines, books, and Web sites targeted to vertical markets

Focus groups and user group meetings

Surveys of customers and Web site visitors

Inquiries handled by customer service and technical support staff

Joining sales calls and visiting a customer site

Comments from beta users

---

*Figure 4.1 Potential sources for researching the content for a marcom project.*

## Interviews

Whether conducted in person, by telephone, or through an email exchange, interviews are an important means of gathering input for most marcom projects. Several techniques can help you save time and headaches when interviewing and garner the most useful information from your sources.

**Do your homework.** Learn as much about the subject matter, the source (as an individual and as a company, if relevant), the customer's applications for your products and relationship with your company, and other relevant background that will make you an intelligent interviewer.

**Develop an interview strategy.** List the most essential questions to cover in the interview; then list optional questions to cover if you have time. But don't stick rigidly to your prepared list. Ask other questions as they come to mind in the interview, especially if the source provides an interesting angle or new information.

**Set the framework for the interview.** Ask all participants for permission to tape record the interview. (This permission is usually mandated by law if the interview is conducted by telephone.) If it will be helpful to the person's readiness or understanding, submit your questions in advance.

**Ask open-ended questions.** These questions will help you get the high-level view, the most interesting quotes, and the most useful information. "Why?" and "How?" questions are good for this purpose.

**Confirm facts and details.** Ask questions that are specific and direct to verify the essential information you want to obtain from the interview.

**Encourage sources to speak informally.** Ask them to give examples and tell stories. You will get a better quote that you can polish if necessary.

**Ask with sensitivity.** Carefully handle questions that cover proprietary and sensitive information. Abide by a source's request to keep remarks "off the record."

**Set the stage for follow-up questions.** It always seems that you remember the "question I *really* should have asked" soon after you have hung-up the phone or returned to your office. Before ending the interview, ask the source for permission to call or email follow-up questions throughout the writing process.

### Writing and Review

The writing and review stage is when most of the work is done and most of the headaches arise. A marcom project usually has multiple iterations of the write-review-revise cycle, with the copy produced in multiple drafts. The amount of time you spend in this stage—and the amount of aggravation you experience—depend on several factors:

**Quality of the input.** Pay attention to the clarity of the document plan, outline, and other instructions given to the writer at the beginning of the project. If the input is vague or incomplete, the first draft is likely to be off-target and the amount of revision will increase accordingly. However, in some cases seeing the first draft of a brochure helps the product and marketing teams figure out what they really want to say in terms of messages and positioning.

**The document type and its role in the sales process.** A glossy showcase brochure that is targeted to executive-level decision-makers will receive more scrutiny and require more writing and revision cycles than a simple update to a data sheet.

**The number of reviewers involved.** In general, the more people who look at a draft, the more comments you will need to incorporate and the more conflicting opinions you will need to referee.

**The number of writers involved.** For newsletters or other projects that use contributions from multiple writers, you may need to spend time revising certain parts to ensure consistency of tone and style.

As these factors indicate, you can gain better control of the time, effort, and expense involved in the writing stage if you plan before the writing begins and clearly state expectations for both writers and reviewers. Issues and considerations for the review process are discussed later in this chapter.

## *Publication*

After the copy has been approved and given to a graphic or Web designer for layout, the publication stage involves all activities for producing and distributing the document. This activity may be a simple matter of photocopying a few laser-printed pages or posting a PDF file, or the more complex tasks of coordinating with a full-color printer or testing a multimedia presentation. Distribution may require its own planning and management effort, such as building the mailing list for a direct-mail project. Additional production activities are required for materials that are localized for international markets (see Chapter 9).

## *Evaluation*

One element of any document plan should describe the method you will use to measure how well the material met its objective. Example measurements include counting the number of product orders or conducting surveys of customers or salespeople. At a suitable point after publication, take the time to conduct the evaluation and identify lessons that can be applied to similar projects in the future.

## THE REVIEW PROCESS: JUGGLING EGOS, INPUT, AND SCHEDULES

For many marcom projects it seems that an enormous amount of time, effort, and political negotiation go into the review process. You must continually juggle different levels and types of input from reviewers against project schedules and budgets. While the review process is determined by the unique requirements of each project, you can apply certain techniques that will make it more fruitful and manageable.

**Circulate a quality draft.** Make each draft as complete and accurate as possible. Run the spell checker, proofread a printout, and check the accuracy of product names, trademarks, and other easy-to-verify text. Highlight the comments or questions for reviewers in a different color so they can be easily distinguished from the body copy.

**Manage the review process.** Determine in advance how you will control the review process by identifying who will serve as reviewers and how they will work with drafts. Typically, more reviewers (and at higher levels) will be involved with pieces that are key for marketing a product or giving visibility to your company.

Not all reviewers will need to see the copy at every stage of its development. Some will see the copy only in early draft form and not again until they receive the final printed piece. Other reviewers will not see early drafts but will review the copy and visuals when the document is in preliminary layout.

Giving the copy to different reviewers at different stages of development offers several advantages for managing your projects. First, you can ask the subject experts to review copy in the draft stages, when extensive revisions can be made easily and inexpensively. Second, some people have trouble visualizing how draft copy, which is usually printed as straight text without any formatting, will appear in the final document. For these reviewers, presenting the copy in the preliminary layout can help them make more constructive comments. Finally, reviewers such as company executives may need to see the final layout—with text and visuals together—in order to verify that the piece will convey the desired product or company positioning and brand image.

A frequent hurdle in managing reviews is motivating reviewers to complete their work on time. As one way to approach this situation, tell reviewers that if you do not receive their comments by the due date, you will interpret their silence as implied approval of the copy in its current form.

**Instruct reviewers.** To obtain more useful comments from reviewers, provide a checklist or cover memo of instructions that accompanies each draft (Figure 4.2). Without guidance, reviewers may assume that any and all aspects of the draft are open for comment. You'll likely receive feedback that is irrelevant or inappropriately focused, or that contradicts comments from others.

---

**Checklist of Essential Copy Reviews**

---

Compliance with the document plan and creative brief

Technical completeness and accuracy of information

Critical details, e.g., product names, trademark notation, mathematical equations, code examples

Audience understanding

Messages and brand

Writing style and copy editing

Captions and images

Legal review

Production testing for Web content and electronic media

---

*Figure 4.2 At a minimum, you will want to ensure that all marcom documents receive these essential reviews.*

You may want to identify an "information freeze" date in the document plan—a point past which you will not accept major changes to the content. Make sure reviewers understand the relative costs—in time and expense—of changes made at each point in the document's development (this explanation can go a long way to discourage last-minute "tweaking" by a company president).

## *Handling Reviewer Comments*

Different reviewers will likely provide different types of comments (Figure 4.3). Realize that reviewers won't always provide the type or amount of comments you may want for a piece. Some reviewers may never look at the draft, some will read only a portion, while others will wait until the last minute and give it only a cursory look. Comments may be vague and incomplete, or at the other extreme, the reviewer may return a complete (and usually poor) rewrite of the text.

You will need to make a judgment call when selecting which reviewer comments to incorporate in the document. It is usually helpful to have another person (often the product manager) designated as the "referee" who can negotiate with reviewers who make conflicting inputs to the draft.

Of course, like any writer who works in an organization, you'll need to develop a thick skin when reading comments. Understand that a draft returned with a substantial amount of edits may not be an indicator of poor writing. Instead, the product positioning or information may have changed between the time you wrote the draft and when it was reviewed. Learn to accept suggested changes as an opportunity to strengthen your knowledge or writing skills.

---

**Typical Reviewers for Marketing Materials**

| | |
|---|---|
| Project Owner | A product manager, marketing communications manager, marketing director, or other person who has primary responsibility for developing and managing the project. Checks the draft against the document plan or outline; reviews overall quality and completeness of the information presented. May negotiate with other reviewers to resolve conflicting inputs. |
| Subject-Matter Expert (SME) | Product managers, engineers, sales reps, and other company personnel who are knowledgeable about the product, issue, or topic. A project may have multiple SMEs who make different types of reviews. SMEs check for accuracy and completeness of the information presented in the piece. |

---

| Typical Reviewers for Marketing Materials (*continued*) | |
|---|---|
| Copy Editor | Verifies adherence to company standards for grammar, usage, style, brand presentation, and similar issues. |
| Marketing Manager | Marcom or PR manager; sometimes head of marketing. Checks for presentation of key messages and brand for product and company. Also may verify suitability of the piece for the target audience and communications objective. |
| Customer Contact | A person at the customer site who can review and approve case studies and other projects that include customer information. Verifies accuracy of information and adherence to the customer's company standards. |
| Corporate Attorney | In-house or external attorney. Checks text for inappropriate claims, correct trademark usage, and compliance with laws or company standards. |
| Company Executive | In large companies, approves high-visibility pieces; in small companies, approves all marketing materials. |

*Figure 4.3 Reviewers can play many roles and provide many types of comments for marketing materials.*

## THE CONCEPT: IDENTIFYING APPROACHES TO CONTENT

*The obscure we see eventually,
the patently obvious takes a little longer.*
—*Edward R. Murrow*

You have created a document plan and completed the research and interviews. You are ready to start writing. But how can you work with your notes and background information to find an approach that will best translate this raw content into a first draft of the document's copy?

Begin by looking at the document plan. Which document type have you selected? What is the objective and purpose for this document? What is the target audience, their knowledge and interests? Clear answers to these questions will help you choose the most relevant information from the source material, and organize it effectively.

Another approach is to look at what the raw information is telling you. Does it have a theme, repeating motifs, a stream of events, an anecdote or phrase that really caught your attention when you first read or heard it? You may be able to use this theme, story, or language as a focal point for organizing the document's content. Use this technique to generate several ideas for a document's concept.

In some cases, an appropriate concept will be determined by the document type. For example, sales materials need a concept that will deliver the key messages with the greatest impact. In addition, consider the synergy between copy and visuals or multimedia elements in developing a strong concept.

Blundell suggests several techniques for identifying a good concept:[1]

**Extrapolation.** What is the real underlying story? What could this mean? What non-obvious conclusions could be drawn from this information?

**Synthesis.** This technique is like working a jigsaw puzzle. Look for the commonality in the inputs; identify how to bring them together into a cohesive whole. Find a theme.

**Localization.** Tailor the material to the audience's particular interests, motivations, problems, and needs. Describe the microcosm. Look for personal drama and human interest. (*Note*: This use of "localization" does not mean translation and adaptation of materials into another language, which is the common definition for this term in relation to high-tech products. See Chapter 9.)

**Globalization.** Show the big picture. Describe the larger trends that influence specific circumstances. Show the range or evolution of events.

**Projection.** Describe where a trend or situation could lead.

**Viewpoint Switching.** Show the different views on an issue in a point-counterpoint format. Identify the different players in an event. Describe differences in impact or results of a plan or activity.

**Progression.** Show a chronology or sequence of events, ideas, or other items. What sense of movement can you detect in your material?

In addition, Marra suggests these techniques:[2]

- Make associations based on features, form, content, size, applications, selling factors, benefits, behaviors, or reversal (i.e., describe what something is not).
- Make connections based on one or more senses, either through direct or reverse association. Use analogy and metaphor.
- Create a framework, then see how the information fits.
- Go from this to that; show change and movement.

To spark your concepts, see Chapters 5 through 7 for more ideas on specific techniques used in high-tech marcom materials.

### Recognizing a Good Concept

When you have identified several possible concepts, don't judge them immediately. Instead begin writing some text as a way to explore each concept until you find one that best fits the content, audience, and document plan.

A well-defined concept makes any writing task easier because it helps you select the best material for the document and ignore the remainder. These criteria will help you evaluate the suitability of a concept:

- Does the concept fit the medium, messages, objective, and purpose of the document? Does it work for both text and visuals?
- Will the concept be appropriate and understandable to the target audience? Does it reflect the right style and tone?
- Is the concept compatible with the marcom plan, creative platform, and document plan?
- Does the concept help you identify information that fits the document's focus? Present information accurately? Eliminate irrelevant information?

In addition, check your own interest level and ease when you are writing text to explore a possible concept. If the words come easily and if you become excited about what you are writing, you may have found a successful concept.

*Caution*: When choosing a concept, watch out for your own biases, whether they are based on too much knowledge about the subject matter or on your own opinions and life experiences. An easy way to check for bias is to ask: Will this concept makes sense and be acceptable to the target audience?

### Deciding What to Leave Out

While it may seem contradictory, deciding what to leave out of a particular piece can help you decide what to put in. Use these factors to select information appropriately:

- Is the information extraneous to the main theme or focus of the document? Eliminate it completely or place it in a sidebar.
- Does the information appear in another document in the collateral set, or is it widely known or easily obtainable from another source? If yes, provide references to print sources or Web links.
- Is the information appropriate for the target audience or for the role of the document in the sales cycle? You may have perfectly wonderful information that just needs to find a better home.
- Would the information be better presented in a different format? If yes, does that mean putting the information in another document, or adjusting the format of the one under consideration? Is the information best suited to electronic presentation only?

While you want to ensure that a document is tightly focused, remember one caution when selecting text to eliminate: What will readers assume about the information you don't present? Consumer marketing research has shown that when readers make inferences about missing information, they will exaggerate the importance of information they don't know, or will underestimate the strength or benefit of these missing factors. And, for better or worse, readers may assume something about a product based on their knowledge of competitive products or the product category.[3]

## *Learn from Others*

One good way to learn new approaches and techniques for content is to mimic what someone else has done. Keep a clippings file of example pieces and Web pages that you think show good forms of marketing writing. Even materials for products outside of your industry can be sources for inspiration. Also, keep the drafts you have rejected in earlier projects. For example, a paragraph that is too obtuse for a sales brochure may be perfect for a technical article.

## WRITING STYLE FOR HIGH-TECH MARCOM

Style is your choice of words, the way you structure a sentence, and how you organize information. However, as a marketing writer, you will likely develop a repertoire of styles, using them as appropriate for different audiences and different pieces. Sometimes your writing will be very formal, with a defined structure and word choices that are based on very precise meanings. In another piece, the style will be more informal, with sentences and word choices that are close to spoken conversation.

Your company may already have a publication style guide or standards for print documents and Web content. A style guide specifies the standards for writing and design style, as well as tone, word usage and other creative issues in print materials and Web content.

## *Choosing a Writing Style*

When choosing the writing style for a particular document, consider the purpose, audience, and subject matter. By necessity, the writing style will vary to accommodate the differences among the three marcom purposes: motivation, information, or persuasion. Writing style may also need to reflect the communication style of the target audience or your company's standards for formality.

The nature of a document's subject matter also will be a significant factor in the choice of writing style. After all, you would not use the same style to present highly technical research findings in a white paper as you would to describe the features of a software program for children in a sales brochure.

For projects such as image advertising or a corporate capabilities brochure, the writing style may reflect the company's personality, such as highly technical, business-oriented, or creative. For example, think of the differences in corporate personality that are typically attributed to IBM (conservative, businesslike) and Apple Computer (innovative, fun). In contrast, a non-promotional style is required for press materials. This writing style must be straightforward, focused on facts, clear, precise, and more neutral than the style used for sales materials.

No matter which writing style you use, apply it consistently throughout the piece. For example, switching from a very formal, corporate style to an informal style within a brochure or distinct area of a Web site would be very disconcerting for the reader. The change in style would prompt him to focus on how the information is presented, not on what it says. This guideline also applies to the tone of your writing. For example, don't use a very serious tone in one paragraph, then make an attempt at irreverent humor in the next.

A project plan should specify the writing style in order to:

- Ensure the style is appropriate for the document's purpose, audience, and content.
- Provide a reference point for checking draft copy.
- Avoid the discontinuity of style that occurs when multiple writers contribute to a document or when Web content is written separately from print material.

Figure 4.4 shows examples of how writing style might be defined for typical projects.

|  | Sales Brochure | White Paper | How-to Article |
|---|---|---|---|
| Audience | Consumers | Technical staff | Business customers |
| Structure and usage | Informal | Formal | Formal to somewhat informal |
| Tone | Friendly, personable, upbeat, helpful | Knowledgeable, dispassionate, analytical, factual | Informative, educational |
| Emphasis | Information and motivation | Information and persuasion | Information |

*Figure 4-4  Example definitions of writing style.*

To learn how to write in different styles, analyze an effective document and determine how to apply its style to your material.

### Structure and Usage in Marcom Style

Many people describe writing style as the degree of formality in grammar and word usage: from very rigid to very casual or anywhere between. For marcom, writing style is usually described as formal or informal.

**Formal.** A corporate, academic, or journalistic style that is informative, educational, or analytical. A formal writing style often uses third person to convey objectivity and sometimes makes heavy use of passive voice. Sentence and paragraph structure adhere strictly to the rules of grammar. Material organization is logical and consistent, and may follow a defined format for document elements. Word choices are careful and precise, with consistent usage of a selective vocabulary. *The worldwide restructuring of businesses and business relationships... further promotes the adoption of internetworking technology.*[4]

**Informal.** A casual, sometimes unconventional style that often resembles the patterns of conversation. An informal writing style typically uses first and second person with active voice to address the reader directly. Sentence and paragraph structure can vary within a document, usually with less rigid adherence to the rules of grammar. Material organization is determined primarily by the overall creative plan for the piece, including tight integration of copy with visuals. Word choices allow flexibility for using synonyms, colloquialisms, and emotionally charged words based on creative appeal and effectiveness in conveying the document's messages. *The result? A line of applications designed to work the way you do.*[5]

### Tone in Marcom Style

Tone is what Cappon describes as "the inner music of words... clusters of associations and images that lurk just below the surface."[6] Tone describes how the text will resonate for the target audience—how your writing will "feel."[7] It can be described by words such as *upbeat, empathetic, knowledgeable, precise,* or *conservative.*

Tone is achieved cumulatively through the combined effect of the content itself, its presentation format, and your specific word choices.

The tone of your writing must be compatible with the structure and usage in the document's defined writing style. For example, a very formal structure and usage would dampen the impact of a tone that was intended to convey excitement and energy. In a persuasion or motivation piece, it is especially important to match tone to the nature of your message and expectations of the audience in order to gain acceptance.[8]

Tone also must be congruent across Web and print material as well as consistent with the purpose of each document (Figure 4.5).

| Purpose | Tone |
| --- | --- |
| Motivation | Confident, upbeat, friendly, inspirational. *And we're prepared to offer you PhotoStyler – and MORE – at exciting savings.*[9] |
| Information | Knowledgeable, businesslike, instructive. *AutoInstall enables the router to learn its address and host information automatically... in a process that can be controlled by a network administrator from a central location.*[4] |
| Persuasion | Dispassionate or aggressive, advocative or empathetic. *At Microsoft we recognize the strategic importance of the messaging infrastructure in solving our customers' current problems and meeting their long-term communication and workgroup application needs.*[10] |

*Figure 4.5  Examples of how tone can reflect a document's purpose.*

## Emphasis in Marcom Style

The final element of a marketing writing style is the choice of what is emphasized in the document's content, whether it appears in print or online. For example, content in a data sheet typically emphasizes technical details, while a capabilities brochure might emphasize the company's overall messages. Like the choice of tone, emphasis also varies according to the document's purpose (Figure 4.6).

| Purpose | Emphasis |
|---|---|
| Motivation | Clear statement of the benefits, call to action, offers, and incentives. *And since it's backed by our 30-day money-back guarantee, you have nothing to lose by giving Saber LAN Workstation a try!*[11] |
| Information | Clarity, accuracy, and completeness of the subject matter and its appropriateness to the reader's interests, needs, and prior knowledge or experience. *Keep track of your images with a built-in file management system – you can add keywords and descriptions, browse through thumbnails, retrieve files, and more.*[12] |
| Persuasion | Delivery of messages or advocacy of an issue or viewpoint. *But let me give you the specifics about these new programs, and then you'll understand for yourself why I'm so excited about them.*[13] |

*Figure 4.6 Emphasis in selected text can convey the document's purpose.*

## Writing Style for Web Content

Brand and positioning considerations usually make it important to maintain a consistency of writing style in both print materials and Web content. Some Web marketers—consciously or not—apply a very different style and tone to the content of a Web site than they use in print materials. When writing or adapting content for a Web site, ask these questions to determine the appropriate style and tone:

- What are the expectations and sensitivities of the target audiences?
- What sense of the product, program, or organization do you want to create in the visitor's mind?
- Is this the same sense that you create with print materials?
- Do you want to carry over the same style and tone from print materials to Web pages, or create a different sense on the Web?

### WORKING WITH GRAPHIC AND WEB DESIGNERS

Designers and writers often work together through the development of a marcom document, from searching for the initial concept to performing a press check or testing the Web pages. This development process usually involves three stages: visual concept, text draft and comprehensive (comp) layout, and final artwork or Web pages. Expect many iterations of ideas and drafts in each stage, with many joint brainstorming sessions in person, by phone, or by email.

The *concept stage* defines the overall approach to the layout and organization of the project. For a print document, choices are made for format, size, and major visual and copy elements. For Web content, this stage determines text, images and multimedia elements, links to other pages or sites, and programming requirements such as data forms, customized displays, or scripts.

At the *comp stage*, the writer and designer develop this concept further with a detailed layout for a print document or storyboards for Web pages. A rough sample of the final document or Web content may be produced at this stage.

At the *draft stage*, the headlines, body copy, visuals, and other elements are complete. In a print document, the designer makes a trial layout to test for copy fit. For Web content, the designer makes a preliminary layout of the page(s), with placeholders for links, scripts, and multimedia elements. Additional text elements such as pull quotes may be identified at this point; so too, different or additional visuals or multimedia elements. In successive drafts, the designer and writer cooperate on a continuous refinement of copy and layout; for a Web site, links and content flow.

*Tip*: Before a document goes to press or is posted online, proofread the final layout carefully and completely. Missing text, incorrect symbols, misspellings in last-minute edits, and reversed images are among the errors that can be introduced in the layout stage.

Writers and designers can work together to ensure the copy and visuals reinforce each other. For example, an advertisement that shows a photo of gears used the words "gear up," "mesh," and "whole works" in the headlines or body copy.[14]

For writers, working with a designer is an interactive, give-and-take process. Don't be afraid to offer suggestions on layout or visuals, but watch for your own subjectivity and respect the expertise and judgment of the designer. In return, be gracious about accepting a designer's suggestions on copy elements or content. If appropriate, offer to support the designer's presentation of concepts to company management. A joint presentation with a well-considered rationale for a concept can substantially defuse the subjectivity of the managers who must approve the project.

## RESOURCES

The recommended books and other resources listed below provide additional information on the topics discussed in this chapter. For an updated list, visit **writinghightech.com**.

### *Books*

Michael Schumacher: *Writer's Complete Guide to Conducting Interviews.* Writer's Digest Books, 1993. Covers interview techniques for book authors and writers of general-interest magazine articles. Contains useful information on structuring interviews, working with quotes, and legal and ethical considerations for using information.

## REFERENCES

[1] William E. Blundell: *The Art and Craft of Feature Writing.* New York: Plume, 1988

[2] James L. Marra: *Advertising Creativity: Techniques for Generating Ideas.* New York: Prentice-Hall, 1990

[3] Ruth Ann Smith: "Inferential Processes in Consumer Response to Marketing Communications: Review and Directions for Research" in *Marketing Communications: Theory and Research.* Chicago: American Marketing Association, 1985

[4] Article in customer magazine, Cisco Systems, Inc.

[5] Product brochure, Microsoft Corp.

[6] Rene J. Cappon: *The Associated Press Guide to News Writing.* New York: Prentice-Hall, 1991

[7] Bruce Bendinger: *The Copy Workshop Workbook.* Chicago: The Copy Workshop, 1988

[8] Theodore A. Rees Cheney: *Getting the Words Right: How to Revise, Edit & Rewrite.* Cincinnati, OH: Writer's Digest Books, 1983

[9] Direct mail letter, Aldus Corp.

[10] White paper, Microsoft Corp.

[11] Direct mail letter, Saber Software Corp.

[12] Product line brochure, Wellfleet Communications, Inc.

[13] Direct mail letter, Citadel Computer Systems, Inc.

[14] Product ad, Alcatel Network Systems

# PART 2

# WRITING A HIGH-TECH MARCOM DOCUMENT

The chapters in this part cover techniques and ideas you can use every day in developing marketing materials. The information presented here will guide you through all components of a marcom project:

- Determining the best way to organize and communicate content.
- Using techniques that will add power and impact to your words.
- Handling legal and ethical concerns.
- Adapting your materials and messages for international markets.

You may first want to evaluate your existing materials against the section "Common Mistakes in High-Tech Copy" in Chapter 7. If you find that your materials contain any of these problems, the information and guidelines presented in this part will give you many ways to overcome them.

# 5

# DOCUMENT ELEMENTS

## PACKAGING INFORMATION FOR GREATER IMPACT

This chapter describes how to organize content to make the best use of the different document elements available in a printed piece or on a Web page. Not all of these elements will be appropriate for every document. Use the information in this chapter as a selection of ideas from which you can pick and choose based on the objective, purpose, audience, content types, and visual design for each project.

The document elements are described in this section in the same order in which they appear in most marketing materials. Many of these elements can be adapted for Web content, but this chapter also discusses elements that are unique to online presentation.

### CHOOSING DOCUMENT ELEMENTS

Some decisions about which elements to use in a particular document will already be made for you, typically by constraints of corporate style, document design, a trade publication's requirements, or production factors. But when you have a choice of which elements to use, select them carefully for each project based on these factors:

- Type of document, overall document design, and length
- Clarity of presentation; maintaining a flow of ideas while presenting necessary but tangential information appropriately
- Continuity of the document's theme or story
- Impact of visual or multimedia elements and their ability to present a message with richer meaning

Another approach is to consider which messages or parts of the story you want to emphasize through repetition. Then choose the document elements that will best present those points in multiple, compatible ways.

## HEADLINES AND SUBHEADS

Headlines (or titles) and subheadlines (subheads) are your first opportunity to "sell" a piece to the reader. These elements catch a reader's attention, enticing her to stop and read more.

Considering that readers often skim sales materials, a fresh headline is especially important for ads, Web content, brochures, articles, and direct-mail letters. Sometimes the headline and subheads may be all she reads, making it even more important they do a good job of conveying a high-impact message. With careful use of the headline and subheads, you also can guide the reader through the document and build multiple messages (see Chapter 3).

A headline or subhead can accommodate any type of information, but several types are common.

**Feature/benefit statement.** Present the product's most important feature or benefit. *The customizable interface makes working in Aldus FreeHand quick and easy.*[1]

**News announcement.** *HP Expands Its Planet Partners Printing Supplies Return and Recycling Program.*[2]

**How-to.** *A Guide to Planning a Wide-Area Network.*[3]

**Call to action.** *Give Us a Few Minutes and $199.95 and We'll Network Your Small Business.*[4]

**Reason-why.** *Ten reasons to choose…*

**Testimonial.** *"I was so blown away by Norton Desktop."*[5]

**Teaser.** An approach where you use the headline to setup the teaser, then deliver the payoff or punchline in the opener of the body copy. *If You're Looking for the Best Solutions to Your Computing Needs, Just Look Inside.*[6]

Subheads are an effective way to guide a reader through the document by serving as section labels for lengthy blocks of body copy. Subheads also can:

- Expand on the major message presented in the headline.[7]
- Explain the topic of an article or white paper, or state a benefit the reader can gain from the document.
- Present secondary messages or incrementally build the primary message. Look at just the subheads, separately from the rest of the text, to determine if they will be engaging and understandable to a skimming reader. Apply this same technique to other elements that stand-out when viewing a document, such as captions, callouts, pull quotes, visuals, and links.
- Carry through the tone and theme set by the headline.

Another type of headline is an overline, which provides a lead-in to the main headline. Also called a cutline, it usually appears above the main headline, set in a smaller type size, with a different color, or an underline.

Use the following techniques to create high-impact headlines and subheads.

**Keep it short.** Make both the headline and the subheads short, in active voice, and use a verb. Watch out for lengthy headlines and subheads; the purpose of these elements is to draw in the reader, not deliver the entire message all at once.

**Direct or indirect?** Decide whether the headline should make a direct statement or an indirect allusion to what you're selling or its benefits.[8] While the examples earlier in this section show a variety of ways to make a direct statement, this example shows the use of indirect allusion in a headline for an appointment-book software product: *Seize the Day.*[9]

**Connect the content.** Look for words or phrases in the body copy that summarize the section or the entire piece. Repeating those words in the headline and subheads will add emphasis to their meaning. Also look for ways to match the text in the headline to what is depicted in any visuals in the document. This technique can yield the kind of creative synergy that makes a piece memorable. For example, a brochure that uses the headline: *Explore the World of Connectivity with Reflection Software* included images of cruise ships, maps, and passport stamps as well as other navigation references in the copy.[10]

Look at the text techniques in Chapter 7 for ideas on adding interest to headlines. For an ad or other sales document, try one of the highly creative techniques such as imagery, alliteration, word play, humor, or emotion. Techniques such as parallelism and asking questions can be effective for subheads. To find the best technique for a particular piece, experiment with different headlines to identify which technique is most effective for the document.

The number of headline levels can affect the clarity and visual appeal of a document. For most marcom documents, use no more than three levels for headlines and subheads. If you think you need more levels, determine whether the text can be formatted into a bullet list, placed in a sidebar, or presented in a table.

## OPENERS

In a marcom piece the opener must capture the reader's interest immediately with clear, enticing prose that leads naturally into the body copy. A good opener also sets the mood and gives the reader a preview of the document's information. Whether it is a sentence, a paragraph, or a section, the opener is usually the most important, yet always seems like the most difficult part of the piece to write. Try the techniques below for writing a seductive and fluid opener.

**State the key message or benefit.** Tell the reader immediately your most compelling sales point. This is a common opener for ads, brochures, and other sales pieces. *QuickTime software makes it as easy to incorporate dynamic data into documents as it is to paste graphics into text.*[11]

**Summarize the theme or discussion with the 5Ws.** Use the opener to present information like a news story—any combination of Who, What, When, Where, Why, and even How. *ADC Kentrox will demonstrate a new broadband RF access and transport system at Wireless '93 in Dallas TX, March 2-4, 1993.*[12] The 5Ws is the opener for the inverted pyramid technique, a staple of press releases and news articles.

This technique gives the reader a clear, high-level snapshot of the content in the piece. It moves the story from the broad overview of the opener to greater levels of detail in the body copy—from most important to least important. Be careful to include only the most essential information in this type of opener; you don't need to tell the reader everything in the opening sentence or paragraph. Also, use the opener to emphasize the most important W—usually the who or what—before explaining the when, where, why, and how in the body copy.[13]

**Make an announcement, indicate a change or new development.** *A new IC that can bring compact disc (CD)-quality sound to broadcasting, multimedia, and other audio/visual applications has been introduced by Texas Instruments.*[14] As shown with this example, state the most important message first—don't let the reader get distracted by a subsidiary clause that contains less important information. If you announce something new in the opening sentence, you may want to compare that with previous versions later in the piece.

**Describe a problem or challenge.** *Too many people, too much equipment, and not enough space. These were the challenges facing...*[15] This type of opener is particularly effective in case studies or other documents where the description of a problem and solution or application is the primary content type.

**Give a new definition.** Defining a term or idea in a new way can be a fresh approach for presenting a message or product that may have become so commonplace it seems nothing new can be said about it. *There are many definitions of open computing. Digital's definition is the broadest: open computing means open technology, open business practices, and open services.*[16] The trick is to create a new perspective in the opener that will cause the reader to say "I hadn't thought of it that way before." An analogy or metaphor may be appropriate for this type of opener (see the section "Using Imagery" in Chapter 7).

**Pose a question.** Questions are a great way to stop a reader's roving eye and prompt him to read on to find the answer. But don't word the question so that the answer is glaringly obvious. You want to intrigue the reader, not make him feel like he's about to take a quiz. Ask open-ended questions such as *Have you ever … ?* or *What if … ?*

**Lead with a quote.** Use an incisive quote from a customer, industry analyst, or a product review. *"Ever since I was put in charge of fund-raising for the zoo, the Microsoft PowerPoint presentation graphics program has become my most important partner."*[17]

Storytelling techniques make for great openers in articles, case studies, and sometimes backgrounders and white papers.

**Set the scene.** Describe a work place, the circumstances around an event, the difficulty of a person's task, or other elements that depict a situation, activity, idea, or challenge. Help the reader visualize what has happened, or the environment in which the story takes place. *Paper-making machines, three stories high and as long as a football field, turn hundreds of thousands of tons of pulp into fine writing, copy, computer, and tissue paper each year at Boise Cascade's St. Helens mill.*[18]

**Present a history.** Summarize the previous developments, events, or decisions that have led to the current situation. This type of opener should answer the questions: Why this topic? Why now?

**Show a diary.** Present a log or timeline to describe events or activities that occur in a sequence or over time. You can make the whole first section a diary, or sprinkle log entries throughout the piece. Just be sure to state the chronology of events correctly. *9:05 p.m. Field technicians work carefully, aware they must perform flawlessly. 9:18 p.m. The moment of truth. The first cell site is online.*[19]

**Tell a human-interest story.** Open with an anecdote based on a real person, activity, or situation. If you use a composite or hypothetical tale, identify it clearly as fiction (see Chapter 8). Choose an anecdote that is relevant to the audience and message. *When Don*

*Glor came to work on the morning of September 15, he'd never used a database before. Two hours later he'd developed his first application…*[20]

How long should the opener be? It can be anywhere from a single sentence to two or three paragraphs—whatever length you need to create a context for readers and hook them into reading further. Be careful that you don't pack too much information into the opener. Remember that other elements of the piece can present your points with just as much impact. These are other problems to avoid in openers:

- Dull recitations of fact.
- Generalities: Broad, bland statements won't give the reader sufficient clues about the subject of the piece, or an interest in continuing to read it.
- Unbelievable claims or scenarios.
- Clichés and vulgarity.

It can be very difficult to write a powerful opener when you begin a project. One trick is to write the opener last. When the draft is complete, look through the text for a phrase or sentence that could make a great opener.

## BODY COPY

In every marcom document (with the exception of some ads) most of your writing effort will be focused on the body copy—the narrative text that provides the detailed information about the product, service, event, announcement, or viewpoint.

For the most part, write the body copy in a clear, straightforward, expository style. Use active voice, present tense, and specific language—but also pay attention to sustaining a style and tone that is unified with the other elements in the piece (see Chapter 4). You also can apply a reasonable mix of the ideas suggested in this chapter and in Chapter 7 to make the body copy more interesting to the reader.

Several additional guidelines are also effective for writing body copy.

**Connect your points.** The lead sentence or paragraph should specifically connect the idea or message of the headline or sub-head with the body copy in that section.

**Show importance.** Structure the body copy so it presents the points or messages in order of importance. Remember that a reader may not read the entire piece, and indeed won't if the first few paragraphs seem boring, irrelevant, or difficult to understand.

**Show the direction of the piece.** Give the reader an idea of where the ideas are going through the subheads or lead sentence of each paragraph or section. The information in the body copy should flow logically from one sentence or paragraph to the next.

**Use transitions.** Phrases such as *More importantly, In addition, However,* and *As an alternative* help the reader move from one sentence or paragraph to the next and provide a continuity as the focus or message shifts. This type of transition is usually internal to a section of a document. An "external" transition helps the reader shift from one section to another, usually because of a change in topic, content type, narrator, time reference, setting, or story focus.[21]

## PULL QUOTES

Pull quotes typically appear in a box that is embedded in the body copy. They highlight an interesting or controversial statement or quote from the text and are designed to entice a skimming reader to stop and read the entire piece.

Pull quotes are a good way to emphasize key messages, benefits, customer testimonials, or applications. You can adapt pull quotes to marcom documents such as sales materials, articles, and case studies.

## SIDEBARS

Sidebars are very useful elements for presenting information that supplements or amplifies the main content of a document. A sidebar can present information that doesn't quite fit into the body copy but which will be of interest to readers. For example, a technical analysis article may include a case study in a sidebar to show how the technology has been applied in a customer's environment.

Sidebars can present information targeted to a specific category of readers. They are also ideal for short glossaries, resource listings, event timelines, specifications, and other detailed information that would be cumbersome to read in the document's body copy. In layout, a sidebar is often presented in a box with shading, a different color, or other design that visually distinguishes it from the body copy.

It is important not to overuse sidebars for two reasons. First, sidebars distract readers from the main document and make it more difficult to follow the theme or story. Second, it is tempting to include extraneous sidebars. For example, an article might benefit from a resource list, but it may be easier for the reader to use the resources if they appear in the most appropriate place in the body copy. Or, instead of including product specifications as a sidebar in a white paper, it may be better to refer the reader to a data sheet.

## BULLET AND NUMBER LISTS

Bullet and number lists are useful elements for a variety of purposes:

- Breaking up long blocks of narrative text, making it easier to read (bullet or number lists).
- Presenting related points that would make a sentence too long and difficult to understand (bullet lists).
- Specifying sequences, rankings, or priorities (number lists).
- Summarizing key points in the section or the brochure as a whole (bullet list).

As much as possible, use the same sentence structure within the list. For example, start each list item with an action verb or an adjective. Avoid using the same word to start each item; this will distract readers. Instead, put that word into the lead-in phrase for the list.

Give the reader a clear indication of the list content. This indicator can be a title (when the list appears in a sidebar or table):

*Ten Methods for Processing Transactions More Efficiently*
Or the lead-in text (when the list is in body copy):
**Methods for processing transactions more efficiently include the following:**

## INVOLVEMENT DEVICES

Worksheets, checklists, and questionnaires are examples of involvement devices—elements that encourage active reading of the piece. Involvement devices are very effective for helping the reader understand how a product could be applied to her own situation. They are commonly used in brochures, direct-mail packages, and as a salesperson's tool for a face-to-face customer meeting.

## CLOSERS

> *I always know the ending; that's where I start.*
> —*Toni Morrison*

You have a snappy opening, well-crafted body copy, attention-grabbing headlines, and... and... no idea about how to close the piece. The closing sentence, paragraph, or section of a document can be nearly as important as the opener because it is often one of the few parts of the document that a reader will actually read. You don't want to waste the excellent opportunity that a closer provides to reinforce key messages and make the piece memorable.

The type of closer should be determined in part by the purpose of the piece. If the purpose is information, use the closer to restate the key message. If the purpose is persuasion, the opener and closer must be strong and work together. Don't use the closer to present a new argument or bit of evidence. Instead, use the closer to restate your position or to summarize your arguments and evidence.[22] Finally, if the purpose for the document is motivation, use the closer to present a call to action (see the next section for details on this document element).

Writing a closer can be tough, especially if you actually put off writing it until five minutes before deadline. The techniques below will help you write closers that ensure the text carries a punch right until the very end.

**Echo the opener.** Repeating the language or structure of the opener creates a sense of verbal echo that reinforces the key message and makes it easier for the reader to remember. If you use one of the techniques for openers described earlier in this chapter, using the same technique for the closer can be very effective. In the example below, notice how the words *answers, puzzling, questions,* and *growing* in the opener are reflected in the closer with *solved, challenging, puzzle, grow.*

Opener (in the form of a headline): *How Q&A Answers the Puzzling Questions of a Growing Business.*

Closer: *"You know, when I think about it, Q&A was the most valuable investment we ever made. Because it solved our company's most challenging puzzle: how to get organized and grow."*[5]

**Use a quote.** Presenting a quote from the subject or source in the piece is one of the most common forms of a closer. To be effective, the quote must be a powerful statement that summarizes or ties together the points made in the body copy.

**Review the key messages.** A summary of key marketing messages can be presented in a sentence, paragraph, or a bullet list.

**Wrap it up.** Take the final discussion presented in the body copy to its logical conclusion or tell the end of an anecdote that appears elsewhere in the document.

**Present a call to action.** An action closer won't be appropriate to all document types, but it is the most common for sales collateral.

**Look to the future.** Discuss potential trends, outcomes, or directions that could result from the topics or examples covered in the piece. Your projections must be reasonable; if you indulge in unrealistic speculation you could cause a reader to view your earlier assertions or information with skepticism.

**Offer an opinion or give advice.** Stating a position or making recommendations is a common closer in analyses, how-to articles, and white papers.

The following tips will make writing closers an easier task.

**Write the closer first.** "But wait," you say. "How can I write the closer if I don't have the rest of the piece written yet?" It doesn't matter. Writing a closer early in the process can help you structure the body copy, or at the very least, give you something to work with once the rest of the piece is complete.

**Write the closer at the same time you write the opener.** This is a great way to ensure that you come full circle in a piece by rephrasing the opener, referring back to it, or presenting its logical conclusion.

**Adapt one of your rejected openers.** Remember that writing an opener is no picnic either. Save all your rejected ideas about openers and revisit them when writing the closer. Can you use any of the phrasing or approaches contained in the rejected openers?

**Look at the last paragraph or two of the document.** Could you simply end the text there? Is good closer text already somewhere else in the document?

## CALL TO ACTION

Every sales piece (and many other marketing documents) should have a call to action—a phrase or sentence that encourages the reader to buy the product or take the next step in the sales process. Otherwise, the reader may not be motivated to take that step or, worse yet, not know how to do so.

The call to action typically appears as the closing text in a piece, although it can also appear:

- In a separate box or graphical element
- In the same format as a subhead
- As a *P.S.* on a sales letter

Particularly in a sales letter, direct mail package, or Web page intended to motivate a purchase, the call to action will appear in multiple places and forms. This repetition reinforces the value of the product or offer and can accelerate a purchase decision by the reader.

Typical actions include calling a toll-free number to order the product, contacting a salesperson or dealer, visiting a specific URL on a Web site, or sending email to request more information.

A call to action becomes more powerful if it reinforces the key benefit or message. For example, this call to action reinforces a key benefit: *Let us tell you more about how our product can solve your financial problems. Call us today at...*.

All too many call to action statements read like this: *For more information call (800) 555-DULL.* To be effective, the call to action should give readers something specific to do, and good reason for doing it. A call to action typically has two parts: an offer and instructions on what the reader must do to accept that offer (see Chapter 6 for more information on offers).

In any call to action, present telephone numbers, an email address, and a Web URL. This choice will allow readers to use their preferred means of contact, and will serve both domestic and international prospects. On a Web page, the call to action can link to an online order form, inquiry form, or email address.

*Caution:* Many ads and sales documents include a toll-free telephone number that a reader can call to place an order or request product information. But toll-free numbers present two problems for international prospects. First, many toll-free numbers work only within the home country, meaning they are unreachable by cross-border callers. Second, because of time zone and language differences, many international prospects prefer to make inquiries by email or a Web form.

Always include all the ways a potential customer can reach you: local and international toll-free, direct-dial, and fax numbers; Web URL and email addresses; and postal addresses for the company headquarters or local sales office.

### Call to Action on a Web Page

On a Web site, state the call to action on every page that leads to the online sale, event registration, or other action you want the visitor to take. For an e-commerce Web site, the call to action is usually presented with a simple button or link. But the text in and around this button or link can strengthen a visitor's motivation to make an online purchase. For example:

*Upgrade today to Adobe PhotoShop CS for only $169*[23]

## VISUALS

Should a writer be concerned only with words? Not if you really want to inform, persuade, or motivate a reader. Knowing how to use visuals effectively can enhance the words in any document.

Creating and presenting visuals in a document is both a distinct talent and an area for in-depth study. In most cases, you will work with a graphic designer to select and create visuals. A large number of graphic design books, magazines, and Web sites (see Resources) offer ideas and techniques that can help your knowledge of visual communication.

This section will help you understand how to use visuals effectively and how to write captions and other accompanying text. When working with visuals, keep in mind the legal and ethical considerations described in Chapter 8 and the international considerations described in Chapter 9.

### *Types of Visuals*

> *Neither text nor graphic needs to tell*
> *every aspect of the story.*
> *Each can present what it tells best.*
> —Eric K. Meyer

In sales materials, visuals can be as important as the words in conveying information, creating a perception, or representing a brand. For any given document, there are many possible visuals: from "beauty shot" product photos and illustrative artwork to the more mundane—but often highly useful to readers—diagrams, flow charts, and data tables.

If your company has defined standards for marketing and PR documents, the number, type, size, placement, and style of visuals may already be defined for the project. Visuals may also be determined in the document plan or creative platform. In any case, the choice of visuals must consider audience needs and understanding, as well as appropriateness for print and online publication. Factors for budget, schedule, and production may also constrain the choice of graphics.

When using any visual, verify that its appearance and placement is correct on its own and in relation to the copy. Ensure that the image has the correct orientation and colors, and that all text in the image and caption is complete and accurate.

Be especially cautious when using stock images and text written to represent a fictitious customer or scenario. For example, an advertisement used a stock photo of Seattle to represent a generic city, but the accompanying text listed street names and other invented "facts" that simply do not exist in Seattle. (I know this because Seattle is my hometown.) Readers who see through this invention may, as a result, view the rest of the document with skepticism.

### Photographs and Illustrations

Photos may be sharp, realistic pictures or manipulated into a softer or more abstract depiction. Line drawings, schematics, sketches, and paintings are examples of illustrations.

**Product.** An image of hardware, a software screen shot, or an image of product code or example output.

**Use and application.** Visuals that show the product in operation or illustrate typical customer environments.

**Problem or need.** Representation of the common issues faced by a target customer.

**Metaphor.** Images that support any metaphor used in headlines or body copy.

**Abstraction.** You may want images that make an indirect or symbolic representation of the subject. Abstract images can set a mood, convey a style, or express subtle cultural cues. Icons are another form of abstract imagery.

**Positioning.** Visuals that subtly tell the reader the type of positioning you want to create for the product. These images may have little or no relation to the product itself, instead using visuals to make a positioning statement, reinforce the product or company brand, or explain a new technology concept.

**Logos**. Although not necessarily a photo or an illustration, present the company logo, product symbols, and other images that make up the organizational identity in a way that is consistent across both Web and print materials. Verify that logos meet any company brand standards for size, appearance and color, especially when appearing in a Web page or electronic document. This consistency can be important for protecting the trademark registration of the logo symbol.

### Diagrams

It seems no document about a technical product is complete without some sort of diagram. Whether showing a system or a network, a potential design or an actual deployment, diagrams can give an "at a glance" understanding of a product, its environment, or its use.

**Product design.** Product block diagrams to show architecture, components, or integration with third-party products.

**Network or system design.** Show the multiple components in a customer solution; also used for "before and after" scenarios.

**Installation, configuration, or application.** Show examples of implementation or options for use.

**Processes.** Show sequences or flows of processes or activities.

### Charts and Tables

Consider using a chart or table anytime you need to present a large amount of detailed information. Work with the designer and read the recommended books in the Resources section to identify the type of chart that will present the information clearly, accurately, and fairly.

**Data charts.** Bar, line, and pie graphs or data tables to show financial and other types of quantitative information.

**Organization charts.** Show company structure or job roles.

**Word charts.** Also called a matrix or table, a word chart presents categories of information in a structured, easy-to-reference format. A word chart can organize lists of features, benefits, specifications, options, pros and cons, or comparative information. They are often useful in brochures, ads, and backgrounders.

**Sidebars.** Although a sidebar may contain only text, it appears to readers as a visual because it is usually presented with a distinct, graphical layout. See the section earlier in this chapter for ideas about making the best use of sidebars.

### Infographics

Infographics combine pictures and words to tell a story. Popularized by the *USA Today* newspaper, infographics are now used in a variety of publications, marketing materials, and other documents. While infographics can take many forms, the following are common examples.

**How it works.** A pictorial depiction of a process, product, or system that shows operation for a particular task.

**Maps.** Geographic, structural, system design, or environment for installation.

**Event sequences.** Schedules, timelines, or event cycles.

**Processes**. A sequence graphic or flowchart showing steps, activities, and perhaps involved systems or personnel.

**Icons and symbols.** Focused depiction of a function, task, location, or other element in the visual.

## CAPTIONS AND CALLOUTS

You know that everyone looks at the pictures first, right? Sometimes the photographs, diagrams, charts, or other visuals are the only thing a reader may look at in the piece. Captions and callouts for visuals can be a great way to reinforce a message and entice a skimmer to read the full text.

A *caption* is a line of text that appears alongside or underneath the visual. On a Web page, captions and callouts can appear as a pop-up when the mouse pointer moves over an image. A *callout* is a small block of text with a line or arrow that points to a detail in the image. Both elements can be useful with images such as product pictures, configuration and architecture diagrams, charts, data tables, and schematics. *Legends* and *labels* define parts of visuals, such as the product type shown by a symbol or the meaning of differently colored lines. These elements are typically placed within the visual, although they may also appear in a boxed area adjacent to the image.

*Tip:* Attach a caption to all visuals you submit to a publication or include in press materials. This will make a journalist's job easier and increase the likelihood that your caption will be used verbatim.

Several guidelines are helpful when writing text for visuals.

**Keep them short.** Captions can be more than one line, but more than three lines may lose the reader. Callouts can be as short as a single word, or as long as a single sentence.

**Keep them relevant to the image.** You will confuse the reader if the caption or callout introduces new or conflicting information. The caption should motivate the reader to look more closely at the image and reinforce information presented in the body copy.

**Focus on one topic or information type per text element.** Text for visuals, especially a caption or callout, can present several types of information (Figure 5.1).

---

**Information Type**

---

Feature and benefit statements for the product, configuration, or application depicted in the image

Identification and description of items, people, or actions

Description of information presented on a screen display

Product names, including trademark symbols

Numbers for steps in a process or flow diagram, or dates on a timeline

Credit and copyright line for the photographer, designer, or illustrator

Source of data depicted in a chart (this may be presented separately in notes after the caption or elsewhere in the document)

Source acknowledgment if the visual was reproduced by permission from a work published by another person or company. For example, this type of acknowledgment is often required by market research firms for data reproduced from one of their reports

---

*Figure 5.1 Information types for captions, callouts, legends and labels.*

When submitting a visual to a publication, include a label or file identifier with the name, telephone number, and email address of a PR representative for your company. In most publications, visuals are handled by a designer, not an editor, and the illustration or disk may become separated from the other materials.

## DOCUMENT ELEMENTS ON THE WEB

Web pages can reproduce many of the elements used to organize text in print materials. But Web pages have two unique element types that are not used in print materials: microcontent and navigation links.

### *Microcontent*

Microcontent includes elements such as:
- Menus, navigation bars, buttons, and links
- Headlines and subheads
- Lead-in text for bullet points
- Sidebars or boxed text
- Field labels on forms
- ALT text that appears when the mouse cursor is placed over a visual
- Any text that is highlighted with a different size or format

Readers tend to focus first on microcontent when scanning a Web page. This means when writing microcontent text, clarity and consistency are more important than creativity. Ann Wylie suggests two questions for evaluating the effectiveness of this text: Is the microcontent clear and self explanatory? Can the reader understand the meaning of the page simply by scanning the microcontent?[24]

### *Web Links and Navigation*

You have an idea for how visitors should explore the Web site: first looking at the home page, then a brochure page, then a services page, and so on. However, given the flexible navigation that is inherent to the Web, visitors can explore the site by following almost any path.

Visitors understand that any link which appears on a Web page is an invitation to explore. But does the content and navigation associated with that link deliver what visitors want to see? Figure 5.2 shows visitor expectations when they follow certain types of links.

Consider these visitor expectations when defining the navigation paths through a site or creating links on specific pages. Matching visitor expectations will not only give them a positive experience with the site, but it will encourage them to stay longer and explore further.

| Type of Link | What the Visitor Expects to See |
|---|---|
| Word or phrase | More information on that topic or a glossary definition |
| Names: Product, person, company, course, events | Brochure, catalog page, profile, seminar description, events calendar, or email form that provides more information or a way to communicate with the subject |
| Call to action | Order form, email form, or other page for taking the specified action |
| Help or questions link | FAQ document, inquiry form, or page with relevant instructions or detailed information |
| File or multimedia placeholder | Download of the full file or multimedia element |
| URL of a page within the site or on an external site | Navigation to that page |

*Figure 5.2  Visitor expectations for links.*

### Guiding Visitor Navigation

Although visitors expect to freely explore a Web site, they also look to menus, buttons, and links for navigation help. Figure 5.3 shows typical navigation paths for common types of promotional activities conducted on a Web site. These paths can be defined in a navigation flowchart, as described in Chapter 1.

*Caution:* Don't force visitors to view multiple layers of pages, going through all of the sales or communication steps you've defined, until they reach the information or action they want. They may lose their way, lose their patience, or forget what they wanted before they reach your intended destination.

| Promotional Activity | Navigation Path |
| --- | --- |
| Selling a product online through a catalog or brochure | Link to an order form from each brochure or catalog page |
| Announcing a new product or service | Link to a brochure from the press release page |
| Cross-sell and upsell | Link to any relevant pages for options or accessories from any product information page and the order form |
| Promoting a course, workshop, or event | Link to a registration form and seminar page from an events calendar |
| Attracting clients for a consulting or service business | Cross-link brochure, profile, and services list pages |
| Encouraging visits to a dealer or retail store | Cross-link brochure, coupon, and locator pages |
| Providing general company information | Link to a FAQ and a newsletter from a company profile page |
| Gathering feedback from visitors | Link to a visitor survey from any page |

*Figure 5.3  Examples for defining Web site navigation to match promotional goals.*

### Navigation to Other Sites

You may want to create links from certain pages to other sites maintained by sponsors, business partners, or dealers as well as to industry or topic sites. Visitors usually consider these links valuable because they lead to additional information. However, consider carefully the number and type of external links. These guidelines will help you make appropriate choices:

- Minimize the number of links to external sites. When you send visitors to other sites, they may not recognize the change and may not remember to come back.
- Write an explanatory sentence or paragraph adjacent to the link text that describes the content on the site and why you think it is worth a visit.

- Select only links that are relevant and create a positive association for your company. For example, if you are trying to promote the advantages of a product's underlying technology, links to sites for relevant standards bodies or developer groups.

*Tip:* An alternative to linking to other sites is to place some of that content (text or images) on your pages. However, obtain permission from the source before doing so.

## RESOURCES

The recommended books and other resources listed below provide additional information on the topics discussed in this chapter. For an updated list, visit **writinghightech.com**.

### Books

William Horton: *Illustrating Computer Documentation: The Art of Presenting Information Graphically on Paper and Online.* Wiley, 1991. Although focused on technical manuals and user interfaces, provides a good primer on visual communications.

Eric K. Meyer: *Designing Infographics: Theory, creative techniques & practical solutions.* Hayden Books, 1997. Written for journalists, this book can give you good ideas for graphics in newsletter articles, white papers, and reports.

## REFERENCES

[1] Product brochure, Aldus Corp.
[2] Press release, Hewlett-Packard
[3] Janice King: "A Guide to Planning a Wide-Area Network," *NetWare Technical Journal,* October-November 1993.
[4] Product ad, MainLan, Inc.
[5] Product ad, Symantec Corp.
[6] Product line brochure, Compaq Computer Corp.
[7] Erica Levy Klein: *Write Great Ads: A Step-by-Step Approach.* New York: Wiley, 1990
[8] Philip Ward Burton: *Advertising Copywriting, 6th Edition.* Lincolnwood, IL: NTC Business Books, 1990

[9] Product ad, Contact Software International

[10] Product brochure, Walker, Richer & Quinn, Inc.

[11] Product brochure, Apple Computer, Inc.

[12] Press release, ADC Kentrox

[13] Ann Wylie, *Revving Up Readership* email newsletter, May 29, 2003

[14] Article in customer newsletter, Texas Instruments, Inc.

[15] Customer case study, ADC Kentrox

[16] Product brochure, Digital Equipment Corp.

[17] Product brochure, Microsoft Corp.

[18] Customer case study, Microsoft Corp.

[19] Janice King: "Sleepless in Seattle," *TE&M Magazine,* December 1, 1993

[20] Product ad, Lotus Development Corp.

[21] Ann Wylie, *Revving Up Readership* email newsletter, October 22, 2003

[22] Lauren Kessler and Duncan McDonald: *Mastering the Message: Media Writing with Substance and Style.* Belmont, CA: Wadsworth Publishing Company, 1989

[23] Adobe Corporation Web site (adobe.com), August 4, 2004

[24] Ann Wylie, *Revving Up Readership* email newsletter, March 3, 2004

# 6

## CONTENT TYPES

## PRESENTING HIGH-TECH INFORMATION EFFECTIVELY

It would be impossible to cover all the different types of information that could be presented in a marcom document for a technology product. However, this chapter describes how to handle the types of subject matter and other content typically found in marketing materials for technical products, services, and companies.

You won't use all of these ideas every time. Choose among them to find it the most useful and effective combination for each project.

### PRODUCT INFORMATION

Detailed information about features and capabilities is the major content type in most marcom documents for high-tech products. Yet you need to determine the appropriate level of technical detail based on the document's audience and purpose. This section describes how to present technical information when describing a high-tech product, upgrade, or service.

### *Product Announcement*

Announcing a new product, model, or version usually involves a flurry of communication activities. The guidelines below will help you provide complete and useful information in a product announcement, whether it is in the form of a press release, direct mail piece, Web content, or customer newsletter article. But remember that not all of these guidelines will be applicable to each product type or for each marcom project.

**Product identification.** Give the complete, official product name and model number.

**Product description.** Provide information on the product's features and functions (e.g., a "How it Works" section), key customer benefits, typical user applications, and sample processes or output. Compare the new product or model with earlier versions, with other products in the same product line, with competitive products (cautiously, and usually without naming competitors), or with nontechnical methods of achieving the same results.

**Quotes.** Include quotes from a company official (president, vice president, or product manager) and, if available, from a customer such as a beta user.

**Platforms.** Specify the platforms required or supported by the product, both hardware and software as is relevant.

**Compatibility.** Describe the compatibility, integration, or interaction of the product with others. If the product is an add-on to another product, describe the base product;[1] don't assume the reader will already know the base product in intimate detail.

**Demonstration.** Provide details on when and where the product will be demonstrated, such as at a trade show or press conference, or indicate if an electronic demo or evaluation unit is available.

**Product packaging.** Describe the product's components, options, and configuration choices where applicable. Specify what the product package contains, for example, hardware, software disks, documentation, tool kits, training videos, and other items.

**Availability.** Specify when the product will be available: either "immediately" or at a date in the future. You may need to indicate separate dates for when customers can begin to place orders and when the product will begin shipping. List contact information for retailers, dealers, distributors, and Web sources where customers can purchase the product or obtain more information.

**Replacement plans.** Give information on phase-out plans for earlier models or versions; specify whether and for how long older models and versions will be sold and supported. Describe any upgrade or trade-in options.

**Company information.** Include a description of the company, its product lines, capabilities, services, or positioning. In a press release this is typically a single paragraph called "boilerplate."

**Trademarks.** Include trademark notations and references for all product names—from your company and others—where appropriate (see Chapter 8).

**Standards compliance and certifications.** Indicate if any portion of the product's technology is patented, compliant with published industry standards or certified, and by which government(s), laboratory, standards body, or certifying agency.

One challenge for high-tech copywriters is explaining a technology or product that is completely new in the market. For example, consider how Amazon.com has explained to customers and the media its many innovative technologies, such as automated book recommendations.

Several techniques can be effective for explaining new technologies and unfamiliar product concepts.

**Develop a single clear explanation, in both text and visuals.** When using variations of that description, make sure they amplify the reader's understanding.

**Use analogy, metaphor, or direct comparison.** These techniques can help the reader better understand what the product is or what it does (see Chapter 7). Make sure these comparisons are fair and won't confuse the reader.

**Describe applications.** Sometimes a prospect can readily understand the technology explanation, but can't immediately grasp why she would want the product. In this case, a realistic and interesting description of applications can make the product or technology come to life in her mind.

## *Features and Benefits*

> *It's not what is the killer app,*
> *it's what is the killer benefit?*
> —Mark Lantz

Readers will look to any marcom or PR document for information on a product's features and benefits. Most advertising and marketing experts will tell you to emphasize benefits instead of features in a marketing document. But for high-tech products, many prospects have a strong interest in detailed information about product features. This is especially true for product categories where there are relatively minor distinctions between competing products. For high-tech marcom documents, this means you must strike a careful balance between product-centered feature statements and reader-centered benefit statements.

Balancing features and benefits can be a difficult writing task because sometimes it's hard to tell which is which. In a simple definition:

- A feature describes a product capability, characteristic, or function. It focuses on the product, not the user.
- A benefit describes what the product or feature will mean to or produce for the user. It focuses on the user, not the product.

The guidelines in Figure 6.1 will also help you distinguish between features and benefits.

| Feature statements describe: | Example |
| --- | --- |
| Product functions (what the product does) | **The Line Recognition feature converts slightly angled lines into perfectly straight horizontal and vertical lines.**[2] |
| Capabilities (what the product enables the user to do) | **Run the same software with different keyboards.**[3] |
| Specifications (details about what the product has or does) | **500 MHz central processor with interfaces for additional, task-specific processors.** |

| Feature statements describe: | Example *(continued)* |
| --- | --- |
| Applications (where or how the product can be used) | *This voice and data transfer capability is also valuable for conference calls.*[4] |
| Components, equipment, facilities, etc. supported by the product | *If your computer has any of the Windows supported sound devices, you can directly play MIDI, Digital Audio, and CD ROM Audio.*[5] |

| Benefit statements describe: | |
| --- | --- |
| What the product feature will mean for the reader | *This [feature] means there's more time to concentrate on ideas, rather than worrying about styles.*[6] |
| Enhancements to the reader's environment | *The new lower frequency beeper is easily heard even in noisy industrial environments.*[7] |
| Solutions to the reader's problems | *Mosaix solves the [problem] of the inbound call center: answering calls in a timely manner while consistently maintaining high levels of agent productivity.*[8] |
| Results (what the product or user can generate; or the value of capabilities gained from using the product) | *As a result [of this feature], People's improved the answer rate for inbound calls by 15%.*[9] |
| | *Paradigm increases the efficiency and accountability of your support organization, reduces the cost of operating your network, reduces training costs, and enhances the service provided to your end-users.*[10] |
| Actions and outcomes | *Users can change the color of the display's background and foreground attributes* [feature] *to enhance readability or to highlight specific screen areas or different applications for greater user productivity* [benefit].[11] |

*Figure 6.1 Guidelines and examples for correct use of feature and benefit statements.*

Feature and benefit statements can highlight the differences or uniqueness offered by the product. Use words such as *first, one-of-a-kind, only, unmatchable, specialized,* or *patented* (if this is indeed true for the product or its underlying technology). Emphasizing the product's unique aspects is especially important in categories with many closely competitive products, where the reader may see your product as no different or better than the others. For example:

> *Now when you want to cut, move, paste, or insert data, you simply select a range with the mouse, and drag the data wherever you wish. It's the fastest way to work and only Microsoft Excel 4.0 has it.*[6]

Arrange the features and benefits in order of most importance to the reader. You may have a different perspective on this ranking than your technical experts. But if readers are most concerned about a product capability that you would otherwise find trivial, you will want to elevate its importance in the text. It also may be appropriate to segment product benefits that can be obtained immediately from those a customer receives with long-term usage.

### Writing Feature and Benefit Statements

Feature and benefit statements may appear separately within the text, or as a combined statement, for example:

> *Windows Messenger is the easy way to communicate with your friends and family in real time.*[12]

Within a sentence, you can present a feature first and then its resulting benefit, or the benefit first and then its associated feature. This example shows a feature-benefit structure:

> *Resident memory can be doubled to 4 MB to manage more demanding documents.*[13]

This example shows a benefit-feature structure:

> *And, to handle sophisticated print jobs, you can choose from a wide range of options including a font cartridge and letter, legal, and envelope cassettes.*[13]

One technique for writing a benefit statement is to remember the acronym WIIFM: *What's In It For Me?* Answering this question will help you focus on the results, advantages, and values that will be meaningful to a customer or prospect. The major benefit statement is often called the "value proposition" of the product.

In most cases, the benefit-feature structure will be more effective for capturing a reader's attention. After all, benefits answer the key WIIFM question. Once you have appealed to a prospect's self-interest, then you can explain the features that deliver the stated benefit.

The feature-benefit structure can be effective in several circumstances.

**Promoting a product upgrade.** Most customers will want to know first about features: the new capabilities and components of the product and how it differs from earlier versions. The benefits statements then provide the compelling reasons for purchasing and installing the upgrade.

**Marketing to a specialized or highly technical audience.** Some engineers and other experts consider benefits statements as irrelevant "fluff." These audiences want the facts presented by features and specifications. But presenting benefits—albeit in a more subtle form than for other audiences—is an important way for technical audiences to fully understand your promotion or message.

**Presenting competitive differences.** When prospects choose between two closely competing products, specific features can be an important decision factor.

### Using Document Elements

**Subheads.** The subheads can present feature or benefit statements for the first time, or restate and reinforce the statements that also appear in a bullet list or table elsewhere in the document. Another approach is to present the benefit statements in a bullet list, then use the subheads to highlight key features. Create a subhead for each feature or benefit and follow it with one or more body copy paragraphs to provide a detailed explanation.

**Body copy.** Present the features and benefits in sentences or paragraphs.

**Bullet lists.** Use a single bullet to show each feature and benefit statement in matching pairs. Whichever lead-in approach you choose (e.g., starting each bullet with a verb), use it consistently within a bullet list.

**Word charts.** Create a table with separate columns for features and benefits. This is an effective way to show a one-to-one, one-to-many, or many-to-one relationship between a feature and its associated benefits.

**Callouts and captions.** Use these elements to highlight a feature or benefit that is depicted in a visual.

### Using Parts of Speech

Consider how the various parts of speech can help you structure feature and benefit statements for greater consistency and impact.

Benefit statements typically start with a verb; when using a verb, distinguish between what the product does and what the customer does:

Product: *[This service] Requires no capital investment to install and maintain a router-based network.*[14]

Reworking this statement from the customer's perspective:

*Avoid the capital expense of installing and maintaining a router-based network.*

Use a verb when a customer action is necessary to fully gain the benefit.

Feature statements often start with an adjective. Use an adjective when something about the product or the customer's environment or circumstances is changed by the feature. Also use an adjective if the result or benefit is an indirect outcome of implementing or using the product.

A benefit statement may also start with an adjective if the text is not addressing the reader directly. For example, in a bullet list of customer benefits in a sales guide:

* *Increased network system protection, simplified management, and reduced costs.*

A noun can provide a lead-in to a benefit statement that is longer than a short phrase or single sentence:

*Scalability—VPNs allow corporations to utilize remote access infrastructure within ISPs. Therefore, corporations are able to add a virtually unlimited amount of [network] capacity without adding significant infrastructure.*[15]

## Cross-Sell and Upsell

Sometimes buying technical products is difficult because of the variety of models—with options, add-on products, and services—among which a customer must choose to obtain a complete solution. Promotional materials for these products must present the choices clearly and take advantage of opportunities for cross-selling and upselling.

You may have heard sales representatives use these terms but never understood the difference. They can sound vaguely suspicious, like manipulative sales tactics for extracting more money from customers. However, if handled correctly, cross-selling and upselling can help customers choose the best products for their needs and generate a stronger customer relationship for your company (and of course, more revenue too).

**Cross-selling** promotes an add-on or accessory product or service that, when combined with the primary product, makes a better or complete solution. A classic example of cross-selling is the question, "Do you want fries with that?" For high-tech products, cross-selling typically involves helping customers assemble a tailored product from a variety of options. An effective cross-sell presents these options clearly and makes it easy for customers to choose among them.

**Upselling** promotes a more powerful or higher level model than the one the customer is considering. To use the fast-food metaphor again, an up-sell would be "The deluxe burger is not only bigger, but it includes the special sauce and only costs a little more. Would you like that instead?" In high-tech, a product model that offers greater capabilities, flexibility, or capacity might be suitable for upsell. In this case, the seller's job is to make sure a customer is aware this model exists and to encourage consideration of both models before the purchase decision.

Both cross-selling and upselling can be done in print materials and on the Web. The following ideas can be used for print materials such as data sheets, catalogs, and selection guides:

- Include a brief "Related Products" section that lists the names or model numbers of upsell and cross-sell products.
- Present a chart of available options, describing the target application or environment for each.
- Describe typical packages or product combinations, especially when a customer must purchase multiple components. This can be done with a simple bullet list that describes the content of each package.

Because of the dynamic links between pages, cross-selling and upselling are especially easy to implement on a Web site. For example, you can create links among catalog pages to show related products, or link to a services page from a product page. The navigation process you define for purchase transactions on a Web site can also guide a visitor through pages that present cross-sell or upsell options.

Your materials must handle both cross-selling and upselling carefully to avoid confusing, overwhelming, or turning the customer away from making a purchase. Upselling presents a particular writing challenge because you need to present both products as valid and attractive choices. Emphasize the key benefits of each product, but indicate that these benefits are best achieved within the right environment.

## *Specifications*

In the case of technical products, the old saying "the proof is in the details" holds particularly true. Detailed product information in the form of specifications supports broader product messages. Readers want specifications because they help eliminate from consideration products that don't meet the need or that would require an expensive investment in additional equipment, services, or other resources.

Product specifications are more useful when they present the details a reader needs to make an informed decision about buying or implementing the product. Specifications can include a variety of information such as:

- Hardware and software requirements
- Operating environment requirements such as rack space, temperature, and power needs
- Size, weight, and other physical characteristics
- Compatibility with other products
- Performance ranges, capacity limits, and other parameters that distinguish models within a product line
- Packaging, options, and other variations in the product's configuration, delivery, or implementation
- Certifications and compliance with standards

Specifications are typically placed at the end of a brochure or data sheet, but also can appear in a sidebar or in tables placed in the main body of the piece.

### Technical Jargon

> ... to paraphrase Gatsby, "The very technical
> do not talk like you and me."
> —John A. Barry

Technical jargon is a favorite target of scorn among journalists, customers, and the general public alike. Indeed, sentences that contain dense jargon are difficult to read and understand, even for readers who know the terms.[16] Certain technical terms are accepted as proper names or descriptors for a technology, product, or function. In contrast, jargon is an informal language that emerges and gains gradual acceptance through conversations, analyst and journalist comments, online exchanges, etc.

It's hard to get away from jargon when writing about technology. In many cases, you will include jargon in marketing material because it is commonly used and understood in your industry.

However, you must be aware of a "classism" that can creep into technical materials: a condescending attitude toward those who may not be in the industry or who may be intimidated by technology and its language. Or, as Barry describes it, "Inherent in technobabble is the assumption that everyone else knows what the users of the technobabble are talking about."[17] In addition, jargon in your native language may not be understood by international readers. Consider whether the amount and type of any jargon is appropriate to the audience.

Fortunately, there are ways to deal with jargon so that it does not overwhelm, obscure, or confuse the messages you want to present in a document.

**Use jargon only as needed.** Sometimes jargon is the best way to accurately identify a technology or concept. Consider whether a simpler, more commonly used term would be an appropriate substitute. Define any technical terms or jargon upon first use in the copy, usually by placing the definition in parentheses.

**Present relationships clearly.** Watch out for noun clusters and long strings of modifiers that confuse the subject-action-object relationship. This sentence provides an example:

*Users can modify all system configuration parameter values.*
The sentence becomes easier to understand when revised to:
*Users can modify the values of all parameters that control the system configuration.*

**Consider localization.** If you are writing a document that will be translated into another language, determine whether the technical terms are the same or different—and widely understood—in the target language (see Chapter 9).

## Acronyms

Acronyms are so prevalent for some industries and technologies that marketing materials look like something written by a child playing with alphabet soup. Especially if the product addresses multiple markets or technologies, verify that any acronyms will be understood correctly by readers.

Acronyms can be adopted quickly into common usage by people in that industry, often to the extent that you no longer need to show the component words when using the acronym. However, remember that the same acronym can have two or more different definitions—even within the same industry. For example, in telecommunications the word POP can be an acronym for *point-of-presence* or an abbreviation of the word *population*.

One ad reviewer advised: "Easy on the acronyms ... I feel like I'm reading over speed bumps."[18] These guidelines can help you handle acronyms appropriately in marketing materials.

**Show the full name or component words with first use of an acronym in a document.** For example: *asynchronous transfer mode (ATM).* If the document is lengthy, or if there is a substantial amount of text between uses of the acronym, show the full name again later in the document to help the reader remember the meaning.

**Use a more common word if possible to avoid an acronym.** For example, use *memory* instead of *RAM* (random access memory) or *ROM* (read-only memory) unless you need to identify the specific memory type.

**Include a brief glossary of acronyms at the end of the document or as a sidebar.** A glossary is especially valuable if the product is in a new technology area where the jargon and acronyms aren't widely known.

**Consider using a legend to define all acronyms that appear in a diagram.** This is especially important if the diagram contains acronyms that are not explained in the body copy.

**Verify the correct spelling for the acronym.** One ad used *SCUZZI* in place of the actual acronym *SCSI* (Small Computer System Interface), which is pronounced "scuzzi." Use a print or online dictionary for the technology or industry to verify the component words and definitions of acronyms.

## Background Information

Some products are easy to understand on the basis of reading a single ad or data sheet. Other products require more explanation—from the detailed view provided by specifications to the high-level view provided by a backgrounder or white paper.

Background information can describe a product's design, architecture, or underlying technology. It should help the reader understand the concept or logic behind the product's functionality, or how the product fits into a larger environment, trend, or strategy. You may need to present definitions and classifications to explain a new term, application, process, or technology in the background information. In this case, using an analogy or metaphor as part of the definition or classifying by type or some other common attribute can help the reader understand important product concepts.

While most background information can be presented in body copy, other good methods for conveying technical concepts include decision trees, architecture diagrams, comparison charts, and flow charts.

## Applications

Application information helps the reader understand potential uses for the product or technology. This information can address improvements in a work environment, operations, tasks, information availability, or in standardizing equipment, systems, and work processes. Applications can be organized by industry, type of company or user, operation type, information need, or any other relevant factor.

Application information should describe in very specific terms how the product will meet a reader's needs and requirements. It should also address a reader's concerns about adopting the product such as hidden costs, implementation effort required, training needs, and ongoing support and management activities. Also describe the benefits the reader can realize from the application, especially if it replaces a method of achieving the same result that does not involve the use of technology.

## Upgrade Announcement

Promoting upgrades to current customers is a special form of a product announcement. These guidelines cover the special issues to consider when writing about a product upgrade.

**Availability and eligibility.** Specify the product name and version number, supported platforms, system requirements, eligible markets or customer types (if relevant), and availability date.

**Motivation.** Use reason-why copy to describe the new applications or capabilities that are possible with the upgrade. *One of the handiest new printing features is the ability to print pages in any sequence.*[19] (More information on reason-why copy is presented later in this chapter.)

**Value proposition.** Describe the value delivered by the upgrade and the features or guarantees that minimize the customer's risk in purchasing or installing the new version. For both your own users and those using competitive products, show the value of the new features delivered by the upgrade, especially in comparison to current product versions. Emphasize the limited risk of purchasing the upgrade by describing satisfaction guarantees, customer service programs, online help, or other product features that will support users.

**Upgrade details.** Present detailed information on the new features and the benefits of implementing the upgrade. Customers need to understand the differences between the new version and their current version. Describe the existing product functions that will be continued in the new version. Describe any changes to training programs, service plans, or support procedures that will accompany the upgrade.

Indicate whether the upgrade is a one-time offering or part of an ongoing maintenance program. Describe any prerequisite service programs, hardware, operating system versions, and other components the customer must have in place before purchasing or installing the upgrade. Describe any installation or customization services that are available for the upgrade.

Provide complete information on how the customer can obtain the upgrade; many companies use a reply card or online order form for this purpose. Include pricing and shipping details; indicate if the product is available through dealer or retail channels; describe what information (such as a registration number) the customer must supply with the upgrade order; specify any time limits, conditions, or incentives attached to the upgrade offer.

**Supporting evidence.** Reconfirm the reader's initial decision to purchase the product by restating key messages, emphasizing your company's commitment to providing improvements, or providing quotes from product reviews or other satisfied users.

## SERVICES INFORMATION

Some technology companies are primarily service providers, offering consulting, integration, or other assistance. Selling high-tech services involves several considerations that are different from those for selling products.

**Difficult to evaluate.** It is difficult for prospects to evaluate the quality and applicability of services for their particular needs before they actually make a purchase. Buying services is perceived as a high-risk activity because there often is no substantial way to perform a "test drive" or see the projected results in advance.[20]

**Reputation.** The service company's reputation and presentation are critical marketing elements. The prospect will make judgments based more on subjective factors—especially about the "feel" of the potential relationship with the service provider—than on the objective comparison of features or specifications that can be made with tangible products.

**Vendor promises.** Customers must rely more heavily on vendor promises about the nature and quality of the service; your text must ensure those promises reflect a realistic relationship with your company. Service promises are both explicit (statements of deliverables) and implicit (unstated assumptions about quality or nature of the service experience).

**Deliverables.** Thoroughly explain the concept behind the service in order to give prospects a reasonable sense of what they are buying. Indicate the delivery timeframe and mechanism for the service—e.g., through a personal site visit by a consultant, via remote access to a customer's systems, by telephone contact, or by access to specialized Web content.

**Options.** Describe optional service components, prerequisites, and variations of service offerings for different platforms, environments, or other factors. Promote service bundles or cross-sell related services for customization and consulting, support plans, training courses, and certification programs.

**Differentiation.** Describe the distinct value-added aspects of the service: What will a prospect get from the service that he couldn't produce himself or obtain from another source? Be clear about the differences of your service over that provided by competitors. Prospects must be able to recognize and value these differences. Describe the capabilities, facilities, staff expertise, clients served, quality guarantees, or other factors as supporting evidence and a form of differentiation.

Even if your company is not primarily a services provider, you may need to communicate information about the service and technical support programs associated with your products. This information is often presented in brochures and data sheets and can include:

- A description of technical support programs, such as initial and extended warranties, on-site or telephone support, or differences in response-time guarantees or cost packages.
- Hours available; phone and fax numbers; unique Web URL; email addresses.
- Limitations, prerequisites, or other factors that define what type of customer is eligible for the service, how the service is delivered, or pricing.

## PURCHASING INFORMATION

Print materials and Web content can facilitate a sale by providing the right information to help customers place an order and take all other necessary steps in the purchase transaction.

**"Where to buy" options.** Indicate where the product can be purchased: from a dealer, retail or online store, or from your company's Web site. If the product is sold through many varied channels, this statement may be high level: *PrimeWidget is available from many local and online electronic retailers*.

Provide the URL for a list of local sales channels or a store locator tool if available on your company Web site. If the product is sold only by your company or through a small number of dealers or partners, consider providing full contact information on each document.

**Sales terms and conditions.** Multi-user licenses, phased implementation, installation prerequisites, and many other terms and conditions may affect a customer's purchase of a high-tech product.

At a minimum, these terms and conditions should be presented clearly and in a distinct manner on the order form and other sales documents, both print and online.

Local laws that cover commercial transactions and consumer protection may specify when and how this information must be presented to customers and what action the customer must take in order to accept the terms and conditions. Work with a qualified attorney to develop standard text that can be used in most sales materials.

**Payment methods and terms.** In addition to price (discussed in the next section), buyers want to know the available choices for payment method and whether the payment is due upon order, upon product shipment, or on another date. For products sold to consumers, specify accepted payment forms such as personal check and credit card types. For sales to a business, indicate whether full payment, a deposit, or a purchase order is required with the product order; also specify standard terms for invoice and payment due dates (e.g., *invoiced upon shipment, Net 30 days*).

**Shipping options.** Describe all choices for product shipping, including carrier and typical delivery times for standard and expedited shipping. Specify the applicable shipping charge for each option.

**Return policies and procedures.** State your company's complete policy for product returns, including terms such as acceptable product condition (e.g., *seal on disk package must be intact*) and limited time period (e.g., *Returns allowed within 30 days after purchase*).

Provide complete information and instructions for obtaining a refund, such as a special shipping address for the return, how to obtain a return authorization (often called a "RMA number") by telephone or on a Web site, and how to package the product for return shipment.

## Pricing Information

One product may have several prices:

- Manufacturer's Suggested Retail Price (MSRP) for direct sales by the company

- Typical retail price (called "street" price), set by the retailers or dealers who sell a product to customers; often less than the MSRP
- Wholesale prices granted only to dealers for products that will be resold to customers
- Upgrade prices for current customers
- Quantity discounts available to dealers or customers

In press releases and sales literature, the MSRP may be the only price listed, but an indication may be given that dealer and quantity-discount prices are available upon request to the manufacturer.

In a catalog, direct-mail piece, or Web page that sells the product directly to the customer, clearly state the product price, applicable discounts, expiration date of special offers, eligibility requirements, and the price of additional options or fees such as shipping costs. Also describe any additional purchase or prerequisite conditions that may be necessary for a customer to qualify for a promotional price.

Any published information on pricing may be subject to local commerce laws or trade regulations. These vary by country and sometimes by local market (see Chapter 8). In the U.S., the most common practice is to present only the MSRP on all information produced by the product manufacturer, perhaps with a footnote stating "actual retail prices may be lower." This technique is a way to indicate that the product may be available from a reseller at a more attractive price, while staying in compliance with trade laws that prohibit price-fixing.

It is especially important to follow legal and ethical guidelines when comparing prices. Comparisons are typically made in any of three ways:

1. To the price of a competitor's product:
   *PrimeWidget costs less than any comparable solution!*
2. A current price to a previous price:
   *Same great features, new low price!*
3. Or, to a price increase planned for the future:
   *Order by December 1st to lock-in this year's prices!*

The total cost of ownership (TCO) measure can be an effective way to side-step a direct price comparison between competing products. A TCO analysis can include any or all of the expenses associated with the product, such as options, additional products or services required to obtain a complete solution, implementation and operation costs, and ongoing maintenance or support fees.

## *Offers*

An offer statement describes any incentive to the prospect for responding to a sales document or purchasing a product. Offer statements are used extensively in advertisements, brochures, and direct mail materials and on Web sites.

The specifics of the offer will vary substantially based on the product and how it is marketed. However, offers generally take one of two forms: a purchase offer or an information offer.

A **purchase offer** describes pricing, conditions, or options intended to motivate an immediate purchase decision. A purchase offer may be included in retail materials, ads, direct-mail pieces, and Web content.

Purchase offers can be either a hard offer (the prospect must buy the product to receive the offer) or a soft offer (the prospect can try the product before paying). An example of a hard offer is: *Buy Q&A Before 10/3/92 and Get QuickBooks for Free!*[21] A free trial period or use of an evaluation unit are the most common soft offers for high-tech products: *If you're comparing word processors, order your free working model of Ami Pro 3.0 today by calling ....*[22]

In direct mail, a hard offer encourages prospects to call a sales center, visit a dealer, or agree to be contacted by a salesperson. A soft offer moves the prospect to the next step in the sales cycle, through actions such as requesting a white paper, visiting a trade-show booth, or registering for a seminar.

In any purchase offer, state exactly what is included such as:
- Guarantees and terms
- Expiration date for a hard offer or trial period
- Any add-on product, other merchandise, or services packaged with the product

To strengthen the offer's appeal, use words that will increase the prospect's confidence, especially if your company is not well-known. These words include: no risk, guaranteed, unconditional return, or free trial period. However, make sure these statements accurately reflect what your company will deliver.

When selling a product in other countries, different regulations may apply to what a purchase offer can encompass and how it must be stated.

**Information offers** include literature packets, white papers, evaluation guides, demo CDs, and other materials that support a lengthy, complex sales cycle or promote attendance at an event. For example: *... call your local distributor or Analog Devices at ... for your free selection kit.*[23] Describe the material the reader will receive and the benefits it provides.

## SALES FORCE INFORMATION

Some marketing documents are directed to the people who will actually sell the product, such as sales representatives, dealers, distributors, and value-added resellers (VARs). The purpose of these materials is to help salespeople become more knowledgeable and effective in selling your product. For dealers and resellers who carry multiple products, this material must also motivate them to make the effort to sell yours.

Depending on the complexity of the product and distribution channels, sales information can be packaged in a print or online memorandum, bulletin, booklet, multimedia sales guide, or multi-document sales kit.

Following are ideas on the types of information to provide for sales personnel.

**Market information.** Describe market conditions, present relevant market research data, and identify market segments by customer type, location, operating environment, industry, or other relevant factors.

**Target customers.** Profile typical prospects, whether they are businesses, government or non-profit organizations, or people. Describe the problems and requirements, current situation, decision-making process, and information needs of each prospect group. These groups may classify prospects by application need, job function, industry, company size, current product implementation, or other criteria.

**Sales techniques.** Describe the typical sales cycle, present selling ideas, list typical prospect objections and effective responses, and include examples of worksheets and other tools available to support the sales process.

**Product information.** Include copies of all sales literature, press releases, clips of press coverage, and other material that will give a salesperson a complete resource for product information. This resource may be distributed as print materials, on a CD, or posted in a distinct area of the company Web site.

**Competitor information.** Describe the strengths and weaknesses of competitive products and give advice on how to sell against them.

**Promotion plans and resources.** Provide schedules for advertising, trade shows, seminars, and other activities planned to promote the product. Describe the literature, consulting services, advertising coop programs, and other resources available from your company to assist sales representatives.

**Ordering procedures.** Describe the procedures and timeline a customer or salesperson must follow to order the product from your company or a distributor. Include example order forms or other ordering documents or provide the URL for a Web order site.

## COMPANY INFORMATION

Documents such as corporate backgrounders and capabilities brochures focus on a company instead of a product. Company information also can appear in product materials as part of the product's positioning or to give readers confidence in "the company behind the product."

**Market overview.** Information on markets served by the company, including size, needs, opportunities, trends, company positioning, and competitors. This information may include a profile of typical customers. It can be organized by product line, industry, market size, or location.

**Product information.** A description of products the company develops, manufactures, and sells as well as service and support programs.

**Capabilities statement.** For product companies, a capabilities statement can describe key technologies, development and manufacturing resources, and support operations. For service companies, a capabilities statement typically describes the services offered and special expertise or experience of employees.

**Organizational history.** Information on when and how the company was founded and key events or accomplishments in the company's history; a description of relationships with parent or subsidiary companies; involvement with industry groups and standards bodies.

**Sales information.** A description of the company's sales methods, marketing partnerships, and distribution channels. Separate information may be presented for domestic and international sales, including a list of key distributors or customers.

**Milestones and achievements.** Factual information on company accomplishments such as X units shipped, awards received, top ranking by a market research or analyst firm.

**Patents and certifications**. Information on patents, licenses, or certifications granted by testing laboratories, standards bodies, government agencies, or other entities. This information also can describe compliance with regulations, standards, or military specifications.

**Financial information.** For public companies, materials may include the most recently published financial results. For privately-held companies, a document may list annual sales or the major investors and funding sources (e.g., venture capital firms). Note: Financial data and investor-relations material is a type of company information that marketing writers may produce. This information has special requirements and considerations that are beyond the scope of this book.

**Staff biographies.** Information on the education and experience of key management and technical employees and their roles in the company.

**Facility information.** Description of sales and support offices, manufacturing plants, laboratories, and distribution centers and other facilities including location, type of work performed, specialized equipment, and other resources.

**Philanthropy, sponsorships, and community relations.** An overview of the company's financial gifts, volunteer activity, and sponsorship of organizations or events. May include guidelines and contact information that a non-profit organization can use to apply for funds and in-kind support.

The company area of a Web site can present additional information such as a calendar of upcoming events, links to related industry or topic sites, and content that is localized for distinct markets (see Chapter 9).

## Strategy Discussion

An article, backgrounder, or white paper may present a company's plans or strategies for a technology area or market. Sometimes called a statement of direction, this discussion is intended to give customers broad information about a company's product plans without tipping off competitors about specific designs or implementation details.

**Phases.** When a strategy will be implemented in stages over a lengthy time period, this information describes the activities, deliverables, and schedules for each phase.

**Trends.** A discussion of trends that are influencing this strategy.

**Benefits.** The value of this strategy for customers or the company.

**Competitive positioning.** How this strategy compares with that of competitors and how it fits into the strategies of alliance partners or other key players in the industry.

## Alliance Announcement

Technology companies often form partnerships, joint ventures, or alliances with other companies to develop new products or reach new markets. Information about these alliances can appear in press releases, newsletter articles, or company backgrounders.

**Background.** The reasons for creating the alliance. How the alliance will benefit customers and prospects, and if appropriate, the benefits to dealers and other alliance partners.

**Dates.** When the alliance was formed, when it will begin activities or introduce a product.

**Description.** The structure of the relationship (e.g., merger, agreement to cooperate, or exclusive marketing rights). The products, sales territories, or market segments covered by the alliance agreement. The responsibilities of each partner for sales, support, or other activities.

**Partner information.** A description of each company involved in the alliance: size, product line, capabilities, location, and financial information.

## CUSTOMER INFORMATION

While some companies are very secretive about their customers and the nature of their business relationships, customer information is a valuable component in marketing materials. This information may be a simple list of customers or detailed case studies on select clients. Remember to obtain approval from the customer for all information before publishing the material.

### *New Business Announcement*

Companies often announce major contracts or other high-dollar purchases awarded by significant customers. These announcements typically appear in press releases, dealer and sales force materials, or articles in the company's newsletter. A new-business announcement can describe:

- What the customer bought: usually products, but may include services for design, implementation, training, and support
- Monetary value of the contract or sale; time period and geographic areas covered

- Customer description and information on the customer's environment or application
- Customer reasons for selecting the product
- Information on the product and company
- Information on other parties involved in the project such as a dealer, alliance partner, or other vendors

## *Testimonials and Case Studies*

Testimonial is the general term for any positive customer statement about a company or its products. A testimonial is a brief endorsement quote that is used in marketing materials (specific legal guidelines apply to endorsements; see Chapter 8).

The key to writing an effective testimonial is to be specific in describing problems, solutions, and results. Don't use a bland quote such as "Your company makes an excellent product. We're very happy with our choice."

A case study is an article that fully describes a customer's use of the product. The case study describes the customer's need or prior situation, why the product was selected, how it was implemented, and the results or benefits the customer has obtained. Case studies can be used in the promotional materials for a product, in a customer newsletter, or be submitted as an article to a trade publication (see Chapter 11 for detailed guidelines on case studies).

## EVENT INFORMATION

Marketing and press materials can be developed for events such as user group meetings, seminars, and conference presentations. These materials can include announcements and invitations, audio/visual materials for a presentation, and follow-up articles or reports. Event information can include:

- Date, time, location, and cost of the event; URL for a Webcast
- Registration and travel procedures
- A description of the event's purpose, target audience, and agenda

- An outline or description of the presentations or discussions at the event
- Benefits or incentives for attending the event

Technology users may receive many invitations to events each year, and must choose among them while allocating their time and budgets carefully. Prospective participants may also dismiss seminars and other company-sponsored events as "just another vendor hard-sell." Materials promoting an event can increase its appeal through techniques such as emphasizing the value of the content and interaction with presenters, and merchandising the materials, free products, and other items that will be given to participants.

## SUPPORTING EVIDENCE

Text that supplies supporting evidence for messages, views, or claims is essential when the document's objective is persuasion. When making product claims or discussing features, be sure to clearly show the "why" or "how" behind it with supporting evidence. Types of supporting evidence include:

**Past performance.** *Over the past 30 years, in fact, IBM Microelectronics has developed many of the industry's most significant "firsts" in semiconductors, packaging and electronics manufacturing technologies.*[24]

**External validation.** *The product's superiority was recently endorsed by MIDRANGE Systems readers, who voted it the most reliable and innovative of its type.*[25]

**Research.** *Mobile consumer applications will drive the takeup of data services and generate traffic and revenues for mobile operators, according to a new study by IDC.*[26]

**Product tests or reviews.** *PC Magazine independently defined and ran a battery of real world performance tests to compare database server software.*[27]

**Lists of satisfied customers.** Named with their permission of course.

Any presentation of supporting evidence from external sources must be honest and fair. Clearly state the source of the information and the relationship of that source to your company, particularly for company-commissioned research or surveys. See the guidelines for citing sources later in this chapter and for endorsements in Chapter 8.

Association is another form of supporting evidence, for example, using customer case studies in ads when those customers are well-known and highly respected. But make sure this association represents fairly the relationship between your company and the customer.

### *Statistics and Numbers*

Market research studies, opinion polls, survey findings, and test results can all provide supporting evidence for messages in a marcom document. But, as the writer Mark Twain once said, "There are lies, damned lies, and statistics." Choose data and statistics carefully, then present them accurately and fairly. Be especially careful about the language you use to describe the statistics—don't use words that will convey an inappropriate interpretation.

These techniques can improve the impact of the statistics you cite:

- Place the statistic in close proximity to the idea or message that it supports. State the numbers clearly and simply to give readers an accurate understanding.
- Consider the question "Is the glass half empty or half full?" Look at a statistic to see if it will be more favorable or meaningful if you present its inverse. For example, instead of saying *almost 25% of subscribers still have not opted for the additional services* you can present a more positive message with *more than 75% of subscribers have already signed up for the new services.*
- If the statistic is particularly favorable, use it as the clincher for an argument, placing it at the end of the sentence or paragraph.
- When citing a group of statistics or evidence from multiple sources, start with the least significant and build to the most significant. Or, frame the evidence by both starting and ending with a good statistic.

- Show the equations or calculation procedures if appropriate to the document's audience.

To increase credibility (especially with journalists), cite the source of the statistic either directly in the document text or in a footnote. Figure 6.2 presents guidelines for citing sources.

| Source | What to Cite |
| --- | --- |
| Publication | Name and date as well as URL if online |
| Survey or test | All sponsors, the testing organization, and all participants (if appropriate) |
| Quoting a person | Name, title, and company or organization |
| A statistic drawn from a sample | Sample size and nature |
| Test results | Product model, configuration, platform, and other factors covered by the test |

*Figure 6.2  Guidelines for citing sources of statistics and other supporting evidence.*

When presenting any type of numerical information, Blundell suggests these techniques for making it easier to read and understand:[28]

- Don't place too many numbers too close together within a paragraph. Consider placing them in a table or chart instead.
- Round and shorten the number if precision isn't critical, for example, stating *$2.6 million* instead of *$2,611,423*.
- Show a ratio of a complex number, for example, *1 out of 4* or *one-fourth* unless it is important to state the exact number.

## Test Results

Product tests, especially those conducted by independent labs or other third parties, are a common source of supporting evidence for marketing technical products. These guidelines can help you present test results accurately and fairly:

- If the results are preliminary or need additional confirmation, use qualifiers such as *preliminary, appear, indicate, unconfirmed.*
- Clearly distinguish between those results you believe are fully proven and those that require additional validation.
- Specify the product model, configuration, platform, or other factors relevant to the test procedures or outcomes.
- When quoting test results achieved by an independent testing lab or a trade publication, be very careful that the quote presents the information completely and accurately. Cite the source and give a date where possible, acknowledging copyrights and permissions where appropriate (see Chapter 8).

## QUOTES

There is nothing like a positive quote from a third party to enhance the believability of what your copy says about a product or company. Quotes are valuable for many reasons.

**Credibility.** Adding credibility to claims, especially if the quotes are from customers, trade publications, or industry analysts. *"If you can click a mouse, you can create stunning presentations with this program." PC/Computing, 11/91.*[22]

**Implication.** Presenting the perspective of an authoritative source who can say things that you should not say yourself.[9] For example, this quote from a customer contains a negative message about the company's competitors: *"We selected Wellfleet because they were the only ones who honestly presented their protocol suite and could offer the partnership approach that we required."*[29] However, a negative message such as this can create both legal and positioning problems; see the guidelines about negative messages in Chapter 3 and comparisons in Chapter 8.

**High praise.** Stating your message or information more forcefully or eloquently than you could in the narrative. *"OS/2 has been tested over and over again in real-life environments and it has consistently demonstrated an unbeatable reliability."*[24]

**Informal speech.** Emphasizing a key point or stating it in everyday language. *"When you pull up a report, you see a figure and say `What was that for?' Hit QuickZoom, you go right to the transactions and there's your answer!"*[30]

**Human interest.** Humanizing the information with real-world stories and examples. *"I've never taken a computer programming class in my life, yet I was able to get the results I needed with NOW!"*[3]

Among the things that can weaken a quote:

- No attribution or only a vague reference to the source. Include full names, titles, and affiliations.
- Lack of relevance because of the source or the content of the quote.[31]
- One that states generalities instead of specifics: *"We were very pleased with [the product's] performance".* This quote would have more impact if it described a measurable result: *"The product increased our performance by at least 30 percent."*
- A lengthy quote (more than three sentences). The reader will forget a person is talking and the points could probably be made more powerfully and succinctly in the narrative text.
- One that merely repeats an idea that is presented elsewhere in the body copy.[31]

Collect positive quotes made by customers, reviewers in trade magazines, test lab reports, market researchers, and industry or financial analysts. The specific quotes you use in a particular document will be based on its objectives, the nature of the quote, and the relevance of the source to your target audience. As a result, it is unlikely that you will use every quote from every source. Instead, choose only the most cogent, concise, provocative, or captivating quotes to use in the document. Think of quotes as the spice for the text, not the meat.

When using a quote, present it within the correct context. For example, if a quote about the product's performance is taken from a test report, your context should not imply that these results were achieved by an actual user. In parentheses or a subordinate clause, explain acronyms or technical terms that may be unfamiliar to the reader.

In addition, verify all references to names, places, dates, and other facts that are included in a quote to ensure they are still current and accurate. This practice, called fact-checking by journalists, is important to avoid presenting inaccurate information and embarrassing your company, or worse, a customer.

### Creating Quotes

For some projects, you will write a quote for a person who will approve it as part of the review process for the draft document. When writing a quote for someone, make sure it sounds like something the person would actually say instead of something that was borrowed from the marketing text of the piece.

### Editing Quotes

There is a certain amount of editing you can perform on a person's quote. Hardly anyone speaks in concise, carefully crafted, grammatically correct sentences. Your job is to take the person's direct statement—with its stumbles, excess verbiage, and incorrect grammar or word usage—and turn it into an understandable, coherent quote.

While the primary purpose of these changes is to make the quote easier to read, you must be very careful when editing. The modified quote *must* remain true to the original in meaning, emphasis, and spirit. Minor tweaking to correct grammar, remove excess and unnecessary words, to make a complete sentence, or to improve the clarity of the quote are acceptable. But more extensive editing may change the meaning of what the person actually said—something you must avoid, both to be fair to the source and to avoid the potential for legal trouble (see Chapter 8).

You also may need to rearrange quotes that appear in different parts of an interview to fit into the continuity of the written piece. This situation can arise when your interview subject goes off on a tangent, then comes back to the main question, or when you collect quotes at different times or from different sources. Again, verify that this rearrangement will not change the meaning or impression given by the speaker's words.

Paraphrasing quotes is another form of editing. For example: *According to Sastri of MediaVision, OEMs should expect to see integrated graphics/video capture/compression chip sets and boards from several different companies as early as mid-1994.*[32] This technique is useful for summarizing several direct quotes that are not strong enough to appear by themselves. Again, be sure that your paraphrase correctly reflects the context, meaning, and actual words of the quote, and don't add information to the paraphrase that wasn't in the original quote.[31]

Paraphrasing also can break-up a lengthy quote that may otherwise bore the reader or make the source appear too verbose. It also lets you put framework information around the quote, such as to explain the topic discussed in the quote itself. In this case, quote only the most powerful statement directly and paraphrase the rest.

*Caution:* Be aware of what happens when you use a partial quote. You may raise questions in the reader's mind about the part left out—that you may be quoting only the complimentary part of the statement.

### Quotes from Customers

Statements from current customers about your product or company make a powerful endorsement. But these quotes must be handled with care to avoid damaging valuable customer relationships.

The guidelines below can help you avoid problems when using customer quotes. They apply to all types of customer quotes, whether they appear as standalone statements or in a case study, article, news release, or other document that provides extensive customer information.

**Ask the right person for permission.** Your customer contact may not be authorized to make public statements on behalf of her company. Discuss with your contact whether an executive or PR manager must approve the proposed use of a quote or other customer information. This may add time to the interviewing stage, but will help you avoid problems later in the approval cycle, or worse yet, when the document has been published.

**Create an approval form.** As a minimum, the approval form should include or reference the customer information to be used, list all approved uses and restrictions, and provide a line for the customer's signature. Include the date, customer name, and contact information.

**Renew approvals as needed.** Circumstances in which you should renew the customer's approval include publication in a new document or medium, significant change in the customer's business (such as a merger), or continued use of a quote when your company releases a new version of the product. For quotes that are more than a year old, verify that all customer information is still correct and determine whether a new interview is appropriate to update the material.

**Follow-up.** Send a thank-you letter and copy of the published material to your source. This simple follow-up can go a long way toward cultivating future cooperation on new quotes, journalists' interviews, prospect references, and other endorsement activity.

### Quotes from Analysts and Third-Party Material

Most of the guidelines presented in the previous section also apply to quotes derived from product reviews, market research studies, or other information published by an analyst or other source that is independent of your company. Some analysts and market research firms may require payment of a fee before granting permission to use a quote or publication excerpt in promotional material.

However, restrictions may apply to use of this material, including:

- Considerations of copyright and fair use, especially for published material (see Chapter 8).
- Limitations on the type of material where the quote may appear, how the source is credited, the time period for which the quote may be cited, links to the source's Web site, or other usage factors.
- Whether you can name the person or company providing the quote or citation from a source document.

Verify that your use of these quotes is in compliance with the source's requirements before publishing the document.

## *Citing Sources*

Always credit the source when using any quote or excerpted text, whether directly or in a paraphrased form. There are two primary ways to give credit where it's due.

When quoting a customer or other individual, include the person's name, title, and organization as part of the quote statement. *"Using T1 lines has been the most economical way for us to handle combined voice and data applications," said Mel Morrison, Manager of Network Systems for Alaska Airlines.*[33]

When quoting a published source, cite the publication, survey, article, or report where the original information appears. *"The Raidion's low price alone makes it worth considering"—Byte, August 1992*[34] or *PC Magazine states, "Oracle7 was the hands down winner on our performance tests, outperforming the others by a wide margin."*[27]

When using verbs of attribution, pick a tense and stick with it, either present tense (she says) or past (she remarked). Present tense is typically used for profiles or other materials that are not time-related. Past tense is used for reporting an event or interview.[35]

Sometimes a customer or other source will allow you to publish information only if the source is unnamed. In this case, use language such as *one company ... , a customer in the banking industry ... ,* or *a study from a leading market research firm indicates... .* However, these anonymous sources weaken your message, and may cause the reader to think the information is fictional. Use a quote from an unidentified source only when you have no other way to present the information.

**Note:** Verify that any person quoted in a PR document is willing to be contacted by journalists or others when the material is released. Reporters may call for an interview or to verify the information provided by your source. Competitors or other customers may also call as a way of "fishing" for information; you will want to prepare your source to handle these calls correctly.

## OTHER CONTENT TYPES

The remaining content types described in this chapter are generally applicable to almost any subject matter found in technical marketing documents.

### *Comparisons*

Comparative information can be presented in several forms:

- Between a product and its competition, commonly called "comparative advertising." As these examples show, competitors may be named or unnamed:

  *A spreadsheet that's easier to learn and use than 1-2-3 and Excel!* [36]

  *No other network laser printer ...* [37]

- Among different models within a product line.
- Contrast of a product's capabilities with a non-technology method for achieving the same result. Or, to state it differently, describe the problems the reader will have without your product.

One disadvantage of making comparisons with competitive products is that readers may not have known about competitors until they read your material. This new insight may cause them to postpone a purchase decision until they have explored the competitive product. In addition, comparative advertising of any type is not allowed in some countries (see Chapter 9).

Comparisons are typically based on features, specifications, or performance measurements presented in the form of a point-by-point matrix or chart. Any comparison should be specific and objective so the reader will not see it as being unfairly slanted in your favor. And, to stay out of legal trouble, the comparison must be absolutely accurate and defensible (see Chapter 8).

Indirect, general comparisons can help you avoid a lawsuit, but a reader may not find them believable. Vague comparisons such as *This technology yields superior performance* are made stronger when followed by supporting evidence such as a chart of actual performance data.

Use comparison to:

- Show differences or similarities among products based on features, performance, application, or price.
- Show alternatives for product applications, configurations, or other decisions.
- Deliver a negative message, especially about competitors (see Chapter 3).
- Show scope or ranking of the product or company.
- State what a product is not. X *is not an operating system.*[38] This form of comparison can be an implicit way to highlight the product's key differentiating factor or a reader's problem.

While focused on ads, the guidelines in Figure 6.3 are useful for making appropriate product comparisons in any type of marketing material. They were developed by the American Association of Advertising Agencies (annotations added).

---

**Guidelines for Comparative Advertising**

The intent and connotation of the ad should be to inform and never to discredit or unfairly attack competitors, competing products or services.

When a competitive product is named, it should be one that exists in the marketplace as significant competition.

The competition should be fairly and properly identified but never in a manner or tone of voice that degrades the competitive product or service.

The advertising should compare related or similar properties or ingredients of the product, dimension to dimension, feature to feature.

The identification should be for honest comparison purposes and not simply to upgrade [your product or company] by association [with a perceived market leader].

If a competitive test is conducted it should be done by an objective testing source, preferably an independent one, so that there will be no doubt as to the veracity of the test. [Note: See the discussion of test results and product reviews in the section "Supporting Evidence" earlier in this chapter.]

In all cases the test should be supportive of all claims made in the advertising that are based on the test. [In other words, don't misstate or distort the test results to be more favorable to your product.]

---

**Guidelines for Comparative Advertising *(continued)***

---

The advertising should never use partial results or stress insignificant differences to cause the consumer to draw an improper conclusion [in favor of your product or against its competition].

The property [feature] being compared should be significant in terms of value or usefulness of the product to the consumer.

Comparatives delivered through the use of testimonials should not imply that the testimonial is more than one individual's thought unless that individual represents a sample of the majority viewpoint.

---

*Figure 6.3 Source: American Association of Advertising Agencies, with annotations by Janice King.*

## Problems, Needs, and Solutions

Describing a problem or need and how it was solved by a product or service is a very common content type in case studies, articles, and brochures. Use the ideas below to describe problems, needs, and solutions effectively.

**The "Before" Story.** Describe how the task or problem was addressed before the customer purchased the product. What were the dimensions of the problem? What did the customer want to do but couldn't given the situation? What issues, barriers, or other circumstances prompted the customer to consider your product?

**The "After" Story.** Describe the changes that occurred as a result of implementing the product. Relate these changes back to the problems or needs identified in the "before" section of the document. For example:

> *Problem: A component supplier to a medical instruments firm needs access to a materials list on her HP 3000, her client's inventory system on a VAX, and word processing files on her UNIX server.*
>
> *Solution: 3000 Connection—gives simultaneous access to HP 3000, VAX, and UNIX-based hosts along with LAN services.*[39]

A solution can be described by the results delivered by a product, both quantitative and qualitative:

- *Financial:* Increased revenues, reduced costs, or avoided expenses (quantitative).
- *Operational:* Increased efficiency, greater ease or flexibility in performing tasks, reductions in errors or unproductive work time (qualitative and quantitative).
- *Marketing:* New customers or product sales, new markets, new product offerings, increased customer satisfaction (quantitative and qualitative).
- *Organizational:* Improved employee retention or morale, improved information and decision making (qualitative).

## Reasons

Often presented in a bullet or numbered list, reason-why copy typically appears in ads, direct mail pieces, and brochures. Reasons tell the reader explicitly the major benefits of a product and are a great way to keep your writing focused on the reader's interests:

Headline: **10 Great Reasons to Upgrade to Stacker 3.0 for Windows and DOS!**

Reasons (abbreviated list):

**1. New Stackometer™... you can monitor the space on all your disk drives as you work.**

**2. New Flexible Setup gives you more control and more choices.**

**3. New Stacker Tuner™ gives you unequaled flexibility in managing your system.**[40]

## Issues

High-tech marketing communication isn't always focused on a product or company. White papers, backgrounders, and articles often present a company's viewpoint on controversies or issues in a market or technology area. These documents provide analysis and interpretation of what the issue means for the reader. For example, this excerpt discusses a set of issues:

**Whatever their situation, organizations should consider three primary issues affecting their email strategies. These issues are the rapid growth in the number of email users, the proliferation of PC LANs, and the emergence of new productivity-enhancing workgroup applications.**[41]

Writing about an issue can be tricky because the nature of the debate can change so quickly. In your copy, be careful about content and phrasing in discussing the issue, and how you present assertions and supporting evidence.

You may want to create material that defines the parameters or nature of the discussion about an issue. This technique is called "setting the agenda" in the reader's mind. For example, with this statement the company was apparently attempting to change the debate from a comparison of specific products to a higher-level view of customer requirements:

> *The new era of internetworking is characterized not by the merits of a single device, but by the robustness of an entire internet—and the resulting gains in an organization's productivity.*[42]

## Trends and Developments

Market or technology trends are another common topic for white papers, backgrounders, and articles. For example, this passage describes a trend:

> *A major trend of corporate information systems in the 1990s will be downsizing—using smaller, cheaper, yet powerful processors to support corporate application requirements.*[41]

When describing a trend, you may need to cover different types of information to help the reader understand the trend and its importance.[28]

**Scope.** How big is the trend? How many users have already adopted it? What do the market forecasts predict?

**Locale.** Where is this trend being developed or adopted? What is its breadth of coverage?

**Diversity.** How does the development reveal itself? Is it affecting multiple markets, applications, or platforms?

**Degree.** To what level are people, places, or things involved with or impacted by this trend?

**Perspective.** What other trends or developments are contributing to or impacting this one? These factors could include economic, social, political, legal, psychological;[28] and more specifically for high-tech products: business conditions, market activity, technology evolution, and competitive factors.

**Alternatives.** Describe the other choices available or counter-moves to this trend or development.

When writing about a trend, use a variety of sources for quotes, viewpoints, and explanations; include both direct participants or affected parties and external, neutral observers. Talk to people who are close to the action, not just the executives several layers up who can describe something only in very broad, lofty terms.

### Anecdotes

Anecdotes add human interest to any subject matter, helping the reader personally relate to the information. They are appropriate for case studies, articles, and brochures. When presenting an anecdote, consider using fiction techniques such as dialogue, foreshadowing and flashbacks, or cutting between scenes. Create a sense for the reader of immediacy, of being there, of being able to feel or visualize the circumstances or actions.

*The air smells of sweet flowers as you drive through the gardens, bypassing traffic and admiring the spring colors. Without warning, your car shakes violently for an instant, smoke rising, then comes to a complete standstill. You try in vain to restart the engine. Frustrated, you reach for the car phone and call the service station whose number you unfortunately know all too well.*[43]

Where can you find a good tale to tell? Talk to customers or beta users about their experience with a problem, with the product, or at an event. Talk to the behind-the-scenes people—the developers, installers, and support personnel who go through heroic or creative measures to accomplish a task or meet a deadline. Look for stories, ideas, or activities that are coincidental to your primary message, but help to show the value of the product, service, or activity.

*11:05 p.m. A lonely stretch of highway near Bellingham, Wash. Technician Tom Brosman, who just changed the nearest cell site, came upon a serious highway accident and reported it by placing one of the first calls on the new switch. Then he called the Changeout Control Center. "The new system just paid for itself," he said.*[44]

## Examples

Examples can be critical for clarifying topics, supporting assertions, illustrating concepts, or supplying evidence that reinforces key messages. Use examples to show:

- How a technology, product, or service can be applied in a typical user environment
- Potential benefits or results from the technology or trend
- A function or process of a product or service

Choose examples carefully, making sure they indeed support the point you want to make. Match examples to the interests of the audience for the piece, and be sensitive to varying cultural interpretations (see Chapter 9).

## CONTENT TYPES FOR THE WEB

A Web site can accommodate any of the content types discussed in this chapter. You may also become involved in writing the content types listed below. Because these are considered legal documents, work with the company attorney to develop the appropriate text.

**Terms and conditions for Web content.** Describes how a visitor may use the site content and services. May also cover license terms for software downloads available on the site, as well as disclaimers for site security, links to external Web sites, and other issues. If children are a target audience, you may need to include terms that specifically address their use of the site.

**Privacy policy.** Describes how your company (or the site owner) will collect and use personal information submitted by site visitors or tracked automatically during a visitor's session.

**Other legal information.** Typical content includes a copyright notice, a list of company trademarks, and the official company address and other contact details. This information may appear in multiple places throughout the site.

### Web Content for Wireless Devices

The idea of "anytime, anywhere" access to email and the Web via a wireless phone or personal digital assistant (PDA) has great appeal to users and marketers alike.

Consider whether you will provide content to mobile devices as part of the planning process for any Web project. Example content includes:

- Promotional offers, often made through a text message, electronic coupon, or an interactive ad
- News updates and alerts, targeted to journalists or investors
- Condensed versions of company or product information
- Personalized text messages based on customer requests or interests
- Surveys or polls

The reality of very limited screen space and awkward input methods has been a major barrier to full realization of text and graphical communications on a hand-held wireless device. Display capabilities and presentation technologies are changing rapidly to address many of these user interface issues. And while writing techniques will be determined in large part by the display capabilities of the device, the principles below provide common guidelines for adapting Web content.

- Short text messages with a link for accessing additional information
- Very short commands on menus (typically, 1-3 words)
- Audio narration instead of or in addition to on-screen text
- Minimized layers in menus to help users avoid getting lost. This guideline may mean that each layer has many options, requiring the user to scroll the display to view them all.

## RESOURCES

The recommended books and other resources listed below provide additional information on the topics discussed in this chapter. For an updated list, visit **writinghightech.com.**

### Books

Bill Carmody: *Online Promotions: Winning Strategies and Tactics.* Wiley, 2004. Detailed guidance for contests, special offers, and other promotional activities conducted on the Web or via email.

Kim M. Bayne: *Marketing Without Wires: Targeting Promotions and Advertising to Mobile Device Users.* Wiley, 2002. A good primer for the concepts of presenting email and Web content on wireless devices. However, supplement this book with more current readings on wireless technologies, presentation techniques, and promotion types.

Shayne Bowman and Chris Willis: *Designing Web Sites That Sell.* Rockport Publishers, 2002. A clear discussion of what goes into an effective, large-scale e-commerce site, with many example screen shots.

### Web Sites

The following sites provide articles, reports, and other resources related to promotional content, issues, and copywriting techniques:

Advertising Age Magazine (**advertisingage.com**)

Ad Week Magazine (**adweek.com**)

American Association of Advertising Agencies (**aaaa.com**)

Direct Marketing Association (**the-dma.org**)

## REFERENCES

[1] Dee Kiamy: *The High-Tech Marketing Companion.* Addison-Wesley, 1993

[2] Product brochure, Adobe Systems, Inc.

[3] Product brochure, Attachmate Corp.

[4] Product brochure, Northern Telecom, Inc.

[5] Product brochure, WordPerfect Corp.

[6] Product brochure, Microsoft Corp.

[7] Product brochure, John Fluke Manufacturing Co., Inc.

[8] Press release, Digital Systems International, Inc.

[9] Customer case study, Digital Systems International, Inc.

[10] Product data sheet, Networx, Inc.

[11] Press release, Wall Data, Inc.

[12] Screen tip, Microsoft Corp.

[13] Direct mail brochure, Digital Equipment Corp.

[14] Brochure, Ameritech Corp.

[15] Article in *Broadband* Magazine, Second Quarter 2001, Cisco Systems, Inc.

[16] David Nadziejka: "Term Talk," *Technical Communication,* 4th Qrtr 1992

[17] John A. Barry: *Technobabble.* The MIT Press, 1991

[18] "Ad-Vantage," *Marketing Computers,* December 1992

[19] Direct mail letter, Aldus Corp.

[20] Leonard L. Berry and A. Parasuraman: *Marketing Services: Competing Through Quality.* The Free Press, 1991

[21] Product ad, Symantec Corp.

[22] Product ad, Lotus Development Corp.

[23] Product ad, Analog Devices Corp.

[24] Product ad, IBM Corp.

[25] Press release, Andrew Corp.

[26] Press release, IDC, May 21, 2004

[27] Product ad, Oracle Corp.

[28] William E. Blundell: *The Art and Craft of Feature Writing.* Plume, 1988

[29] Customer newsletter, Wellfleet Communications, Inc.

[30] Product brochure, Intuit

[31] James L. Marra: *Advertising Creativity: Techniques for Generating Ideas.* Prentice-Hall, 1990

[32] Bernard C. Cole: "The Art of Blending Video and Graphics," IABC *Communications World,* December 1993

[33] Customer case study, ADC Kentrox

[34] Product ad, Micropolis Corp.

[35] Marshall J. Cook: *Leads & Conclusions.* Writer's Digest Books, 1995

[36] Product ad, Borland International, Inc.

[37] Product ad, Compaq Computer Corp.

[38] Product booklet, Tektronix, Inc.

[39] Product brochure, Walker, Richer & Quinn, Inc.

[40] Direct mail brochure, Stac Electronics

[41] White paper, Microsoft Corp.

[42] Article in customer magazine, Cisco Systems, Inc.

[43] Product brochure, TeleSciences, Inc.

[44] Janice King: "Sleepless in Seattle," *TE&M Magazine,* December 1, 1993

# 7

## TEXT TECHNIQUES

### ADDING POWER TO YOUR COPY

High-tech copywriting can be creative and fun, but it also can be frustrating and challenging to do well. On one hand, you are free to explore a range of writing styles and forms of expression. On the other hand, you face high expectations from audiences for the appeal, readability, and relevance of the piece. In a marcom document you can use a broad vocabulary, loose sentence structure, metaphors, even humor. But you must also deliver a realistic, informative, and convincing presentation about the product, service, or company.

Good copywriting skills require continual practice. You will find yourself constantly striving to improve the clarity, power, and impact of your writing. Look at a marketing piece that does well at holding your interest and delivering its message. You are likely to find the piece is successful because it uses a variety of techniques such as:

- Language that is easy to understand yet is potent and expressive.
- Phrasing that follows the natural, varied rhythms of speech.

---

- Short paragraphs, incomplete sentences, and other deviations from the traditional rules for good writing.
- Formatting devices that guide a reader's eye through the key points.
- Verbal imagery that amplifies a message or clarifies a concept.

This chapter describes a variety of techniques that will help you transform your content into an interesting, polished marcom document. Some of the techniques presented here may seem contradictory or inappropriate to certain projects or media. Some will not be appropriate for documents that will be adapted for international markets.

Indeed, if you tried to apply all of these techniques to each marcom document, you would not be successful. Instead, think of these techniques as ingredients you can selectively add to your typical writing style to create the unique recipe you will need for a particular marcom document. Just as you wouldn't combine certain flavors when cooking, you will want to blend these techniques carefully.

## GETTING AND KEEPING ATTENTION

Catching a reader's attention is the first task of any marcom document. It involves more than just a headline set in 72-point type or blinking on a Web page. But how do you pack your words with the right kind of punch? This section presents a range of ideas for getting and keeping a reader's attention.

### Power Words

Power words grab the reader's attention immediately and keep it until the end of the key points you want to make. Power words are lively, specific, and concrete; they are active verbs, descriptive nouns, and vivid modifiers.

**Nouns**. Use the most specific nouns you can find for the subject of the sentence. Examples of power nouns include: *tasks, results, efforts, answers, islands [of computers].*

**Verbs**. Use vibrant verbs to express an action. Examples of power verbs include: *yield, synergize, escalate, generate, maximize.*

**Modifiers**. Use adjectives and adverbs that add a vivid punch or flavor to the sentence or phrase. Examples of power modifiers include: *keener, staggering, foremost, enduring.*

The opposite of power words are qualifiers such as *somewhat, almost,* or *possibly.* You may use qualifiers when the subject or assertion is in doubt or if you indeed want to temper or hedge a statement.

Another type of qualifier is any form of the auxiliary verb *can;* the reader may ask "so does it or doesn't it?" Use forms of *can* only to indicate that options or choices are available for the action described by the primary verb.

### Evocative Language

> *How do I know what I think, until I see what I say?*
> —W.H. Auden

Words that conjure a sensory meaning for the reader can have a very strong impact. To find evocative language, think of words that will create a vision, a sound, or a feeling in the reader's mind. For example: *VoiceView: A Sight for Sore Ears.*[58]

Did you get the picture of someone who has been talking on the telephone for too long? This example is effective not only because it evokes an image, but also because it talks about a problem familiar to almost anyone. This attention-getting technique intrigues the reader to continue further into the document. When using evocative language, be sure the phrasing paints a complete and accurate picture.

Here is another example of this technique: *Scream Saver for Windows*[1]

Did you hear a scream in your mind? This is an example of onomatopoetic language—words that sound like what they describe. Your goal when using words that create a distinctive sound in the mind's ear is to achieve euphony (pleasing to the ear), not dissonance.

Alliteration is another technique based on sound; in this case, the repetition of the same letter or sound within a sequence of words or phrases. For example: *Protection. Performance. Productivity.*[2]

## Emotion

Suggesting a positive or negative emotion for the reader can add greatly to the impact of your text. Using emotion doesn't mean telling a sentimental story about how the product has achieved triumph against overwhelming odds. Instead, use emotion that is appropriate to the audience and their circumstances, and use it in measured doses.

**Frustration.** This is one of the most common emotions referenced for technical products. After all, everyone recognizes the experience of trying to get this blasted thing to work!... *as I sit here watching my spreadsheet crawl on my PC, I'm thinking to myself, "This is making it easier?*[3]

**Wishes and dreams, ambition or prestige.** *What if you could...* or *Now, the faster processing you've wanted is here.*

**Comfort, ease, and convenience.** *Dallas Semiconductor's digital potentiometers, unlike their mechanical counterparts, can be set remotely. No dials. No screwdrivers.*[4]

**Fear, skepticism, or confusion.** *Downtime could cost you a lot more than just access to your data.*[5]

**Challenges.** *You've got 60 days to create a computer-based training system for 5,000 employees—and you're not a programmer.*[6]

Many marketing messages are designed to evoke FUD (Fear, Uncertainty, and Doubt) in the reader. FUD is an extremely powerful—if tricky—technique for grabbing a reader's attention and motivating a response or action (see Chapter 3). *What else are they slashing when they slash prices?*[7]

*Caution*: Be careful when using any of the negative emotions such as confusion, fear, or anger. When you do, always show how the reader can overcome or avoid this negative situation with your product. And, make sure your use of positive emotions doesn't imply a promise that is more than the product can deliver.

## Relevance

Think about what catches your eye—the ads or brochures that describe a familiar problem or situation, right? The more tangible, the more "real life" you can make the information in a marcom document, the more the reader will relate and respond. Examples of familiar problems or situations include:

**Time pressures.** *Downloadable configuration files save many hours when connecting multiple PCs to the application.*

**Industry or business trends.** *One result of this trend [an increased demand for remote access] is that many Cisco customers are adding remote offices and small sites to their internetworks.*[8]

**Preparation for disasters or for the future.** *Whether it's a crashed disk or an unretrievable file, computer failures seem to occur at the worst possible times.*[9]

**Financial concerns.** *You need to create a local presence, but you're wondering whether you can afford to open a branch office.*[10]

Draw the reader into the document by addressing her directly with "you" words throughout the copy. Put the reader into the scene:[11] *... which meant [you had to] weave the cable up, over, around and through office obstacles ... .*[12]

Copy that conveys relevance is effective for grabbing a reader's attention when used in a headline or opener, and for holding that interest when it appears throughout the document.

## Emphasis

Two techniques can help you improve the emphasis of text: where you place the key message, and the use of formatting devices.

Put the message or point you want to emphasize either at the beginning or the end of the sentence. Place the emphasis at the beginning to help the reader understand the topic or message immediately. Place it at the end to deliver a "punch line" or to help the reader remember it as the last thought in a paragraph, section, or document.

Formatting devices are a way to make individual messages, phrases, or words stand out from the rest of the text. These devices include use of a second color, exclamation points, commas, boldface and italic type, bullets, em dashes, ellipses, and uppercase (but don't use uppercase if the document includes acronyms). Formatting devices are especially useful for highlighting benefits, quotes, definitions, or to deliver the payoff for a teaser or anecdote. They can draw a reader's attention to key points and improve the rhythm of your writing. The example below incorporates several of these devices:

**Want to get more from your Aldus software?**

More *productivity*?

With practical techniques that reduce time and effort, while improving results.

More *profitability*?

By avoiding costly printing problems and preparing files so they print right the first time.

More *self-reliance*?

Through troubleshooting system, printing, and file-management problems—all by yourself!

How *about all of the above?*[13]

Exclamation points add a sense of excitement or urgency to a message and are especially effective in a headline, pull quote, or call to action: *Remember that this is a risk-free offer!*[14] However, punctuation marks are very difficult to see on a screen display, so don't rely on them as the only form of emphasizing text in Web content.

One thing to keep in mind for formatting devices is that a reader may look only at those words that have received special typographic treatment. Stand back from the printed piece or Web page display and look only at the words highlighted by a formatting device. Are these the right words to highlight for the emphasis you want?

## *Inspiration*

Convey the sense of satisfaction or achievement a reader can obtain with the product or service. Give readers positive, exciting reasons for buying the product or agreeing with your views. Think of this technique as a form of evangelizing the product—a concept that Apple Computer adopted with great success when it launched the Macintosh computer in the early 1980s. You can create inspiration by invoking a variety of motivators.

**Leadership.** After all, everyone likes to know they'll be in good company when they buy a product. *Voicelink is used by the world's most respected companies. [It] gives you the competitive edge you need to succeed.*[15]

**Strategic values.** *With a network that carries new types of traffic, your business can now address new strategies, new service offerings, and new markets.*

**Future opportunities.** *Calling Centers are a New Business Opportunity for Utilities.*[10]

## *Transitions*

Successful direct-mail copywriters are masters of transition... keeping a reader's interest piqued through every paragraph and every page of a long sales letter. Many of the techniques used by these writers—such as suspense and tease—can engage and keep the reader's attention in other marketing materials, especially Web content.

**Words and phrases.** A transition can be made by individual words at the beginning of a new paragraph, such as "And," "Yet," even "However." A staple transition for direct-mail copy is the phrase "But wait, there's more!" These transitions signal the reader that more information is coming and it would be worthwhile to continue reading. A handy list of transition words and phrases is included in the book *Words That Sell* by Richard Bayan (see the Resources section).

**Formatting devices.** Punctuation such as an ellipsis (...), a dash (—), and a colon (:) all signal the reader that the thought presented in a sentence is not yet complete.

**Breaking the paragraph.** You were probably taught that a paragraph should contain one complete point, with each subsequent paragraph making a different, also complete point. But direct-mail copywriters often break a paragraph before the thought is complete, sometimes after only one or two sentences. When using this technique, choose a breakpoint where the reader will instinctively recognize the need to continue.

**Questions.** Ending a paragraph with a question naturally prompts the reader to look for the answer in the next paragraph. This technique can be especially effective for prompting the reader to turn the page on a printed document, or to click on the "Continue" link when an online document is split across several Web pages.

## CREATING RHYTHM

> *Words march to a beat. Sentences have rhythm. Their pace*
> *can be fast or slow; their cadence, soothing or staccato.*
> *The skillful writer controls the dance of words by*
> *carefully manipulating the structure of sentences.*
> *Long sentences can flow gently,*
> *picking up momentum as they go.*
> *Short sentences can create a tense, insistent rhythm.*
> *Repetition can add accent and meter.*
> *—Herschell Gordon Lewis* [16]

The cadence or rhythm of your writing is a subtle form of holding the reader's interest in a document. Text with an even rhythm—created by words with the same number of syllables and sentences of similar length—may be easy to read but may also put the reader to sleep.

When evaluating the rhythm of your copy, consider the overall pace you want to establish for the document as well as for the individual elements, paragraphs, and sentences. Do you want to keep a varied rhythm throughout, or build momentum gradually to a crescendo that is delivered in the conclusion or call to action?

Check rhythm by reading the text aloud. To the reader, your writing should seem like a satisfying, engaging conversation. If it sounds stilted or if you stumble over phrases while reading, the text has a rhythm problem. To get the words back on the beat, write it like you would speak it, but without slipping into grammatical sloppiness, a disrespectful tone, or inappropriate use of idiom.

Paradoxically, one of the best ways to improve the rhythm of your writing is to break it. Use short sentences. Long sentences. Varied paragraph lengths. A mix of active and passive voice. But remember to make your rhythm compatible with the style and tone of the piece. You can change rhythm within a piece by using any mix of the techniques described in this section.

## Varied Sentences

Using different sentence lengths can improve the rhythm of text. However, avoid very long or complex words and sentences that will slow down or trip the reader. For example:

> *SKYLIGHT is a low-cost, easy-to-use, yet powerful database management system designed to give Windows application developers a refreshing alternative to the cumbersome and non-intuitive database managers currently available.*[17]

Without looking, can you remember what this sentence was talking about at its beginning? It would be better broken into two sentences:

> *SKYLIGHT is a low-cost, easy-to-use, yet powerful database management system. It gives Windows application developers a refreshing alternative to cumbersome, nonintuitive database managers.*

When they contain clear, simple language, you can use a mix of long sentences, short sentences, and fragments as well as declarative sentences and those with subordinate clauses. *We handle more applications than all other providers combined. Collect call billing. Suspend, restore, disconnect. Innovative solutions that lower costs, improve customer service, raise revenue—and work perfectly with other databases.*[18]

Another way to vary sentences is to use a mix of active and passive voice. In most cases, it is better to write in active voice because it makes clear the subject-action-object relationship in a sentence. Readers who know English as a second language will find active voice easier to understand; some languages do not use passive voice at all.

However, passive voice may be more appropriate for the following situations:

- When you want to emphasize the act, not the actor or when an action doesn't have an actor.[19]

- When an actor is implied, but unnamed because the actor is unknown or described indirectly in the surrounding text.
- When the act or the thing acted upon (the object) is more important than the actor (the subject).
- When an action doesn't have a specific actor, or the actor cannot be identified for some reason.

The techniques below will help you identify the use of passive voice and rewrite those sentences in active voice.

**Verbs ending in "ed" when the sentence is present tense.** Change the verb to the active, present-tense form, and revise the sentence to imperative or the classic subject-verb-object phrasing. *The management tool is configured via a GUI.* Rewrite the sentence in the imperative form: *Configure the management tool via the GUI.*

**The sentence is missing an actor.** Add an actor: *Network administrators can configure the management tool via a GUI.*

**An actor need not be a person.** For example, instead of: *A test conducted in 2000 confirmed these results,* write: *In 2000, an automated test system confirmed these results.*

**Check the sentence construction.** A sentence written in the form "the [verb] of" always indicates passive voice. Use the active verb form instead:

Passive: *This network enables the transport of video.*
Active: *This network transports video.*

Use active voice to present facts, assertions, conclusions, summaries, or supporting evidence. Use passive voice to indicate indirectness, uncertainties, or complexities: *Notification of critical problems is escalated to all levels of your organization.*[20]

Passive voice is one way to vary the rhythm of a text. In addition, if the document needs an academic writing style, passive voice may appear more often.

## Rhyme and Wordplay

Rhymes, a clever turn on a familiar phrase, and other forms of wordplay can add rhythm to text. Consider these headlines: *Unmiring Wiring*[21] (rhyme), or *High Performance for disk, DAT, and the other things*[22] (wordplay). Wordplay often means giving new meaning to familiar phrases, such as *Welcome to the LAN of plenty.*[23] Wordplay also can incorporate product or company names, such as this tag line for a set of sound chips called JAZZ: *It's time to JAZZ up your designs.*[24]

To develop ideas for wordplay, look at the product's features, benefits, or applications; you can also consider the behavioral characteristics of the target audience. Look for words that can have different meanings in different contexts.[11]

Rhyme and wordplay are most effective in sales pieces; they may not be appropriate for white papers or other serious editorial material. While these techniques are often used in headlines, rhyme and wordplay also can be applied with positive results to other document elements.

When creating wordplay based on sound, make sure the meanings of the words you select are truly appropriate for the message you want to convey. Also, consider whether readers will understand your wordplay, especially if the document will be translated or read by an international audience.

### Parallelism

Parallel structure creates a sense of rhythm within a sentence or paragraph, between paragraphs, or in a bullet list. Parallelism means using the same sentence structure for related topics, such as starting each sentence in a paragraph with a subordinate clause, or each item in a bullet list with an adjective.

One form of parallelism is to use word combinations that have balanced sounds, syllable counts, placement, or meaning: *The Way It's Packed, Stacked, and Backed.*[25]

Another form of parallelism is repeating key words, messages, or phrases like a mantra:

*Easy to Buy*
*Easy to Install*
*Easy to Use*
*Easy to Expand*[26]

This example shows how using a combination of repeated structure and repeated words can create a sense of rhythm.

*Cautions:* First, repeating unusual words or inappropriate jargon may trip the reader, especially if those words are defined poorly or not at all in your text. The reader may skip over the unfamiliar word or phrase the first time, but become annoyed when she encounters it again and again.

Second, too much repetition of the same words or phrases in a piece can lead to staleness and lessen the impact of your message. Watch for overuse of favorite words when you review the drafts of a piece. Use the search capability in your word processor to find these words, then replace them selectively with carefully chosen synonyms.

### Document Elements

Look at how you are using the different elements in the piece. Subheads, pull quotes, sidebars, callouts, and captions can all be effective tools for improving the appeal and rhythm of a document, especially for breaking up lengthy blocks of body copy (see Chapter 5).

## ASKING QUESTIONS

Questions are an especially effective technique for headlines and closing statements. For example, the headline *What Does it Take to Get High-Quality, Obsolescence-Proof Electronic Publishing?*[27] could be followed by the closing statement, *Can you afford cheap publishing software?*

Use questions to prompt the reader to analyze a problem or to reconsider a competitive product or viewpoint. Questions are also key to building the FUD factor (see Chapter 3). This technique is most effective when the questions are directed to the reader or when they are written from the reader's perspective. Using first or second person in questions helps the reader's understanding and is more likely to encourage him to continue reading in order to find the answer.

You can sprinkle questions throughout the text to build a case gradually, or list the questions in a separate section or sidebar. You can create a sense of mystery or intrigue by posing a question in a headline or opener, then answering it later in the document. A question-and-answer section (Q&A) is an approach that is often used in white papers, press kits, or articles.

When writing questions, don't limit yourself to those actually asked by customers (although these are usually the most relevant to the reader's interests). Questions can highlight product features, reinforce marketing messages, or overcome a reader's potential objections to your arguments. *How can you do more with less? How can you bring your products to market faster? How can you get more out of your existing technology investment?*[28]

*Caution:* When asking questions, make sure they do not exclude or filter out prospects.[16] This inadvertent exclusion is more likely to happen with closed-end questions (answered with a yes or no) than with open-end or "what if" questions.

## CONTRASTING SEMANTICS

The semantic contrast technique creates a juxtaposition of words or phrases that make your point in a surprising, engaging way.

This juxtaposition is typically based on antithesis, the contrast of two words with opposite meanings. But semantic contrast also can create a symmetry between words based on their usage or purpose in a sentence, as in this example: *We give you big-system performance. We give you small-system flexibility.* Here, the direct contrast is between *big-system* and *small-system*, while an indirect contrast is made between *performance* and *flexibility*.

The contrasting semantics technique offers great flexibility for illustrating a product's features or making a selling point. Here are two examples:

*When your systems are complex, your choice is simple.*

*[This truck] is designed to haul loads for your customers, and lighten them for your company.*[29]

## USING IMAGERY

It is always easier for a reader to understand something new when you can compare it with something familiar. Taking a new or highly technical product or issue and describing it in a familiar way is one of the benefits of using any of the imagery techniques: analogy, metaphor, allusion, and personification.

**Analogy** suggests similarity between two things based on a substantial amount of similar or shared attributes. It is a useful technique for describing the characteristics of a product, service, or activity. *This is a Convention Like Woodstock was Just a Concert.*[30] Analogy can be a literal, concrete comparison of things that belong to the same class (convention and Woodstock are both events) or a figurative comparison of two things that are completely different: *Like the owners of starter homes that have become too small for growing families, many users feel their local-area networks are busting at the seams from new, bandwidth-hungry applications.*[31] Analogy may be used to compare things based on a relationship of one-to-one, one-to-many, many-to-one, or many-to-many.

**Metaphor** suggests comparison by using symbolism or describing a technical idea or feature in terms of something that is nontechnical. This technique relies on the power of showing something in a new light or describing something complex in terms that are simpler and more familiar to the reader. Metaphor must use symbolism in a way that the reader can recognize and interpret correctly, such as in this example comparing a network wiring device to an airport: *The first transportation hub that handles more connections than O'Hare.*[32] A few of the many sources of metaphor include current events, sports, entertainment, music, nature, or hobbies. Metaphor compares the similarities of two seemingly different things in a one-to-one relationship.

**Allusion** is an indirect reference to "… a well-known character or situation from literature, history, or popular culture, or to a proverb or topical saying."[33] For example, an article about an all-night installation project in the Seattle area was titled "Sleepless in Seattle," alluding to the film with the same title.[34]

**Personification** gives a human quality to an inanimate object. For example, in one ad the computer monitors it promotes are made to address the reader directly, as if in a conversation: *Pardon* *us, but would you mind if we sat right here on your desk, a mere two feet away from you, for the next few thousand hours?*[35]

These guidelines will help you make effective use of imagery.

**Match language and visuals.** Be especially careful that your language and visuals work together to support the image. For example, an advertisement that shows a photo of industrial machinery can use the words *gear up, mesh,* and *whole works.*[36]

**Use a relevant vocabulary.** Make a verbal connection to the document's subject or story. For example, an advertisement that described the communication needs of the healthcare industry used this headline: *Looking for a specialist in data systems and solutions? I'll refer you to Bell Atlantic.*[37] In this example the words specialist and refer are drawn from the vocabulary of the target audience.

**Consider the document's concept.** Decide whether to carry the image throughout the piece, both visually and verbally. For example, a brochure for a product called Concert displayed the metaphor of a symphony orchestra with subheads labeled *The Overture, The First Movement,* and *Finale,* as well as related words in the text such as *tuning, harmony, movement, tempo, players, unison,* and *orchestration.*[38]

When metaphor is a major concept for the piece, create a list of all the nouns, verbs, adjectives, and adverbs related to that metaphor. Use this list when writing the text to help you convey the image thoroughly and concretely. A terrific resource for this task is *The Random House Word Menu,* which presents word lists by topic (see the Resources section).

The various forms of imagery can be powerful for improving the memorability of a piece. But they also can cause problems if not used carefully.

**Comprehension.** People may not understand the allusion or metaphor, or may have different interpretations and associations with the image. You may be tempted to overextend the image in ways that decrease its usefulness or that are inappropriate to the subject matter.

**Appropriateness.** You may try to make an inappropriate image fit when presenting the information in a straight, expository form would be a better approach. The images may be clichés or rely too much on idiom or fads. The image may perpetuate an unfair stereotype of people, places, or things. An image that may be perfectly acceptable to one audience may be offensive to others.

**Mixed images.** It is easy to create too many images, which then confuse readers and dilute your message. Choose one analogy or metaphor and stick with it. For example, one ad used an image of a *bridge* in both the visual and the headline, but then ignored it in the text, talking instead about *benchmarks, promises,* and *steps*.[39]

**Errors.** The image may be presented incorrectly. For example, this passage alludes to the film *The Wizard of Oz*: *Where Are We? Not in Kansas anymore, Toto. In the summer of 1992, the cyclone of ATM is cutting a swath through the user and service provider landscape.*[40] Well, even Toto (a dog) could have told this writer it was a *tornado* that transported him and Dorothy to Oz. Imagine the surprise of Kansas residents if a cyclone (an oceanic rain and wind storm similar to a hurricane) had indeed struck.

## SHOWING PARADOX

Paradox describes something that seems self-contradictory or to be two things at once. For example, *Recent studies reveal 25 MHz is now faster than 50 MHz*[41] (presumably not feasible), or *We perform field service even when there's no field*[42] (in a story that described a service trip to an offshore oil well). Use paradox as a technique to describe a feature, problem, solution, or need.

Paradox is an effective technique because it catches the reader off-guard and piques his interest in learning how this apparent impossibility can be true.

## ADDING HUMOR

Humor and puns can be a great way to make a point if they are used intentionally and carefully. For example, an article about a company called XLNT Designs Inc. was titled *Totally XLNT [excellent] FDDI Management*[43]—in this case, using idiom to make a pun of the company's name. Or, this statement about a fiber-optic cable:... ***there's light at the end of the bundle***[44] makes a pun out of a familiar proverb. (These cables transmit light through fibers that are bundled together in a sheath.)

*Caution*: An attempt at humor can lead to bloopers that are the embarrassment of any marketing writer. Consider whether the audience will understand the joke. Remember that all forms of humor—including sarcasm, irony, parody, and puns—often don't translate well into other languages. And you must be certain that your humor won't offend readers. Avoid any jokes or puns that imply racism, sexism, or cultural slur.

## WATCHING THE BASICS

This book is not intended to be a review of the basic principles of good writing. However, the principles described in this section have special application to marketing writing.

**Contractions.** When using an informal style in the document, you may want to use verb contractions such as ***it's, won't,*** and ***aren't***. Contractions help to maintain a conversational tone, but they may slow down the reader if used extensively, because of the time the reader needs to decode them.

**Possessives.** Do not use a product name or other trademarked text in the possessive form. Such usage can jeopardize the status of the trademark (see Chapter 8).

**Conjunctions.** In most marketing documents it is acceptable to start sentences with conjunctions such as ***And, Or, But, Yet,*** and ***Because***.

**Slang and Idiom.** Slang and idiom, if used cautiously, can be effective in some marcom documents. You can use slang if you have a small, homogeneous audience that fully understands your meaning. But if readers come from a variety of backgrounds, age groups, or cultures, your slang may not have any meaning, or worse, it may be offensive. Slang also presents a problem for translators, and can make the piece seem dated when the hip slang of today goes out of fashion tomorrow.

**Narrator's Voice.** The narrator's voice in a document can be in first or third person. The use of the second person (you) to address the reader, combined with the first person plural (we), is common in marcom documents because it creates a sense of direct communication between the company or author and the reader. However, many marcom documents are written in the third person in order to create a sense of objectivity. No matter which narrator's voice you choose, use it consistently throughout the document.

## TEXT TECHNIQUES FOR WEB CONTENT

> *Writing is the only thing that… When I'm doing it,*
> *I don't feel that I should be doing something else instead.*
> —Gloria Steinem

Although many of the techniques described in this chapter can be applied to Web content, some will not be comprehensible or appropriate to the site's content or visitors. A wealth of books and Web sites present detailed guidelines and examples for effective copywriting techniques on the Web (see the Resources section). The most common recommendations are summarized here.

**Place important information first.** Write in an inverted-pyramid structure, with the most important information at the top of the page. This is the same style that journalists use when writing a newspaper article. By placing the key information and messages in the first 25 lines on the page, you catch a visitor's attention and encourage further reading to learn about the details. This approach also ensures that you present the essential information to visitors who do not scroll down to view the complete page.

**Write short.** The text for Web pages is more effective if it is shorter and crisper than what you may be accustomed to writing for print materials. Short, declarative, or imperative sentences are easier to understand both for international visitors and when visitors read text on the screen. Write shorter paragraphs—even single-sentence paragraphs. For complex information, use bullet lists and tables instead of paragraphs. Consider the shorter line length of displayed text—usually 8–10 words—and how that may impact a reader's understanding of your text.

**Be consistent.** On a Web page, visitors can be confused by ambiguous and inconsistent wording of any content, but especially menus, links, and other navigation elements. This is one case where you don't want to be creative in your writing, because a confused visitor is likely to abandon the purchase or transaction and leave the site. For example, a *Shopping Cart* should always be a *Shopping Cart* not a *Shopping Basket* or *Your Purchase* depending on which page the visitor displays.

Make sure the terms for buttons and graphical links are congruent with any associated icons; a link that shows a grocery cart icon should use the text *Shopping Cart.*

**Choose specificity over generality or creativity.** For example, instead of *My Stuff* use *Your Account* or *Account Profile* as the button label that links to a visitor's personal information page.

**Format for clarity.** Don't rely on punctuation to convey meaning, as it can be nearly impossible to see on screen.

Avoid using acronyms, or show the component words on each page where the acronym appears. If content on the site includes numerous acronyms or other specialized terms, create a glossary page of definitions, and link to that page from the first appearance of each acronym or term on each Web page.

For more than seven items in a bullet list, group the items into separate lists with subheads to indicate category or topic.

Some writers use underlining to add emphasis to individual words, sentences, or paragraphs. However, on the Web underlining usually indicates the text is an active link. Remove the underline from any text that will not be a link and use bold or italic format instead.

**Use links.** Don't reference other blocks of text or images—even if they are located on the same page—with words alone such as "as described above" or "as shown in Figure 1." Create a link to these items instead, whether they are located on the same page or other pages on the site.

### *Writing Link Text*

<u>What if this entire sentence was a link on a Web page</u>? Would you be able to guess where it might lead, or why you would want to go there? This example illustrates the importance of writing the link text in a way that helps the visitor recognize what to expect when clicking on that link.

Don't write long sentences as links; these make it too difficult for visitors to determine where the link will lead or what type of interaction it will activate. Instead, make the link from a keyword or short phrase (for a topic link) or a verb-object pair (for taking an action). Here are a few examples:

- <u>Order PrimeWidget</u> (emphasis is on the action).
- Check the <u>Locator</u> for a store near you (emphasis is on the page content).
- View details about the <u>Annual User Conference</u> (emphasis is on the topic).

*Caution:* Don't make the link text too short and cryptic or visitors won't be motivated to follow it.

Other guidelines to remember when writing link text include the following:

- When multiple links appear together as a series, place the most important links at the top of a bullet list or at the left on a horizontal line.
- In bullet lists, use a parallel structure for the link text as much as possible. For example, in a product family overview that links to catalog pages, start each link with the product name.
- Users will recognize links more easily when they appear at the beginning or end of the sentence or paragraph.

## TOP 10 MISTAKES IN HIGH-TECH COPY

Sadly, many marketing pieces don't meet the guidelines for good writing that are described in this book. Maybe it is due to the influence of marketers who are too caught up in their promotional zeal. Maybe it is due to writers who don't fully understand what they are writing about. Maybe it is due to engineers who lose sight of customer benefits in their enthusiasm for product features. Maybe it is just the pressure of too much work to do in too little time.

You can avoid these problems by following the guidelines in this book and by checking documents for the mistakes described in this section.

### Mistake #1: Excessive Hype

The word hype is an abbreviation of hyperbole, which means exaggeration or overstatement. Of course the first job of marketing is to make a product, service, or company seem like the best in its category. As a result, it is tempting to use nothing but superlatives such as *best, most, perfect,* or *greatest* when writing about a product. But readers view these superlatives with skepticism unless they are followed by strong supporting evidence.

Overuse of superlatives is where promotional copy can get into the most trouble. It can cause your statements to lose credibility in the reader's mind because she won't find them believable. Or, in the worst case, it can misrepresent a product, causing legal and ethical problems (see Chapter 8).

Of course, no self-respecting marketer will describe a product as "Ralph's Pretty Good System" (to borrow from author Garrison Keillor). Hype can have a place in some materials, such as print and Web banner advertisements, direct-mail pieces, and email campaigns, where your message must compete for the reader's attention in a very cluttered environment. And strong adjectives and adverbs *do* play an important role in conveying message and product positioning.

But not every product needs to be described as the latest, most advanced, proven, complete, sophisticated, integrated, value-added solution to any problem your customers will ever have. Instead, a more realistic presentation will enable readers to draw this conclusion for themselves based on the strength of the document's content and presentation.

One key to controlling hype is to watch the nature and number of adjectives and adverbs you use to describe a product. Some marketing materials read like entries in a "Let's See How Many Fancy-Sounding Adjectives We Can String Together" contest. For example, one ad uses these words in close proximity: *sleek, miraculous, sublime, whopping, cinch, bevy.*[45] All of these words are powerful, but give them some breathing room!

To break gushing words of praise into more palatable chunks, try these techniques:

- Replace multiple adjectives or adverbs with just one that is more evocative or concise.
- Try to find a more precise noun or verb that will eliminate the need for a modifier.
- Limit yourself to a maximum of two adjectives or adverbs for any particular noun or verb.
- Instead of using a modifier, create a separate feature or benefit statement that will present the point more clearly and powerfully.
- Use bullets to break up points. Modifiers are easier to swallow when you dole them out in smaller portions.
- Make sure that supporting evidence backs up any comparative or superlative language used to describe a product or company.[16]

Bendinger suggests this activity: "After adding up all the adjectives… ask one question. Is there one adjective strong enough to build [an advertising] campaign on? It may be the only one you need."[46]

### Mistake #2: Forgetting to Sell

In contrast to ads or brochures that are trying too hard to sell, some technical marketing materials seem to ignore selling altogether. Several factors contribute to this mistake.

**Use of empty phrases where a selling point could be made.** Many marcom documents include a phrase like this: *The following is a list of our product's benefits.* Okay, the reader will know what to expect from the information that follows. But why waste a good opportunity to make another selling point? Instead, you could write: *Here are just some of the ways PrimeWidget can improve your efficiency:*

**A bland or missing call to action.** A product brochure includes this lifeless call to action: *For more information, contact our headquarters or your local authorized dealer.* Or worse yet, the brochure doesn't include any call to action (see Chapter 5). The comparable mistake on a Web page is no link to an order form or other page that guides the visitor to the next step.

**Key messages and benefits not stated clearly.** Without specific and compelling information, the reader may doubt whether the product is worthy of consideration.

**Insulting the reader.** Attempts at humor or cleverness can backfire. A reader who feels insulted may not only be a lost prospect or customer, but may also spread negative word-of-mouth about your product or company.

Always look at your material with this question in mind: "Is it taking advantage of every opportunity to sell the reader on our product, service, or company?"

### Mistake #3: The "Blah, Blah, Blah" Syndrome

> *I try to leave out the parts that people skip.*
> —*Elmore Leonard*

How often have you read a marketing piece that seemed to say the same thing as another—even though the pieces were from two different companies? The reason may be that they use the same trendy words and phrases (remember when everything was *best-of-breed*?). Called *buzzwords* or *jargon*, this language pervades all areas of technology. While some terms have become accepted into common usage, other words may have a much shorter life.

Some marketers feel their materials won't be effective without the latest trendy words. This can lead to the "Blah, Blah, Blah" syndrome, where a document contains all the latest language, regardless of whether it has become cliché, has any real meaning for the product, or has any power for delivering the key messages. As a result, the document may leave an impression that is the exact opposite of what you want—where prospects and journalists discredit or ignore your information as "just another bunch of noise."

To avoid this mistake, make a list of the words and phrases that are currently trendy in the industry or target markets. Identify whether and how you have used this language in marcom materials. Did it really support your objective and strengthen the document's impact? If not, write a list of synonyms or alternate phrasings that would make the text more specific, relevant, and interesting.

### Mistake #4: Lack of Clarity

You shouldn't make readers guess what messages you are trying to convey, why they should be interested, and what you want them to do. For example, could you guess what the headline of this ad is about? *A Klee it's not. But who needs big dots.*[47] (Hint: Paul Klee is an early 20th-century painter.) The accompanying photo is the only initial clue that the ad is for a computer monitor.

A better headline for this ad might be: *A monitor equal to your masterpiece.* This alternative headline clearly states what is advertised and presents a benefit statement—both essential for capturing a reader's interest. The concept, the text, and the image(s) must make sense together, and help the reader understand the key message quickly and easily.

Excessive use of passive voice, overly long sentences, convoluted syntax, striving for conciseness over clarity, and the use of complex words instead of simple ones are the most common culprits when a document is difficult to understand. Here's an example:

> *Reliability, availability, and maintainability is ensured by [the product's] built-in reliability, symmetric multiprocessor architecture with comprehensive redundancy options for no single point of failure, on-line hot swap and dynamic reconfiguration capabilities, and an easily maintainable hardware and software design.*[48]

The clarity of this text could be improved considerably by splitting it into several short sentences and rephrasing the subsidiary clauses:

*[The product] has a symmetrical multiprocessor architecture that is highly reliable, available, and maintainable. It offers comprehensive backup options for no single point of failure. The product's hardware and software is easily maintained. You can even exchange components and reconfigure the unit while it is online.*

On the other hand, emphasizing conciseness can also reduce clarity as readers may not fully understand text written in a very clipped style.

Vagueness, whether intentional or not, is another problem that detracts from the clarity of a marcom document. This example contains so many generalities the reader can't really determine the subject: *Vertical integration helps assure reliable, cost-effective products based on the latest technology.*[49]

Unless you have spelled out elsewhere the meaning of "vertical integration," "cost-effective products," and "latest technology," the reader isn't likely to have much interest in this sentence because it doesn't tell him anything specific. Here's one way this example could be improved: *Our products work together. This makes them more reliable and more cost-effective as your needs change. You can easily add the latest technology without disrupting your operation.*

To avoid ambiguity, check a dictionary and usage guides for help in making the best word choices. When writing a first draft, write the text as you would speak it. Don't worry about being grammatical, polished, or complete on your first try. Then, rewrite this text into a more formal style. Check the text for clarity using the guidelines discussed earlier in this chapter.

Remember that readers can more easily understand shorter text. Take out words, sentences, and paragraphs until you have the minimum necessary to communicate key messages. Then add back the deleted text, a bit at a time, but only those elements that truly strengthen your copy.

## Mistake #5: Jam-Packed Jargon

Your product has many wonderful features, applications, and benefits. That doesn't mean you should tell readers about them all in the same breath. For example, this headline from a press release is a real mouthful that fails to make its point because it is so dense with jargon:

*11 milliOhm, 70 Volt MOSFET with 300 Watt Ratings; New IXYS TO-247 MOSFET Offers Lowest Rds(on) at 70 Volts.*[50]

The message will be more effective if you spread jargon and technical details over several sentences or paragraphs. Build your case incrementally, giving the reader time and brain space to absorb the message.

**Lists.** Avoid squishing a laundry list of product features, benefits, or specifications into a single sentence. Put them into a bullet list or use multiple sentences instead.

**Acronyms.** Watch the number of acronyms, especially in a document that is targeted to nontechnical audiences. Always provide the component words of the acronym on first use. For long documents, you may want to use the full name again at multiple points in the text.

**Cluttered sentences.** Avoid noun clusters, unnecessary verbs (write *monitors*, not *provides monitoring*), and multiple compound adjectives. Write sentences that clearly show the individual subject-action-object relationships. However, check that this technique does not create too many sentences with the same pattern, especially sentences that begin with the product name.

**Legalese.** Avoid terms that are used primarily in legal documents such as *thereby, whereas*, or *henceforth.*

## Mistake #6: "It's All About Us"

When a document is written from the company's perspective, it is easy to forget about the reader's interests. Some sales documents are heavily focused on boasting about the company's mission, experience, wonderful products, expert staff, etc., etc. The reader may feel ignored or distrustful of the company's claims.

Certainly, a company focus is appropriate for documents such as a profile. But for sales materials, it is better to focus on the reader ("you, your") not the company ("we, our").

Condescension or pomposity in the tone or narrator's voice is a symptom that may appear in articles, backgrounders, white papers, and proposals. When discussing issues, problems, trends, or architectures, it is a natural desire to seem as authoritative and expert as possible. But this desire can lead to writing that is a turn-off to readers and cause them to devalue what you say. Want proof? Just look at the letters-to-the-editor section of any trade magazine. There is nothing like condescension to get a reader angry enough to write.

Overimportance also can be expressed as an attitude or tone that implies arrogance. *Ambra. What more can we say besides "call soon"?*[51] While a product may indeed be the best in its category or your company the leader in its market, you still have to convince every reader to adopt this belief for himself. To avoid the mistake of overimportance:

- Keep the document's tone and language familiar and down to earth.
- Don't preach to readers.
- Check the text formatting. For example, a product brochure that uses initial caps on all of the words in a headline: *Take Advantage Of The Widest Variety Of Interface Options Available Anywhere.*[52] In this case, the words alone are strong enough to carry the message.

### Mistake #7: Negativism

Most marketing materials present information with positive, upbeat language. Yet some materials, especially those that present negative messages or comparative information about a product, can suffer from an excess of negativism. This problem can be caused by placing too much emphasis on negative words or messages, or by using too many words that could have a negative association for the reader.[53]

Negative words are demotivators, as Kaplan pointed out: "Readers are more interested in what is than what is not. The key word is not. It is a signal that tells the readers what follows isn't important—don't give it a second thought."[54] For example, this attempt at a clever headline: *Go Ahead ... Add Network Users. See If We Care!*[55] Given the phrase "see if we care!" you might be tempted to turn the page without reading the rest of the ad.

Readers may find negative messages insulting, as in this headline on a direct-mail postcard: *So What's Your Reason?* (for not responding to a previous mailing).[56]

Negative statements are more difficult for readers to interpret correctly than positive ones. Even when a negative message is part of competitive positioning, balance it with stronger positive statements about the product (see Chapter 3).

### Mistake #8: Forgetting the Audience

Given the complexity of most technical products and the fast pace of most marcom environments, it's easy to lose sight of readers when writing the copy for a particular piece. This mistake typically manifests itself in several forms.

**Featureitis.** An excessive focus on the product's capabilities without relating what these features mean to readers. Balance feature statements with benefit statements that answer these questions in the reader's mind: "Why should I be interested in this? What's in it for me?"

**One Piece Fits All.** Don't try to make one piece be all things to all people, unless you are clearly segmenting and identifying the content for each audience. Segmenting techniques include using subheads to identify the audience, identifying text in the body copy such as "For resellers," or isolating information for a specific audience into a sidebar.

**Not watching your language.** No profanity or vulgarity of course, but also forgetting that readers may not understand the latest hip jargon or internal terms used in your company every day. For example, would you understand that *Visit your Prime-Widget value-added channel partner* actually means "go to a computer store?"

**Confusing word choices.** While using synonyms can be effective in a marketing document, they can confuse readers. Choose synonyms carefully, use them sparingly, and verify they will carry the correct meaning in the context. Also, consider whether readers will be confused by closely related words, such as these adjacent buttons on an e-commerce site: *Your List. Shopping Bag. Checkout. Your Account.*[57]

A good marcom plan, creative platform, and document plan can also help you identify how to present information effectively for each target audience (see Chapter 1).

### Mistake #9: Irrelevancies

Information that is irrelevant to the message, objective, and purpose of the document will distract readers. Or, even worse, these irrelevancies will raise unnecessary questions in the reader's mind: "Oh yes, what about that?"

This mistake can creep into your writing when you feel you need just one more bit of evidence to support a message, when you have white space to fill or a quote that is too vague. You want to give readers just enough information to make a decision or take an action—and no more.

### Mistake #10: Errors

After multiple drafts and even more reviews, it is easy for errors of fact or omission to find their way into a marketing document. Not only can these errors be an embarrassment, they may cause legal problems (see Chapter 8). Using checklists of facts and giving the document to an expert reviewer who is seeing it for the first time are two methods you can use to avoid errors in the information.

Another form of error arises from lack of careful proofreading. Misspelled words, improper grammar or word usage, incorrect punctuation, reversed images, and missing text can damage your credibility in the reader's mind. After all, the reader might think, if your company can't put together a simple data sheet correctly, can he trust you to deliver a quality product?

## RESOURCES

The recommended books and other resources listed below provide additional information on the topics discussed in this chapter. For an updated list, visit **writinghightech.com**.

### *Books*

Richard Bayan: *Words That Sell.* McGraw-Hill, 1987. The most-used book on my shelf; an excellent tool for finding modifiers and phrases that add promotional sizzle to any text.

Stephen Glazier: *Random House Word Menu.* Ballantine Books, 1997. Groups words by topic, making it a very helpful tool when writing text that presents a metaphor.

Jonathan and Lisa Price: *Hot Text: Web Writing That Works.* New Riders, 2002. An excellent and detailed (if opinionated) guide to writing Web content and email messages. Includes many before-and-after examples of Web text.

Nick Usborne: *Net Words: Creating High-Impact Online Copy.* McGraw Hill, 2002. Geared more for pure e-commerce sites, but contains useful guidelines for writing promotional content and email messages.

### *Web Sites*

Poynter Online (**poynter.org**). A site for journalists that contains a number of good articles for writers.

*Excess Voice* (**excessvoice.com**). A collection of articles about copywriting for Web sites, written by author Nick Usborne.

The following sites can help you find just the right word:

Plumb Design's Visual Thesaurus (**visualthesaurus.com**)

Phrase Finder (**phrasefinder.co.uk**)

The Word Spy (**http://wordspy.com**)

OneLook Reverse Dictionary
(**onelook.com/reverse-dictionary.shtml**)

Sources for quotations and proverbs
(**http://directory.google.com/Top/Reference/Quotations**)

# REFERENCES

[1] Product ad, ICOM Simulations, Inc.

[2] Product catalog, Central Point Software, Inc.

[3] Product ad, Apple Computer, Inc.

[4] Product line ad, Dallas Semiconductor

[5] Product line ad, CORE International

[6] Product ad, Macromedia, Inc.

[7] Corporate image ad, Hyundai Computers

[8] Article in customer magazine, Cisco Systems, Inc.

[9] Product catalog, Central Point Software, Inc.

[10] Article in customer newsletter, Digital Systems International, Inc.

[11] James L. Marra: Advertising *Creativity: Techniques for Generating Ideas.* Prentice-Hall, 1990

[12] Product booklet, ADC Fibermux

[13] Training program brochure, Aldus Corp.

[14] Direct mail letter, Saber Software Corp.

[15] Product brochure, Digital Systems International, Inc.

[16] Herschell Gordon Lewis: *On the Art of Writing Copy.* The Dartnell Corporation, 1986

[17] Product ad, Harley Systems

[18] Product ad, Perception Technology, Inc.

[19] Emily Skarzenski: "When to be Aggressive with Passive Voice," *STC Intercom,* June 1997

[20] Product brochure, U S WEST NewVector Group, Inc.

[21] Product ad, AT&T Corp.

[22] Product line ad, Silicon Systems, Inc.

[23] Product ad, IBM Corp.

[24] Product ad, MediaVision, Inc.

[25] Product ad, Motorola, Inc.

[26] Product ad, MainLan, Inc.

[27] Company brochure, Prep Publishing

[28] Product ad, Lotus Development Corp.

[29] Corporate image ad, Kenworth Truck Co.

[30] Ad, NAB Multimedia World Conference

[31] Article in *Network World,* November 1, 1993

[32] Product ad, Northern Telecom, Inc.

[33] Elyse Sommer and Dorrie Weiss: *Metaphors Dictionary.* Visible Ink Press, 2001

[34] Janice King: "Sleepless in Seattle," *TE&M Magazine,* December 1, 1993

[35] Product ad, NEC Corp.

[36] Product ad, Alcatel Network Systems

[37] Service ad, Bell Atlantic Corp.

[38] Product brochure, British Telecom Ltd.

[39] Corporate image ad, Sanofi Diagnostics Pasteur, Inc.

[40] Product booklet, Telco Systems, Inc.

[41] Product line ad, Motorola, Inc.

[42] Corporate image ad, Continuum, Inc.

[43] "Totally XLNT FDDI Mgm't," *Communications Week* Magazine, March 15, 1993

[44] Product ad, Amoco Corp.

[45] Product ad, InFocus Systems, Inc.

[46] Bruce Bendinger: *The Copy Workshop Workbook.* The Copy Workshop, 1988

[47] Product ad, Samsung Information Systems America, Inc.

[48] Product line brochure, Wellfleet Communications, Inc.

[49] Corporate image ad, Fujitsu Network Switching of America, Inc.

[50] "Can you put that in English?" *San Jose Business Journal,* May 3, 1993

[51] Product ad, AMBRA Computer Corp.

[52] Corporate brochure, Brooktrout Technology, Inc.

[53] Erica Levy Klein: *Write Great Ads: A Step-by-Step Approach.* Wiley, 1990

[54] Burton Kaplan: *Strategic Communication.* Harper Business, 1991

[55] Product ad, CBIS, Inc.

[56] Direct-mail postcard, AT&T Corp.

[57] Nick Usborne: "Making Wrong Assumptions." Clickz.com, April 5, 1999.

[58] Product brochure, Radish Communications

# 8

## LEGAL AND ETHICAL ISSUES

## AVOIDING PROBLEMS IN YOUR MATERIALS

The information in this chapter is intended to present an overview of the legal considerations involved in writing marcom materials, covering practices that are common in the United States. It is not intended to give legal advice.

Different legal issues and requirements may apply in other countries (see Chapter 9). In addition to national and local laws, promotional materials may be subject to regulation by a variety of government agencies or guidelines from a standards organization. Laws governing e-commerce transactions, Web and email content, and online privacy are evolving and vary among countries.

Copywriters must not only be concerned about what's legal, but also about what's *right*. While ethical dilemmas vary widely with each situation, some are common to nearly every type of marketing communication project. This chapter also presents an overview of ethical problems and suggests a set of considerations that apply specifically to high-tech copywriting.

### WORKING WITH AN ATTORNEY

When it comes to legal issues, the single best thing you can do is consult with a qualified attorney who can address the specific factors that apply to each marketing project. Most companies require that an attorney review all significant marcom materials, including brochures, data sheets, and press releases.

Some copywriters feel that attorneys veto the most creative elements in marketing materials. However, there are solid reasons why legal counsel takes a very cautious approach to the words and images in any marketing document. The potential for revealing trade secrets, creating a liability concern, or bringing up other legal issues is simply too great to ignore an attorney's suggested changes to text or images.

This cautionary approach does not necessarily mean you must incorporate every attorney's edits verbatim. There are often many alternative ways to express the same concept or information that will be acceptable to both the attorney's sense of caution and your sense of marketing impact. Whether it involves a single word, a sentence, or an entire section of the document, you and the attorney can probably reach a compromise.

Here are additional ideas for working effectively with an attorney during the review process:

- Remember that the attorney may not have the technical knowledge required to judge whether a document contains false information or improper claims. A detailed or highly technical document also should receive an appropriate technical review.
- Attach an explanation of the document's objective, purpose, planned use, audience, and relationship to other materials. This will help the attorney understand the context behind the document's content.
- Develop a list of words, phrases, and boilerplate text acceptable to both of you that can be used in any document for the product or company. This agreed-upon vocabulary can expedite both the writing and review processes.
- Create a list of your company's trademarks and guidelines for their proper use, notation, and acknowledgment (see discussion later in this chapter).

## TRADE LAWS

In the United States, business activity in general—and advertising in particular—is governed by a variety of federal and state fair-trade laws. U.S. federal trade laws are based primarily on the Lanham Act, with supporting regulations from the Federal Trade Commission (FTC). State laws and regulations may be administered by a variety of departments, agencies, and commissions. In addition, the marketing of medical and biotechnology products is regulated by the U.S. Food and Drug Administration.

Whether on a national or local level, fair-trade laws cover a variety of practices in advertising and marcom. These practices include statements about a product's functionality or performance, safety warnings, use of testimonials and endorsements, information about pricing and purchase incentives—in short, anything you say about the product and how it is sold.

For e-commerce, different laws and regulations may apply to issues such as sales terms, warranty, liability, and implied contracts created by customer orders placed via an email message or order form on a Web site. Although Web commerce can attract customers from all over the world, trade laws and regulations may restrict the import or export of certain products in individual countries. Because e-commerce law is continually evolving, discuss these issues with a knowledgeable attorney.

### *Product Claims*

U.S. federal law prohibits claims about a product that are unsubstantiated, exaggerated, or ambiguous with a deceptive intent. Product claims cover any statement about features, performance, quality, options, costs, warranties, and other characteristics that may influence a purchaser's decision. State consumer protection laws also cover advertising practices, often with severe penalties for ads that contain false or deceptive claims.

The product capabilities and features described in an ad or brochure must in fact be available at the time of publication. If the capability will be available in the future, the text must indicate this fact clearly: *Expected release date: 4th Quarter 2002.* In addition, you must be absolutely truthful about statements that a product is:

- The first available in its field.
- New. The product must be commercially available for six months or less to be advertised as "new."
- Approved by a government agency, has received a patent or approval from a regulatory agency, or was developed by a recognized research laboratory.

A statement made in an advertisement or other marketing document doesn't need to be an outright lie to be problematic. Also considered an unfair practice are statements that:[1]

- Are false or misleading because they don't disclose complete information.
- Are partially true or true only in certain circumstances.
- May be deceptive by themselves but are clarified by other text that appears in the "small print."
- Are factually accurate but convey a false impression. "Each sentence in an advertisement, considered separately, may be literally true and yet the entire advertisement as a whole may be misleading."[2]

As an additional incentive to ensure the accuracy of marketing materials, the Lanham Act allows a competitor to file suit if you make a false representation about your product in advertising—even if you don't mention the competition.

These restrictions on promotional copy do not mean you need to use only noncommittal language in marketing and PR materials. The FTC recognizes that a company can be expected to praise the features, capabilities, performance, and benefits of its products (called "puffing"). The key to avoiding legal problems is to ensure that all claims are based on a truthful representation of what the product and company will deliver.

Repeated fact-checking is a standard activity for journalists and news organizations. This task is even more important for marketing and PR materials, where information often lands in a document because it was copied from another piece or sent by the first responder to a group email query. Because of the danger for inaccuracies to self-perpetuate, it is essential to proofread and verify all marcom documents, each time they are released. Preferably, this fact verification will be done by multiple people, with one person serving as the final authority.

## Service Programs

Direct Marketing Association guidelines specify many parameters (summarized below) for an ongoing service program. Many of the guidelines in this section also apply to subscription programs for product upgrades. For details, see the document *Direct Marketing Association Guidelines for Ethical Business Practice* at **the-dma.org**.

**Program details.** Information about the program should cover details such as a description of standard and optional services, time frame, all prices and fees, billing terms, minimum purchase requirements, cancellation terms, and refund policy.

**Informed consent.** The customer must explicitly consent (usually in writing) to participation in the program.

## Offers and Pricing

Guidelines from the Direct Marketing Association provide a succinct statement of how all copy relating to offers and pricing should be written: "All offers should be clear, honest and complete so that the consumer may know the exact nature of what is being offered, the price, the terms of payment (including all extra charges) and the commitment involved in the placing of an order."[3] In addition, the overall impression of the copy and images in the piece should not obscure or contradict the nature of the product or offer.

In the United States, FTC regulations contain strict rules about the language that describes the product, offers, pricing, and incentives to purchase. This language includes:[2]

- The words "free," "sale," "clearance," and other language that implies special pricing.
- The words "proof," "evidence," and other language that implies scientific or external verification of product claims.
- Any language that describes environmental claims.

FTC regulations also apply to offers of premiums and contests or sweepstakes that are presented online, in ads, direct-mail pieces, or other media. Consult with an attorney for applicable requirements and to review all text related to the contest or promotion.

Information presented on a Web site for prices, product specifications, and other terms of sale must be current in order to comply with commerce laws. Different legal considerations may apply when the Web site is accessible to international users because e-commerce laws vary considerably among countries.

The following practices can help you comply with the most common legal requirements for pricing and offer information:

- State clearly the countries and currencies in which prices and other sale terms are applicable.
- Indicate whether the stated prices include all applicable taxes and import or export duties. List these amounts separately or include a statement if payment is the purchaser's responsibility.
- Clearly indicate whether the product or offer is from the manufacturer or a dealer/reseller.
- Indicate whether another product may be substituted if the customer's choice cannot be fulfilled.

### Terms of Sale

Any print or online sales document—such as an order form, invoice, or purchase contract—should specify the complete terms of the sale.

**Seller and customer service information.** Name, physical address, telephone number, and email address for the company selling the product. The telephone number and email should be for the customer service department, where a customer may inquire about order status, cancel the order, request a return authorization, or receive assistance with a problem.

**Pricing components and terms.** Specify separately the product price, taxes, shipping and handling fees, and any discounts or rebates applied. Indicate whether the customer must meet any conditions to obtain the listed price and if an expiration date applies.

**Payment.** List the payment due date (e.g., net 30 days) and all forms of payment accepted by the company (e.g., cash, personal check, credit card types).

**Shipments.** Indicate projected shipping date and method, packaging, and separate delivery address if appropriate. If an item must be back-ordered, describe the customer's options for accepting the delayed delivery date or canceling that part of the order.

**Cancellation.** State the company's policies about orders that are canceled before shipment, including any cancellation fees that may apply.

**Returns.** Describe the timeframe, procedures, and conditions that apply when a customer wants to return a product after receipt. Provide an email address and telephone number for requesting a return authorization (if appropriate), list any restocking fees, and specify instructions and payment responsibility for shipping the return. For online sales, these terms must be visible on, or clearly linked from, the page where the customer places an order.

## Quotes and Endorsements

A glowing testimonial about a product from a customer … a favorable comment from a well-known analyst… an endorsement by a celebrity… all of these statements can make a positive impact on product marketing. Yet quotes and endorsements must be handled appropriately to avoid misrepresentation and other legal issues.

**"Fake" testimonials.** Marketing collateral, ads, and press materials may not include a quotation from, or reference to, fraudulent or nonexistent testimonials, surveys, or endorsements.

**From a person.** An "endorsement" by a fictitious person is considered to be an unfair trade practice. In addition, you cannot use testimonials or endorsements if the person no longer uses the product or if the product has changed so substantially since the endorsement was made that it could no longer be considered a fair statement.[2] Obtain a signed consent from the person or company involved before publishing the endorsement quote in any promotional material.

**From a survey.** When quoting a survey or study, especially when comparing competitive products, the survey must be designed properly and the conclusions must be fair and truthful.[4] For a study or other document, cite the source as a part of the quotation or in a footnote. Many market research, consulting, and analyst firms require that you obtain their permission before quoting from a study or report in product or company marketing materials.

**Appropriate context.** Be careful to present the quote in an appropriate context—one that does not distort the meaning or implication of the quote. When quoting a person, verify that the context is fair to the person and the statement.

### Warranties and Guarantees

Most companies offer some form of a product guarantee or warranty. A warranty is a statement that the product is of a specific quality or offers a specified performance level. A guarantee is a statement of what the company will do to repair, replace, or refund a product that is unsatisfactory or defective. Both types of statements can be made with a time limitation on their coverage.

The concept of a warranty or guarantee may seem simple at first: a statement of what your company will do if the customer experiences a problem or is not satisfied with the product. However, beyond offering good customer relations, warranties and guarantees also create legally binding conditions that you should carefully consider when writing any type of marketing material.

Most commercial transactions carry three types of implied warranty that, if they don't apply, must be specifically excluded in written terms that accompany the product.[5]

**Merchantability.** The product is of suitable quality for sale and use.

**Fitness for a particular purpose.** The seller warrants that the product is suitable for a buyer's specific intended use. This warranty is usually excluded for high-tech products because of their broad potential for use.

**Title and third-party rights.** The seller has the right to transfer title in the product to the buyer and warrants that the product does not infringe on copyright or other intellectual property rights owned by other parties. For technology products, these rights are usually described and granted or restricted in a detailed user license.

Within promotional materials, there are two types of warranty statements from a legal perspective: an explicit warranty and an express warranty. An explicit statement is what usually comes to mind when you think of a warranty or guarantee. For example, *No Risk Guarantee! Remember, if you're not satisfied with Quick-Books for any reason, you can return it within 60 days for a full refund.*[6] An **explicit warranty** tells the customer exactly what your company will do and what he must do to receive a repair, replacement, or refund under the warranty. It also must describe any other conditions, limitations, or terms that apply to the warranty or guarantee.

In the United States, the Magnuson-Moss Act spells out detailed requirements for explicit warranty statements made for consumer products. This Act may be applicable to your product, as well as consumer protection laws in each state. Consumer products also may be covered by an implied warranty about their quality and use; consult a qualified attorney for guidance.

The other type of warranty is called an **express warranty**. You may inadvertently create this type of warranty if materials promise more than what your company intends to deliver. Meyerowitz explains: "Express warranties can be created in virtually any advertising, marketing, or packaging materials and can be created without the use of the words 'warranty' or 'guarantee.'"[4]

An express warranty can be created by any written description, specifications, or visuals depicting the product, because a prospect would reasonably expect that the product will conform to the description or depiction. An express warranty also can be created by product samples—in the case of high-tech products, samples include demo disks, trial versions, and evaluation units. In addition to printed materials, an express warranty can be created by a salesperson in an oral presentation.[4]

There are two essential ways to check that your copy does not create warranty problems. First, develop standard text for explicit warranty statements and use that text consistently in all marketing materials. Compare the other text in the document with the explicit warranty statement; are they in conflict? Second, check whether the text in the document implies a greater promise than is covered by the warranty. Are all statements in the text and all visuals accurate in the way they describe and depict the product?

## Disclaimers

As a defensive measure against rapidly changing product features and market circumstances, many companies develop a standard disclaimer statement that appears on all marketing materials. For example, *ADC Kentrox reserves the right to change specifications without prior notice.*[7]

Materials for consulting and other types of services also may contain a disclaimer: *The company makes no guarantees or warranties as a result of the risk analysis service and resulting recommendations.*

Because disclaimers can have significant legal implications, consult an attorney for specific language to use in each marketing situation.

## Product Safety Warnings

Some technical products can be used safely only in certain conditions or by following specific procedures. If your product could potentially cause any health or safety problems for a user, the marketing materials may need to include safety warnings. Consult an attorney with expertise in product liability laws for guidance.

## Marketing to Children

If children are a targeted audience—especially for Web content—you must be sensitive to legal and ethical factors about promotional techniques, messages, and privacy. These factors include:

- Collecting and protecting the privacy of information that could personally identify the child; especially important is information that could lead to off-line contact with the child.
- Collecting information beyond that required to deliver a product or service or to support appropriate market research.

- Obtaining and verifying parental consent for the child to view certain pages or use certain features on the site; also, permission for sharing the child's personal information with third parties.
- Identifying and controlling access to content that is "child friendly" or "family friendly."

For an overview of relevant guidelines, visit **the-dma.org** and **caru.org**, the Web site of the Children's Advertising Review Unit of the National Advertising Review Council.

## POSTAL REGULATIONS

The postal authority in every country regulates any commercial activity that is conducted through the mail. Of particular concern to copywriters are regulations that cover direct-mail materials and practices. For example, some postal authorities allow promotional copy to be printed on an envelope, while others do not. These regulations can vary widely for each country; a direct marketing agency with experience in international mailings may be able to provide appropriate guidance.

## FINANCIAL REGULATIONS

A number of regulations from the U.S. Securities and Exchange Commission cover the disclosure of any information that might impact any stock traded on a U.S. stock exchange. This information includes claims about products and capabilities made in sales materials, if it can be shown that those claims influenced an investor's decision to buy or sell the company's stock. If the stock is traded on exchanges in other countries, additional or different regulations may apply.

As company insiders, many copywriters learn about product plans or other critical information before the public. Do not use a company's confidential information for personal gain or disclose it to others who might improperly gain; such an action could be considered insider trading. Notify your employer or client of any existing or potential conflict of interest as it applies to the company's stock or other financial transactions.

Scandals about improper accounting and financial disclosure have led to significantly stronger laws in the United States about the presentation of a company's financial information. In addition, many companies have strict internal policies about the use and disclosure of sensitive information. Your company's investor relations staff can provide guidance on disclosures and other issues involved in communicating financial information.

## COPYRIGHTS

U.S. laws give the creator of a work complete copyright protection once it has been expressed in a fixed form such as a printed document, image or object, Web content, or software. While you do not need to place a copyright notice on each copy of the work, doing so creates stronger protection under international copyright agreements.

In countries that comply with the Berne convention for copyright laws, the text, images, and other elements on a Web site are protected in the same way as print materials. In other countries, copyright protection may be different.

To reinforce copyright ownership, place a copyright notice on each printed document. For Web content, place the notice on each page and in the underlying HTML file. Ensure that a copyright notice appears on all pages and documents printed from your site.

In the U.S., the strongest form for a copyright notice is: *Copyright©2004, (owner's name). All Rights Reserved.* The owner can be a person, a company, or an organization.

For revised works, the copyright notice needs to include only the latest year in which the work was published; it does not need to include every year in which the work was written, issued, or revised.

For a substantial work that may have commercial value, consider registering the copyright with the U.S. Library of Congress or the appropriate agencies in other countries. Registration may strengthen your ownership claim.

## *Material from Other Sources*

Some marketing documents incorporate text, images, or multimedia elements from other sources that are protected by a copyright. Obtain permission from the copyright owner for any excerpt you use—no matter how small the block of text or how seemingly inconsequential the image. Copyright protection for text includes the original language and any translation.

Text and images are covered in print and electronic form, including Web content. Patent protection as well as copyright may be applicable to Web technologies and scripts.

A simple process is usually all that is required to obtain permission for use of most text excerpts. Contact the copyright owner (usually the company or individual who wrote or published the document). Send a letter that describes the exact text that will be reproduced, provides a sample of how it will appear in your document, and describes the publication circumstances. This letter may include a space for the copyright owner's signature, indicating agreement with the proposed use and terms. In most cases, permission to use brief excerpts on a limited basis are given without payment of a fee. However, the copyright owner may demand a fee for more extensive excerpts or more significant uses of the source material.

*Tip:* If you want to use content from another Web site, it may be simpler to provide a link to the source site instead of obtaining permission to reproduce the content on your own site.

Copyright and usage permissions also are a significant concern for the use of photos and images in any marcom document (print or online), as well as for video and audio clips on the Web or in a presentation. Use of these elements often involves payment of a fee and a very specific agreement on issues such as:

- Planned use in each specific document or project
- Time limitations for exclusive use
- Restrictions on alterations, links, and downloads
- Quantity and distribution of a printed document

In most cases, companies either develop agreements with external creative resources that acquire all rights to the work (including the copyright) or contract (and pay for) usage rights on a project-by-project basis. (This latter practice is much more common for images and multimedia than for text.) When negotiating usage rights, make sure the agreement covers all planned uses for the element.

Permission to use an element in the document does not transfer the copyright. The copyright owner retains all rights to the element and can monitor your use to assure compliance. To prevent misunderstandings, keep copies of all source material, signed permissions and related correspondence, as well as all documents (print and electronic) that incorporate elements owned by other parties.

### "Work for Hire" Produced by Employees

The copyright for any creative work produced by employees as part of their jobs belongs to the employer. In most cases, this definition of "work for hire" covers all print and electronic rights.

### Work Produced by Agencies and Freelancers

Work produced for your company by agencies, consultants, or freelance writers or designers requires an explicit transfer of copyright. Unless the contract or work agreement specifies the project is "work for hire," the creator must sign a separate document to transfer the ownership rights to the elements. Keep in mind the points below for assignments that involve independent creative resources.

**Scope of rights and contract terms.** Your company receives only the rights specified in the contract or work agreement with the resource. Terms usually cover:

- A description of the work product
- The application or use (e.g., the use of a photo in a company brochure)
- The time period covered by the agreement
- Any limitation on print quantities or distribution
- Required credit or copyright acknowledgments

**Print and electronic rights.** Purchase of rights for use in print material does not automatically include use in electronic documents.

For example, you cannot place on a Web site the text or images that appear in a printed brochure unless you have obtained both print and electronic rights from all involved writers and designers.

**Alteration rights.** Separate rights cover the ability to animate an image or make any other changes to a creative work. In most cases, you will not be permitted to make these changes yourself. Instead, the alterations will be made by the work's creator as a separate project with a separate fee.

**Multiple uses.** The creative resource must grant permission for the company to use the work for additional purposes or applications. This means you cannot use a photograph in a different brochure unless you have purchased that right.

Unless you obtain full copyright, the creator can use the element in other projects and grant permission to other companies to use or adapt it. While this freedom may cause you to worry that the appealing image in a brochure may suddenly appear on the brochures of other companies, in practice this concern is usually moot. Purchasing full rights can be expensive, so you may find it more cost-effective to give up insistence on exclusive use.

### Licenses and Permissions

Negotiating rights, permissions, and licenses can be very complex, involving multiple parties and issues, as well as considerable time and effort. Figure 10.1 lists the most common licensing issues. To make your task easier, work with a rights agent, stock house, or intellectual property attorney.

Always assume that any content or element in print material or on a Web site is covered by a copyright, even if no copyright notice appears. These elements include clip-art images, geographic maps, and others that are marked as royalty-free, but in fact may come with restrictions on their commercial use. Also, specific images or recordings may be protected, even if the artwork or music they present are in the public domain. Use the element only if an explicit notice appears with it to allow completely unrestricted use. Otherwise, you must contact the copyright owner to obtain a license or permission.

In general, it is less expensive to obtain only the specific rights you need, for a limited time period, than to purchase a complete set of all rights. If you later decide you want make changes to or additional use of a licensed element, you can obtain those rights from the copyright owner. You must specify all planned uses for the material, even if it is for multiple projects of the same type, e.g., a series of ads that use the same image. In most cases, an additional fee will be required.

| Element | Rights to license or permissions to obtain |
| --- | --- |
| Text | Rights to publish text that previously appeared in print or electronic material, in identical or adapted form. If you plan to localize the text for international visitors, also purchase translation rights. |
| Images | Rights for use and public display of the image itself and to make modifications or apply animation to that image if appropriate. If the image includes recognizable people or celebrities, you must obtain permission for publicity. These permissions apply whether you obtain the image from an artist or photographer, or license it from a stock house or image library. Merchandising rights may apply if you want to use the image on other items that will be sold by your company. |
| Music | Licenses from the composer and the copyright owner for the specific recording; compliance with usage requirements imposed by the performers' unions. |
| Other Audio | Permission for narration and translation of the text; rights from the narrator or actors to use their performances; union permissions. |
| Video | Video and film elements present many of the same issues as music and audio elements, but can involve more people and organizations. For commercial videos or film clips, consider using a rights agent. |
| Software | A Web site may incorporate software elements developed by multiple vendors. Ensure that your company or Web developer obtains and renews the appropriate licenses from each vendor. |

*Figure 10.1 Licenses and permissions for content elements.*

Permissions or permits may also be necessary for filming or photography in a private or public location. For example, when using customer photos to illustrate a case study, obtain permission from the company or property owner to access the location and portray it in the images. Permits from a local government agency may be required for photographing public locations. When in doubt, obtain a signed permission and release form from any person or entity involved with the image.[5]

## TRADEMARKS

A trademark is a word, name, symbol—or any combination—that a company uses to distinguish a product from others that are similar in design, operation, or function. A service mark is the same as a trademark, except that it applies to nontangible services performed by a company. Trademarks are important because they help to create a particular brand name and image for a product or service, and by extension, for your company. The remaining discussion in this section references only trademarks, however the principles apply to service marks as well.

Trademarks can be created for a company's logo or for the company name, but only as it identifies a concrete product or service. For example, Microsoft by itself is considered a trade name that identifies the company and cannot be protected as a trademark. However, Microsoft® Windows™ identifies a specific product and can be protected as a trademark, as can the Microsoft logo. Your company can tell you which products have received trademarks and which services have service marks, and whether those marks are registered.

Trademarks involve two considerations for copywriters: properly using the trademarks owned by your company, and acknowledging the trademarks owned by others.

### Trademark Notation

All trademarks, whether owned by your company or others, should appear with the correct notation in any marketing or PR materials (Figure 10.2).

| Symbol | Use |
| --- | --- |
| TM | For a trademark your company is claiming, but which has not yet received registration with a governing authority |
| SM | For an unregistered service mark |
| ® | For a trademark or service mark that is registered with the U.S. Patent and Trademark Office. Trademarks that are registered in other countries may be covered by different rules for notation. |

*Figure 10.2  Guidelines for using trademark notation.*

Use the symbol on the first or most visible appearance of the trademark in the document; you do not need to include the symbol on subsequent appearances. For example, if the trademark symbol appears with the product name in a headline, you do not need to include it every time you use the product name elsewhere in the document. For newsletters, catalogs, or other documents that have distinct articles or entries, use the trademark notation again with each new article or section. For Web content, use the trademark notation on each distinct page; it is not necessary to repeat the notation within the same page.

Include a statement on each marketing document or Web page (or link to a separate page of trademark acknowledgments) that indicates ownership of each trademark: *Microsoft is a registered trademark and LinkExchange is a trademark of Microsoft Corporation.*[8]

## Trademark Usage

Present the trademark in the correct word form: always as an adjective, never as a noun or verb. The correct word form is a necessity to prevent the trademark from becoming a generic word that can lose its protected status. For example, Xerox Corporation has made extensive efforts to protect its Xerox® trademark to describe a photocopying process. These efforts have been necessary because the word *xerox* has been widely adopted by consumers as both a noun and verb synonymous with photocopying.

The guidelines below will help you avoid turning a trademark into a generic term.

**Use the proper word form.** Always treat the trademark as a proper adjective (starting with a capital letter), and always use it with a generic noun that describes the product or service. For example: *the Windows NT operating system.*[8] Don't use the trademark as a noun, a verb, a possessive, or a plural (if not already a plural).

**Shortened forms.** A trademark can be used in shortened form after first reference within a document. For example, *Microsoft Windows* as the first reference; *Windows* in any later reference in the same document.

**Consistency.** Don't change the spelling or hyphenation, or use the trademark in an abbreviation or acronym. However, you can create an acronym from a multiword trademark, such as *Transaction Monitoring Facility*™ *(TMF*™*).*[9]

**Trademarked company names.** A company name may be a trademark only when it appears with a product or service name (which itself may also be a trademark). For example, *The Microsoft® Windows® operating system* is a correct usage of the company trademark (as an adjective) , while *Microsoft Corporation today announced*…describes the company (as a noun) and thus cannot use the trademark symbol.

Fueroghne suggests this test to determine if you are using a trademark correctly in a sentence: If you remove the trademark, does the remaining sentence make sense?[10]

Develop a guide to proper usage of your company's trademarks or include this information in a marketing style guide. Distribute this guide to employees; outside marcom, advertising, and design firms; resellers and strategic partners; and others who might produce materials about your company and products.

### Using Another Company's Trademarks

If another company's trademark appears in your document, it is best to acknowledge ownership. To determine whether a term or phrase is a trademark, check the source company's Web site or search the database of U.S.-registered trademarks at **uspto.gov**.

Use the appropriate symbol when the trademark appears in the document and include an acknowledgment statement such as:

*Microsoft and Windows are trademarks of Microsoft Corporation.* And, because it sometimes can be difficult to determine if all product names you mention are trademarks, or who owns those trademarks, include a general statement such as: *All other trademarks are property of their respective owners.*

In some cases, your company may license the trademarked name or logo of another company's products. Refer to the owning company's guidelines for proper usage of that trademark or logo. Also, be aware that images can be reflective of a trademark. For example, one company used images from the Star Trek films in its advertising, and included a reference to the trademark's owner, Paramount Pictures, even though the words Star Trek were not used in the ad's copy.[11]

## PATENTS

Check with an attorney before publicly releasing information about a product, process, or design that your company may want to patent. Releasing information too soon could jeopardize your company's ability to obtain a patent in one or more countries. Different countries have different laws that cover whether an idea can be patented after information has been disclosed publicly.

## PROPRIETARY INFORMATION

Because high-tech markets are so competitive, most companies are understandably reluctant to release information that may be considered proprietary or a trade secret. In the U.S., trade secrets are largely governed by state law; a number of states have adopted the Uniform Trade Secrets Act.[5] Internationally, trade secret laws are specific to each country.

Examples of proprietary information include detailed designs, processes, methods, or components in a product; description of manufacturing processes or sources; sales methods, marketing expenditures, and contract details; customer lists or information on customer relationships; and details on alliances.

To avoid inadvertently including proprietary information, all marcom documents should be reviewed by a company executive and attorney before release or distribution. Your company may have written policies or may be subject to government regulations that cover release or nondisclosure for certain types of information.

In some situations, confidential information may be released to a person or company under a nondisclosure agreement. This situation typically occurs when two companies are exploring an alliance or other business relationship, or when a company conducts a press tour in advance of a new product announcement. The person receiving the information agrees to treat it as confidential, and not disclose it to any other party without permission from your company. This limitation usually has an expiration point—a specific date or upon termination of the agreement or business relationship.

In the case of a press tour, giving a journalist information under a nondisclosure agreement allows you to create advance awareness for a product without concerns that the journalist will publish a story before you make a public announcement.

Your company may have an existing nondisclosure agreement that can be used for marketing communication purposes, or contact your company attorney for guidance.

## LEGAL ISSUES FOR EMAIL MARKETING

In the United States, commercial email is regulated by the "CAN-SPAM Act" (Controlling the Assault of Non-Solicited Pornography and Marketing Act of 2003). In addition to governing how and to whom email is sent, this Act has several requirements for message content to consider when writing email text.

- The subject heading must be clear about the message's content and not misleading.
- Each message must contain a valid return email address or Internet-based reply mechanism that will function for at least 30 days following message transmission.
- The physical postal address of the sending or sponsoring company must appear in the message body.

- The message must include a conspicuous notice that identifies it as an advertisement or solicitation.
- The message body must contain an "opt-out" notice and mechanism.

Anti-spam, commerce laws, computer crime laws, and consumer protection acts may also govern email marketing in individual states and in countries other than the United States. When planning an email campaign or developing new types of messages, work with a qualified attorney to assure that this communication will comply with applicable laws.

The American Association of Advertising Agencies, the Association of National Advertisers, and the Direct Marketing Association have developed the "Joint Guidelines on Legitimate Email Marketing Practices," (available at **the-dma.org**) which cover many of the same points as the CAN-SPAM Act. However, two points in these guidelines are of particular interest to copywriters.

First, marketers are encouraged to use company or brand names in their domain address and prominently throughout the message. This practice not only provides brand reinforcement, it may also be a way to help recipients recognize poorly constructed and fraudulent "phishing" messages sent by unauthorized parties.

Second, a commercial email should contain the sender's privacy policy, either within the body of the email or via a link. This practice may also help recipients recognize the message as legitimate, but more importantly, provides reassurance about the information collected by your company during an email exchange.

## PRIVACY RIGHTS

For most high-tech marketing communication that is product-oriented, privacy rights are not a major consideration. However, if any material uses the image, name, or information of an identifiable person or company, you must take the steps to protect the subject's right to privacy.

Copywriters must be concerned with two types of privacy rights: the privacy of information published about a person or company, and the privacy of information collected on a Web site or during the sales process.

## *Privacy in Published Materials*

When publishing information, there are several primary considerations for protecting a person's privacy:

- Using the person's name, likeness, or voice in promotional materials.
- Disclosing information about the person's affairs, beliefs, statements, or actions.
- Exposing confidential data such as credit card numbers, especially when collected on a Web site.

Many states have laws that protect the publicity rights of individuals. These laws require permission for use of any information about or images of a person in any promotional material (including press materials).

You must obtain a signed consent from that person for use of the information or images before the material is published. If a photograph shows a group of people, obtain a signed consent form from every person in the group. Even for employees of your company, obtain a signed consent form before using their photos, names, or other information in any promotional material. Publicity rights also apply to an actor or narrator in a video, audio clip, or multimedia presentation.

The release should specify the form, media, and duration of usage rights the person is granting for the image or information. If you want to use it in another medium or for a different purpose (or make new alterations to an image), obtain a new release whenever possible.

For any type of image or multimedia element, you may need to obtain two types of authorizations for use:

- A publicity release from each person who appears in the element. In many cases, the work's creator will obtain this release for you.
- A use license from the photographer, producer, artist, or other creator who owns the copyright for the work.

If you use content, images, or multimedia elements licensed from a third-party, obtain copies of all signed releases and verify that your use for the material will comply with the source's terms.

### Disclosing Sensitive Information

Another concern of individual privacy is disclosure of a person's sensitive information. As a matter of common business sense, most copywriters are unlikely to publish information about a person that is embarrassing or confidential, or to portray a person's image, statements, or actions in a false context. To avoid problems, always obtain written permission from the person on the specific text to be published and its planned use. In some cases, this permission may apply only to certain media or uses, and apply only to a specified time period.

A variation of privacy rights applies to celebrities, called publicity rights. You cannot use the image, name, or other identifying characteristics of a celebrity without permission from her or her estate. These restrictions apply to celebrities both living and dead and apply also to "look-alikes" or "sound-alikes."

Privacy concerns extend to information you may want to publish about other companies, whether they be customers, alliance partners, or competitors. Disclosure of confidential or proprietary information is a primary concern, as is presentation of their information in a false context. Do not publish another company's information, such as in a case study or press release, without obtaining written permission from an authorized representative of that company.

In some cases, a customer may be willing to let you tell their story, but only if the company is not named. In this case, you can describe the company by a general identifier, e.g., "a large metropolitan hospital." Or, give the company a fictional name, but clearly identify it as such, along with any other fictitious or composite information presented in the text.

*Note:* Some ads or collateral present a fictitious person, company, or scenario. Yet especially for a person, it can be difficult to create a name that will not belong to someone somewhere in the world—causing a problem of privacy rights. Always indicate when names are fictitious, such as in this footnote: *Companies, names, and data used in scenarios and sample output are fictitious.*[12]

## Privacy of Web Information

Another consideration is protecting the privacy of visitor information and activity on a Web site. If you collect any type of personal, financial, or other sensitive data from visitors, describe why you are requesting the information and what you will do with it. If appropriate, reassure the visitor about the confidentiality of the information as it is transmitted over the Internet via the security features supported on your Web server and in the visitor's browser.

Laws that address personal privacy are too complex and changeable to discuss here. See the Web sites listed in the Resources section for more information and work with a knowledgeable attorney.

### COMPARATIVE ADVERTISING

Use extreme caution when writing material that compares a product with its competition. The comparative statements must be factual, complete, and based on verifiable evidence. Otherwise, a competitor may file a lawsuit alleging unfair trade practices under the U.S. Lanham Act, which does not permit materially false representations about another company's goods, services, or commercial activities. The act can apply even if there are really only two leading products in that market and the competitor is unnamed.[4]

Comparative advertising of any type is illegal in some countries outside of the United States. Work with an attorney in each country where your advertising or marketing materials will appear to ensure they will comply with local laws.

### PROPOSALS

Information presented in a proposal can become legally binding if the proposal is incorporated into the purchase contract. In any case, the proposal should contain accurate information on items such as the functionality and performance of products, level and types of services to be provided, schedules, task responsibilities, and costs.

## ETHICS

Ethical considerations always present difficult challenges: Who's right? What's right? What should be said or done? For a high-tech copywriter, these considerations involve the responsibility of the writer to readers, to the employer or client, and to third parties such as customers or journalists. Many of the legal issues covered in this chapter can also describe the need for ethical behavior by marketers and communicators.

The situations where ethical questions arise in high-tech marcom can vary widely, and each requires individual evaluation. A number of professional organizations have developed codes for ethics or standards of practice that are relevant to high-tech copywriters; these codes are reflected in the considerations suggested here. However, these considerations have not been reviewed or approved by any professional organization or other governing body.

In addition, your company may have a set of policies that cover ethics or it may be required to comply with government regulations about ethical practices. Cultural considerations also may play a part in your development of a set of ethical guidelines.

The ethical considerations below may help you produce fair, honest, and ethical materials. Yet, no set of standards can predict every potential ethical problem you may encounter. Remember that you will need to apply common sense, good judgment, and a sensitivity to the people and implications involved to determine the best response to each situation.

### Overstatement

Filled with zeal for promoting a product, a marketer or copywriter may be tempted to make unjustifiable exaggerations about the product's features and performance. This overstatement can appear in many forms, including:

- Misrepresenting a product's design, functionality, or other characteristics in descriptive text, specifications, or images.
- Implying that features, options, or other product capabilities are currently available when in fact they will not be available until a future date.
- Promising certain results that may require additional products, conditions, resources, or activities that are not included in the base product or that are beyond the company's control.

When an inaccuracy is found in any marketing or PR material, the company should promptly take steps to correct the information and attempt to notify those who received it.

### Inappropriate Interpretation

Another problem of information accuracy is making an inappropriate interpretation of fact, data, comment, or description. This problem can occur in a number of forms, in both text and visuals.

**Carelessness.** It is important to verify feature or benefit statements, quotes, and other content with multiple, reliable sources. In journalism, this activity is called "fact checking."

**Unjustified boasting.** Making an inappropriate attribution of your company's involvement in an activity, or the value of the solution or results delivered by the product or company.

**Only good news.** Making inappropriately selective use of facts, comparisons, or comments. For example, including only test results that reflect favorably on your product or company while ignoring other, less favorable results that would be an important factor in the decision-making of a customer or investor.

**False impressions.** Creating a false impression by paraphrasing or excerpting neutral or negative comments to make them seem more positive or at least less damaging.

**Misleading emphasis.** Using formatting devices to add emphasis to text that was not there in the original form to give it a stronger or different meaning. This tactic is typically used to highlight the most favorable part of a review or quote. To be fair to both the source and the reader, include the words "emphasis added" immediately following the altered text. In visuals, a reader may gain a wrong impression if an inappropriate emphasis is placed on a portion of the image or data.

### Altered Images

Graphic design, animation, and editing software for photos, audio, and video can create or alter multimedia elements. While this issue usually is not handled by copywriters, keep in mind the implications of this ability to alter or enhance "reality," especially as they apply to product images, data charts, and recorded audio or video.

**Altered images.** Certain minor modifications to images are acceptable, such as those made to correct visual flaws or improve clarity. However, extensive changes that substantially alter the proportions or appearance of the product may cause problems of misrepresentation or express warranty (see discussion earlier in this chapter). Changes may violate the usage rights granted by the image's owner or creator, and may slander or violate the privacy rights of a person.

In addition, magazines and newspapers may not accept an altered image for publication, or may require that it be labeled to indicate the alteration. These concerns may not apply in cases where the image has been altered so dramatically that it makes only a symbolic representation of the product it depicts.

**Data charts.** Tables or charts that present statistics can be manipulated to distort the meaning or relationship of the data. This becomes especially problematic because many readers give charts only a cursory look, seeking only a sense of the information presented.

**Audio and video.** Editing audio and video clips carries many of the same implications as altered images. These elements also present the danger of context distortion. For example, a "sound bite" taken from an audio file may convey a different meaning on its own than in full context. Video representations can be distorted by animation, lighting, camera angles, and editing. Voice-over narration, captions, and graphical elements added to the video may also affect the accuracy and meaning of what is presented.

### Examples and Fabrications

When promoting a new product or service, you may not have user case studies, test results, or other fact-based evidence that will support the benefit claims or show all potential applications. Describing example scenarios or telling the story of an invented user are common techniques to address this shortcoming. But using a fabrication can create more problems than it solves. Check all examples and fictions against these cautions:

- Clearly label the text or image as an example or fictional representation.
- Use generic names and images that will not be confused with an actual person or company. Verify that you are not impinging on the privacy rights of an actual individual or company (see discussion earlier in this chapter).
- Verify that the image and text work together appropriately. One advertisement used a photograph of the downtown Seattle skyline with text describing streets which don't exist in that city.[13]

### Identifying Sources

Plagiarism involves directly copying or borrowing text, images, or ideas from another source without authorization or acknowledgment. All sources for all content elements in a document should be cited, and externally produced material used only after securing the necessary copyright or usage permissions (see the discussion on Copyrights earlier in this chapter).

Accurate source identification is particularly important for email, some types of Web content, and some partner materials where it may not be immediately obvious to the reader who is sending the communication. Your company may establish requirements about how dealers and other partners can describe the relationship or use your company's materials for their own marketing purposes.

### Interviews

Obtaining and using information from interviews can present several ethical considerations.

**Interview request.** How you represent yourself, your company, and your planned uses for the information in order to get an interview from a customer or other source.

**Nature of the interview questions.** Questions must be worded carefully to avoid prompting the source to make statements that are inaccurate, incomplete, or misleading.

**Accurate context.** Any information or quotes taken from the interview must be presented in an accurate context when published.

**Recording.** Many countries require that you obtain permission from the source before recording an interview on audio or video tape, whether in person or over the telephone. Because many people are simply uncomfortable with the recording process, respect any request from the source that you not record the interview.

### Web and Email Communications

The ethical issues around online marketing and public relations activity will continue to expand as the mediums and their uses evolve. At a minimum, consider the guidelines presented in this section.

**Honesty.** Be truthful about your name, job, and employer when participating in online discussions, Web conferences, and instant messaging.[14] Do not "plant" false or misleading comments, reviews, etc. about your company or its competitors, even if you think you are doing so as a private individual off the job.

**Disclosure of interests.** Indicate any ownership positions in products, services, Web sites, etc. that you recommend or comment upon either as an individual or a company representative.

**Trust.** Trust is an achievement that must be earned with every online communication. Recipients of an email must be able to trust that it indeed came from your company, is for a legitimate purpose, and is sent by permission.

Visitors to a Web site must be able to trust that the content is accurate and current, that e-commerce transactions will function properly, and that personal data will not only be transmitted and stored securely, but used only in the ways as stated by the company's privacy policy.

Participants in a blog, online discussion, or instant messaging exchange must be able to trust that you are who you claim to be, and that you have clearly identified your employer or business affiliation when appropriate.

## RESOURCES

The recommended books and other resources listed below provide additional information on the topics discussed in this chapter. For an updated list, visit **writinghightech.com.**

### Books

J. Dianne Brinson and Mark F. Radcliffe: *Internet Law and Business Handbook.* Ladera Press, 2000.

Graphic Artists Guild: *Handbook of Pricing and Ethical Guidelines, 11th Edition,* 2003. Useful for understanding contracts and rights issues from the perspective of an artist or other media professional. Regularly updated, so check for a newer edition.

Edward Tufte: *The Visual Display of Quantitative Information.* Graphics Press, 2001. An excellent discussion on accurate presentation of statistics.

Lee Wilson: *The Copyright Guide: A Friendly Guide to Protecting and Profiting from Copyrights.* Watson-Guptill, 2000.

Lee Wilson: *The Advertising Law Guide.* Allworth Press, 2000.

### Web Sites

The following sites provide articles, reports, and other resources related to legal issues for marketing:

Giga law (e-commerce issues) (**gigalaw.com**)

World Intellectual Property Organization (**wipo.org**)

U.S. copyright information from the Library of Congress (**loc.gov/copyright**)

The ethics considerations suggested in this chapter are drawn in part from the ethics codes established by several professional organizations:

International Association of Business Communicators (**iabc.com**)

Business Marketing Association (**marketing.org**)

Public Relations Society of America (**prsa.org**)

Direct Marketing Association (**the-dma.org**). The DMA publishes a particularly in-depth and useful set of guidelines for print and online marketing.

American Association of Advertising Agencies (**aaaa.org**)

Associated Press Managing Editors (**apme.org**).

## REFERENCES

[1] Article in *San Jose Business Journal,* November 22, 1993

[2] Philip Ward Burton: *Advertising Copywriting, 6th Edition.* BNC Business Books, 1990

[3] *Direct Marketing Association Guidelines for Ethical Business Practice,* **the-dma.org**

[4] Steven A. Meyerowitz: *An Ounce of Prevention: Marketing, Sales, and Advertising Law for Non-Lawyers.* Visible Ink Press, 1993

[5] J. Dianne Brinson and Mark F. Radcliffe: *Internet Law and Business Handbook.* Ladera Press, 2000

[6] Product brochure, Intuit

[7] Product catalog, ADC Kentrox

[8] Trademark usage guide, Microsoft Corp.

[9] Trademark usage guide, Tandem Computers, Inc.

[10] Dean Keith Fueroghne: *"But the People in Legal Said... "* Dow Jones-Irwin, 1989

[11] Product ad, Boole & Babbage, Inc.

[12] Product brochure, Microsoft Corp.

[13] Product ad, MapInfo Corp.

[14] *Principles for Public Relations on the Internet,* Arthur W. Page Society, **awpagesociety.com**

# 9

# GLOBAL COMMUNICATION

## ADAPTING MATERIALS TO
## INTERNATIONAL AND MULTICULTURAL MARKETS

While the United States remains a major source of and market for high-tech products, no company can ignore the significant sales opportunities available in other countries and cultural communities. Nearly all forms of technology are disseminated globally, and the pace of that dissemination is quickening. Localized products that previously were delivered several months after the U.S. launch are now part of a simultaneous, multi-market introduction.

These market factors are behind a growing volume of international and multicultural marketing communication. Advertising, collateral, press materials, direct mail, and Web content are among the materials being adapted or specially developed for each geographic or cultural market.

This chapter describes the general issues around global marcom, presents an overview of localization practices, and offers writing guidelines for materials that will be localized. While the information presented here is applicable primarily for materials that will be adapted from American English, it also may be useful to writers working in other languages.

Throughout this chapter, most of the references to localization and adaptation apply not only to audiences in other countries, but also to ethnic and cultural markets within a country.

## GENERAL ISSUES

Farinelli describes the most significant issue for marcom targeted to international audiences: "Our international marketing errors are usually errors of omission, not errors of commission. It is not that we misinterpret the culture of a country—typically, we do not do any interpretation at all. We simply assume that international markets are 'pretty much like here, except that people might speak a different language.'"[1]

As these remarks indicate, one of the most important things you can do for an international marcom project is to give it the same high level of attention and quality as any other communication effort. From the reader's perspective, international marcom should not seem like an afterthought to your domestic efforts.

Beyond this general concern for quality, which factors are critical to developing successful international marcom? First, avoid the arrogant assumption that if international customers want a product strongly enough they will accommodate themselves to the same messages and text that are targeted to a domestic audience. This arrogance implies a serious lack of respect for your customer.

Second, learn about—and respect—the linguistic, cultural, and business differences that exist in each market. For example, technologies that are widely available in your home country may not be available at all in certain international markets. As another example, many world cultures do not share the American sense of informality in business interactions, communication style, personal behavior, and etiquette.

Also, don't treat parts of the world—such as Europe or Asia—as a single market and don't think of Europe as just Western Europe; the Eastern European countries are important markets, each with its own characteristics. Market segmentation, audience concerns, buying factors, ability to easily access the Internet, and sales cycles will likely be different in each area, and these differences should be reflected in your materials.

**Company brand and image.** A strong, consistent company brand is important when you are marketing outside of the home country, where your company may not be known at all or may be confused with another company in the same industry or with a similar name. Consider the spillover of information from the American press. Many U.S. publications are read worldwide, especially on the Web.

**Product awareness.** Unless your company is one of the global brands, more time is required in many markets to build awareness of the company and products.

**Direct mail.** Prospects outside of the United States and Canada receive a significantly smaller number of direct-mail pieces than prospects in those two countries. Laws covering direct mail materials vary by country, and can be significantly stricter than laws in the United States. For example, local postal regulations may not permit self-mailers or teasers on the envelope of a direct-mail package. The envelope copy and design also must accommodate the longer line lengths and greater number of lines in most international addresses.

**Email, instant messaging, blogging, and online chat.** A sometimes extreme informality exists in email, listservs and blogs, online chat, instant messaging, and other forms of electronic communication. Remember that all guidelines in this chapter about cultural sensitivity, local business conditions, and company image apply equally to online and printed text.

**Legal guidelines.** Advertising, privacy laws, and Internet marketing laws can vary significantly among countries. Copyright and trademark registrations and notations are often different. Product packaging may need specific types of text, symbols, or other elements. Some countries do not allow advertising that compares a product with its competition. Offers are another content type that is subject to different local regulations.

As a precautionary measure, your marketing and press materials should be reviewed by an attorney who is thoroughly familiar with the laws and regulations in the target country.

**Text organization.** Documents may need to be organized in different ways to accommodate localization or differences in learning styles and reading orientation. Or your materials may need a much greater level of detail for some countries where readers expect this depth of information. In contrast, some cultures place a high reliance on the context of information exchange.[2]

**Visuals and multimedia elements.** Appropriate images, symbols, and colors vary widely among cultures. Multimedia elements may be affected by different considerations for portraying people, using music, choice of narrator's voice, and use of animation.

## WEB SITES AND E-COMMERCE

Marketing to an international audience on the Web presents numerous challenges. Many of the issues and processes described in this chapter for localizing print materials also apply to Web content. But Web sites and e-commerce activity also involve technical issues such as content management. A Web site that targets international markets must address issues such as:

- Maintaining a single Web site in only one language (usually English) or multiple, localized Web sites, each with different languages and content.
- Explaining the online shopping process and encouraging an online purchase.
- Displaying prices in multiple currencies; accepting payment by methods other than credit card (e.g., wire transfer, debit cards, local payment centers); and explaining international shipping procedures, restrictions, and schedules.
- A single Internet access account and email address shared by family members, making target marketing and personalization more difficult.
- Slower connection speeds combined with pay-per-minute access services that cause users to minimize Web browsing. These conditions mandate Web content that is concise and fast-loading, with optional links to images and multimedia elements.
- Web access by cell phone and wireless devices, especially for information and e-commerce transactions.

## COORDINATING MARCOM IN MULTIPLE MARKETS

With all of the different factors involved in international marcom, it may seem impossible to create any level of commonality among promotional materials for multiple markets. Although localization factors must be considered separately for each marketing campaign, some technology companies have successfully created coordinated, global materials. The guidelines below can help you with this coordination effort.

**Legal requirements.** Local laws can vary substantially about issues such as in-person and online commerce, customer privacy, marketing and advertising techniques, guarantees, and liability issues. Work carefully with in-country marketing and legal staff to fully identify the requirements that will apply to your print materials and Web content.

**Single concept.** Develop a single concept for a product or campaign that can be adapted successfully for the different target markets. This concept may be in the form of common text and visuals for the piece as a whole, supported by detailed information, calls to action, and offers that are specific to each market.

While a single concept can work across multiple markets, it may not be successful in all cases. Evaluate each concept individually in light of your communication goals, objective, and purpose as well as the product and market characteristics.

**Coordinated translation.** Coordinate the effort among the different translators and in-country marketing and public relations agencies involved in localization activities to ensure consistency of terminology and messages.

**In-country reviews.** When adapting an existing English-language document, verify with the in-country reviewers that its messages will be understood and its content will meet the needs of the local audience.

**Market-specific information.** The product name and other brand elements may vary among countries, perhaps for competitive or positioning reasons, but more likely because an English brand name may not translate with the same meaning in the local language.

Be clear about the product offering and availability date for each market, especially when describing localized versions of a product. List any regulatory approvals received, in process, or that must be obtained before a customer can purchase or install the product in that country. Specify prices in local currency and country-specific sales terms and delivery options. Indicate any differences in version, product bundles, configuration, packaging, or system requirements.

Incorporate market-specific information: previous successes, local business or regulatory trends, and local applications. Use quotes and case studies from in-country customers and analysts.

## COPY ADAPTATION AND LOCALIZATION

The term *translation* is often used synonymously with *localization*. However, translation is only one part of the activity for developing materials that are appropriate to diverse markets. Going beyond simple translation, localization is the process that both translates *and* adapts messages, text, visuals, and multimedia elements to meet the information needs, interests, customs, and practices of each market. For example, the formality of tone, the choice of words and visuals, even the length of a marketing document can vary substantially when it is localized to accommodate linguistic and cultural differences among international readers.

As Grüber explains, "Copy adaptation works on the premise that today's consumers are highly attuned to advertising copy. If it doesn't ring absolutely true, it loses credibility. Copy adaptation helps to create a strong international image within different national contexts, getting the advertising message across with all the freshness and impact it had in the original campaign.[3]

### Which Materials? Which Languages?

Most technology companies choose to produce localized materials for those markets where any combination of these factors apply:

- A significant sales opportunity exists for the product
- English (or your native language) is not widely understood

- Local laws require translation of product advertising and other materials
- Competitors use localized materials

However, DePalma suggests localizing a core set of company and product information for each market, such as a corporate profile, press releases, FAQs, and the essential product information a buyer will need to make a purchase decision.[4]

Localization can be considered for any marcom or PR materials. The specific materials you adapt may vary by market, based on prospect needs, the sales process, competitive factors, or legal requirements.

An early decision for print materials is whether to produce separate documents for each target language, or a single, multilingual document. (Because of the comparatively lower production costs, Web documents are usually produced individually for each language.) A multilingual document can be produced in multiple formats:

- The complete text appears in one language, followed by the complete text in each additional language.
- The text appears in parallel columns, one column for each language.
- The text appears in alternating paragraphs for each language.
- English or the company's primary language is used in the base document, with a localized appendix or wraparound document.

You may need to consider regional dialects when localizing materials. For example, the English written in the United States is slightly different from that of the United Kingdom; the French language used in Canada is different from that in France; the Spanish language in Spain is different from Latin American Spanish. A language may have additional local dialects within each country. Adapting text for only one market can make a document stand out in a way that will be perceived by the reader as subtly negative. Your translators can offer advice on whether to create a separate version of the material for each specific market or find a version of the language that will be understood by readers in all markets.

## Localized Web Content

English is the most common language for business and on the Web. But your company may already have a significant market presence in one or more countries and your Web site may attract many visitors from certain countries. In either of these cases, local-language content or a linked, fully localized Web site may be appropriate. Many large, multinational corporations maintain several localized sites. Especially if you are conversant in one of the local languages, check those sites for ideas.

Creating localized Web content can require a significant investment of time and money. For this reason, work closely with in-country contacts and translation resources to assure the best results. Among the decisions to address when localizing Web content is whether to develop and maintain a local-language page for key information only or a complete, mirror site of localized content. Coordinating content development and posting also becomes a challenge to assure the timely availability of information and to meet country-specific disclosure requirements.

Place links to local-language sites on the home page and other landing pages to help visitors immediately access their preferred site. These links are important for visitors who find a page on your site in one language as a result of a Web search, but who will want to view the page in one of the other available languages.

## Working with Translators

A major task for localization is actual translation of a document's text. The translation process involves finding a qualified translator, supporting the translation process, and working with local reviewers to verify the accuracy and appropriateness of the translation.

Grüber notes, "Adaptation relies on the skills of professional copywriters, living in their own country, writing in their own language and in touch with local trends. It is also a question of teamwork: between copywriters and technical specialists in the case of technical copy; between the copywriters of the different countries for very creative multi-lingual campaigns; and, whenever possible, between the adapters and the local managers to ensure company terminology is respected."[3]

As Victor notes, "At best, a translation provides an equivalence, not an exact reproduction of meaning. This holds true for all words, even the most concrete of expressions."[5] Because localization means more than just matching words, it will likely involve some amount of rewriting—making it important to find a translator who is also a good writer in the target language.

Copywriting skills will enable the translator to successfully adapt the message and positioning, tone and style, and product personality—as well as the words in the document. Most localization experts also recommend choosing a translator who is a native speaker of the language and who either resides in the target country or visits regularly.

You can make a translator's job easier in several ways. First, provide support materials, in both the company's primary language and the target language, that will help the translator understand the technology, the market, and applications for the product. This material also will help the translator assess how others have handled information similar to what is presented in your materials.

Second, coordinate the efforts of multiple translators and the other international communication resources. This guideline applies whether you are working with the same or multiple languages. An effective way to coordinate the efforts of everyone involved is to appoint a single lead translator or translation company.

Remember the cascading impact of changes made to the text after it is delivered; translation compounds this problem. Finally, write the English text with translation in mind (see the guidelines presented later in this chapter).

### Working with Local Reviewers

Once an initial translation is completed, it should be reviewed and proofread by marketing or dealer staff in the target market. These reviewers should check the translation accuracy for technical information, marketing messages, and appropriate cultural considerations. They should verify the translation of both words and meaning, and the accuracy of hyphenation, punctuation, accent marks, and other notations. However, remind the reviewers that the primary intent of this process is to verify the translation, not to extensively rewrite or add to the document.

In addition to the review by local staff, some companies perform a reverse translation on critical documents. In this process, the translated text is retranslated—by another translator—back into the original language. A reverse translation helps both you and the translators verify the accuracy of the first translation. This step can also identify ways to improve translation quality in future projects.

### Developing a Translation Glossary and Style Guide

Two essential resources for you, your translators, and your reviewers are a common glossary and style guide. These documents become especially critical when you are working with multiple translators, agencies, and reviewers who are located in many countries. Freivalds notes, "Without specific guidelines from the client, the individual overseas agencies would interpret English after their own fashion, or worse, cling to the belief that only a literal translation of what needs to be said will do."[6]

**Glossary.** The translation company may own a glossary of common industry terms that it can apply to your projects. In this case, supplement the glossary with terms, acronyms, and abbreviations that are unique to your products or markets. In projects that involve multiple languages, work with the translators to ensure consistency of terminology and usage across languages and across all materials, including marcom, public relations, Web content, packaging, and documentation. Ask the local reviewers to check the accuracy and completeness of product-specific or company-specific glossaries before translation begins.

When creating definitions in the glossary, define both what a thing does and what it doesn't do. Glossary entries should be as concrete and detailed as possible—even include an illustration if it will help the translator select the correct word. Also, list the terms that should not be translated, such as product and company names, trademarks, publication titles, and technical terms that are widely used and understood in English or another original language.

**Style guide.** An international style guide is one means for creating a consistent corporate identity when using multiple translators in multiple markets. For some technical products, localized style guides developed by the industry leaders (such as Apple, Microsoft, and Sun Microsystems) may be a helpful resource if these are available to your company.

DePalma recommends that a translation style guide also cover the following elements:[4]

- Writing style and tone
- Graphical style standards, covering text layout, font rules, colors, and other design issues
- Processes for copy editing and content review

### Image Library

Many companies maintain online libraries of standard images and graphical elements that are approved for use in promotional materials. These elements include items such as logos, photos of products and company facilities, and symbols for certification and marketing programs. Photos and images that represent product users, applications, and positioning may be placed in the library for use in high-level marketing pieces.

Verify that any image you select will be suitable and relevant to the audience, particularly for images that portray people or make extensive use of a certain color. It may be appropriate to maintain separate image libraries for each target market.

## WRITING GUIDELINES FOR INTERNATIONAL MARCOM

This section lists many techniques for considering the international implications when you write English-language documents. Add your own techniques to the list based on the specific circumstances for your products and markets. In addition, your translation resources may follow different practices.

### General Guidelines

The guidelines presented in this section generally apply worldwide and to all types of marcom and public relations projects.

**Translation spread.** For print documents, consider the translation-spread factor—the differences in physical space required by other languages, especially compared to English. For example, Latin languages such as Spanish and French increase the copy length by 20 to 25 percent while German and Scandinavian languages increase copy length by 25 to 30 percent. In the other direction, Japanese and Chinese characters decrease the space required.

While translation spread may seem to be only a formatting problem, it can be difficult to overcome for document elements such as sidebars, headlines, captions, and callouts, which may have limited space on the printed piece. If you are working with a rigid or tight format, identify portions of the copy that could be deleted from the translated version in order to keep the document at the same overall length or size.

Translation spread can also affect Web content, usually by requiring more scrolling to read a single Web page or by causing line breaks in lengthy link text.

**Document format.** Consider the reading orientation of languages such as Japanese and Arabic, where the text is read from right to left and bottom to top. Can a different reading orientation be accommodated by the layout and document elements in the piece?

**Market-specific information.** Although a Web site can reach a worldwide market, your company may choose to sell a product only in select countries. List all countries where the products and services are available. Health, safety, and environmental laws may impact the sale of certain products in some countries, or specify how those products must be labeled and shipped.

Clearly indicate country-specific differences in product specifications, features, and availability such as:

- Different product names or numbers
- Availability of localized versions
- Variations in features, packaging, or specifications
- List of stores or dealers by country
- Differences in pricing, shipping, currency, and payment terms; warranty and technical support programs
- Who is responsible for compliance with export and import laws and payments of taxes or duties

The call to action should include detailed instructions on how to respond for each country, such as completing an online form or calling an in-country contact for more information.

## *Writing Style*

The writing style used in a document can be just as important as the actual words for building a brand, conveying a message, and achieving a communication objective. International marcom requires some variations from the writing style commonly used for English-speaking, North American audiences.

**Variances in copy styles.** In general, marcom outside of the United States adheres to a formal writing style and may have less "hard-sell" language. American informality is very difficult, and sometimes impossible to translate into other languages and cultural contexts.[7] Identify and adhere to the preferred style for each market, in a way that is authentic and respectful. As noted by information design consultant William Horton, "[It is] better to be a polite foreigner than a phony native."[8]

**Repeat key messages.** Repetition of key messages can reinforce the content and overall impression of the piece, as well as contribute to brand building.

**Keep ideas distinct.** Present one topic at a time to simplify the translation process and reduce the possibility of error. Use active voice to avoid confusion about the subject-action-object relationship that can arise when a statement is written in passive voice.

**Avoid negative statements.** Negatives can be confusing enough in the reader's native language; translation compounds this problem.

**Verbal courtesy.** Adhere to local guidelines for courtesy in written communication. For example, salutations in direct-mail letters are usually more formal in countries other than the United States.

**Local laws.** Advertising laws in some countries do not allow the use of superlatives or hyperbolic claims such as "this product dominates its category."

## *Text Techniques*

The words you choose and how you use them in marketing copy can make the crucial difference between a customer who buys and one who turns away. While choosing the most compelling words can be difficult enough in your native language, different considerations apply for international marcom. The guidelines in this section cover issues that apply when materials are written in English for an international audience. As a model, Eisenberg suggests analyzing articles in the *International Herald Tribune* newspaper.[9]

**Clarity and consistency.** Choose words with the clearest meaning and use them consistently. Reduce your use of synonyms and choose words that have a single primary meaning to avoid mistranslation. Use the appropriate article before nouns. Avoid negative statements, especially double negatives.

**Technical terminology.** Some languages create new words for a technical term and may have multiple words to indicate variations in that term or to handle different parts of speech. Other languages use the English word or a phonetic equivalent. Avoid introducing new words that will be difficult to translate, even if you provide a definition.

Some technical terms are adapted from general words, but given new meaning. For example, when used in reference to a technical product, the term "trap door" usually describes a quick way to gain unauthorized access to a system. A native English speaker might recognize and gain a deeper understanding of this term from its origins on a theatre stage. Non-native English speakers may not know of this association, so the term may seem nonsensical to them.[10]

**Acronyms.** Always include the component words of the acronym when it first appears in the text, and consider using the full words instead of the acronym throughout the document. Be especially careful about acronyms that may have multiple meanings. In addition, a single technology may be referenced by different acronyms in different languages. However, it may be acceptable to use acronyms if they are widely known in the industry, regardless of their originating language.

**Noun strings.** Watch for compound adjectives and noun clusters, for example: *remote access router series*. To facilitate a correct translation, rewrite this noun cluster as: *a series of routers for network access from remote locations*. When using a modifier + noun + noun combination (common in English), identify which noun is associated with the modifier, because in some languages the modifier follows the noun.[11]

Talk with translators to determine which words and phrasing must change in the English-language text to prepare it for translation. For example, the writing style of most American marketing materials makes extensive use of pronouns and inferred relationships among objects and actions within a text. This style can make it difficult for translators to accurately identify the subjects, actions, and objects. As a result, the features and benefits of the product may not be presented properly.

**Ambiguity.** Watch for vagueness and unclear relationships of subject-verb-object in the original text. Any ambiguity will be compounded by the translation process. Use of passive voice is a common cause of this problem and is difficult to comprehend by readers whose native language does not use any form of passive voice.[9]

**Complete sentences.** Write full, but short sentences. Include articles (e.g., the, an) and make sure the pronoun associations are clear. Watch for long sentences that contain multiple prepositional phrases. Long sentences in general can make translation more difficult. Vögele suggests these guidelines: Each sentence should contain a maximum of 15 words and 30 syllables, with an average of 10 to 12 words. Only a few subordinate clauses should appear in the entire text.[12] Bullet or numbered lists are a good way to recast long sentences into a more understandable form.

**Punctuation.** Use proper punctuation, including serial commas (i.e., place a comma before "and"/"or" when they connect three or more words or phrases in a sentence.)

**Single word, multiple forms.** Watch for words that are the same whether they are used as nouns, verbs, or adjectives. For example, *display* can be used in these ways: *display a screen* (verb), *on the video display* (noun), and *install a display adapter* (adjective). Use these words in only one part of speech. Also, avoid using nominalizations—verbs that have been converted to nouns such as *reach a conclusion*; replace with *conclude*.[13]

**Qualifiers.** *Can, may*, and *could* are examples of qualifiers that add a slightly different meaning to their associated verbs. These fine distinctions are difficult to translate because they carry different meanings depending on the context. Whenever possible, state any limitations or differences in meaning implied by the qualifier as a separate phrase or sentence.

**Phrasal verbs.** A verb may be comprised of two or more words, such as *print out* or *set up*. For clarity, substitute a one-word verb with the same meaning, such as *print* or *configure*.[9]

**Possessives and contractions.** Using a mix of possessive and contracted word forms may also confuse readers. Avoid contractions and use the apostrophe only for possessives. Show plural forms without an apostrophe (e.g., *ATMs*).

**Creative writing techniques.** Humor, analogy, metaphor, allusion, and the other techniques for creating imagery through text may be misinterpreted or meaningless to international readers. Many of the creative writing techniques described in Chapter 7 may not be appropriate for documents that will be localized for other countries or cultures. Winters notes, "Has that metaphor been *completely* researched; that is, will it intellectually work, make sense, and have the desired cognitive connection?"[14]

**Casual language.** Avoid idiom, jargon (both business and technical), and local slang. Be especially conscious of the habit of using slang, abbreviations, and a very informal style when writing email or other online messages. Clear, formal language can be just as important in these media to assure clear communication.

**Country-specific references.** When using general terms such as "government," specify which country is involved.

**Gender preferences.** Avoid gender-specific language and examples because they may not accurately represent gender roles in other cultures. Whenever possible, use neutral terms such as *customer* or *user*. If you must specify a person's gender, use the terms *man* or *woman* not *male* or *female*. For adapters and connectors, use the terms *plug* and *receiver*.

## Content Types

Special parameters apply to content types (as described in Chapter 6) when creating a document for an international or multicultural audience.

**Subject matter.** Evaluate a document's subject matter against two essential questions: Are you describing a technology that is considered controversial or unethical in other cultures? Are you discussing issues that affect customers in only one part of the world, or that have different implications in other areas?

**Formats.** Items such as punctuation, units of measure, monetary values and currency notation, dates, times (24-hour clock), large numbers, addresses, and telephone numbers vary in their appearance among countries and may vary even within a country. Specify which measurements and units you are using in the original text. For example, when you state an amount as $5 million, specify whether this is in United States currency (e.g., *US $5 million*) or that of another country that uses dollars (e.g., *CAN $5 million*). For a list of currency codes, visit **xe.net/currency/table.htm**.

**Quotes.** A quote from a person or a source document involves a decision about translation or presenting it in the original language. If you present the original quote, include all special characters and punctuation. Follow the quote with an accurate translation that is placed in brackets or highlighted with another type of formatting device. Also, include in the translation a definition of any specialized terms or slang that appear in the original quote.

## Document Elements

Global marketing factors may also affect the choice of the document elements described in Chapter 5.

**Visuals.** All photographs, illustrations, animations, and audio/video clips must be culturally appropriate. For example, different cultures attach different meanings to colors and symbols; what has a positive meaning in one culture may have a negative meaning in another. The use of cartoon-style drawings may be acceptable in some markets but perceived as inappropriate for business communication in others.

For screen shots and diagrams, place callouts in a separate legend and use only key letters on the image itself to avoid space problems when translating. Photographs of software screen displays should show the localized version whenever possible.

Images of people may present concerns, especially if revealing the body or if the image portrays gender roles. Talk with local reviewers to find visual elements that will have a positive, or at least neutral, meaning in all target markets.

**Audio.** For music, verify that the chosen piece does not carry negative associations for the target audiences. Verify that lyrics and narration will be understood by and acceptable to listeners.

**Boilerplate.** To avoid the cost and problems caused by repeat translations of similar text, develop approved boilerplate and other blocks of text that can be used in multiple documents for each market.

## RESOURCES

The recommended books and other resources listed below provide additional information on the topics discussed in this chapter. For an updated list, visit **writinghightech.com.**

### Books

Donald A. DePalma: *Business Without Borders: A Strategic Guide to Global Marketing.* Wiley, 2002. A general book about international marketing.

Nancy A. Hoft: *International Technical Communication.* Wiley, 1995. A good overall reference for communicating with global audiences.

## REFERENCES

[1] Jean L. Farinelli: "Technology Respects No Boundaries, Why Do We?" *Mass High Tech,* June 14, 1993

[2] Edward T. Hall and Mildred Reed Hall: *Understanding Cultural Differences.* Intercultural Press, 1990

[3] Chapter in Adam Baines: *Handbook of International Direct Marketing.* Kogan-Page, 1992

[4] Donald A. DePalma: *Business Without Borders: A Strategic Guide to Global Marketing.* Wiley, 2002

[5] David A. Victor: *International Business Communication.* HarperCollins, 1992

[6] John Freivalds: "Creating a Verbal Identity," IABC *Communications World,* December 1993

[7] Nancy L. Hoft: *International Technical Communication.* Wiley, 1995

[8] William K. Horton, "Multicultural Multimedia" presentation, 1999

[9] Bryan Eisenberg: "Writing with Global Reach." **clickz.com,** March 7, 2003

[10] "World speaks English, often none too well; results are tragicomic," *The Wall Street Journal,* March 22, 1995

[11] Ad, Berlitz Translation Services

[12] Siegfried Vögele: *Handbook of Direct Mail.* Prentice-Hall, 1992

[13] Edmund H. Weiss, "Twenty-five Tactics to 'Internationalize' Your English," *STC Intercom,* May 1998

[14] Elaine Winters: "Preparing Materials for Use by the Entire World," *Technical Communication,* Third Quarter 1993

# PART 3

# HIGH-TECH MARCOM PROJECTS

The chapters in this part describe common marketing materials and Web content for high-tech products and services. The information for each type of material has a similar structure, presenting a description of characteristics, uses, and content ideas.

Not every company uses all of these materials and your company may use others that are not described here. In addition, as a marketing writer you may focus on a limited range of project types, such as sales materials only or press materials only. Use these chapters, together with Chapters 5 through 7, to spark your ideas and guide each of your marcom and PR projects.

# 10

## SALES MATERIALS

### REACHING PROSPECTS AND CUSTOMERS

The majority of projects for high-tech copywriters involve materials such as brochures, white papers, direct-mail pieces, and related Web content. Often called sales collateral, these materials provide information and support the sales cycle for a product or service. While prospects are the primary audience for sales materials, these documents also may have a variety of secondary audiences including current and previous customers, dealers, alliance partners, journalists, analysts, employees, and investors.

The specific mix of materials will vary for each product, depending on its characteristics, markets, and sales cycle. You may develop different sets of materials for different markets and develop localized materials for international sales (see Chapter 9). You may also post print materials on the Web (in PDF files) or use them as a starting point for writing Web content.

### ADVERTISEMENT

An advertisement is a paid message from a company that appears in a print, online, or broadcast medium. This section provides an overview of the copywriting challenges and guidelines for print and Web ads; radio or television ads are typically developed solely by agencies with experience in those media. Whatever the medium, writing an effective advertisement requires special focus, skills, and collaboration with a designer and other communicators. These topics are beyond the scope of this book; see the recommended reading and Web sites in the Resources section.

Print ads can range from two lines of text with a Web link to a multi-page, full-color spread in a magazine. Most print advertisements for high-tech products appear in trade, business, or consumer magazines; local or national newspapers; distributor catalogs; trade-show programs; and similar publications.

Many technology companies use minimal product advertising compared with companies that produce consumer or other business products. The reason is that most high-tech products are too complex and expensive for a prospect to feel comfortable buying just on the basis of an ad. Instead, these companies often use brand and image advertising to build awareness of the company and its major product brands. In the case of products that have a low price or involve a low-risk decision, a company may use advertising to generate an immediate order from the prospect (called direct-response advertising).

## Content Ideas—Print Ads

A print ad can use any of the document elements described in Chapter 5. Many of the text techniques described in Chapter 7 reflect the creativity required for eye-catching ads. Ads for technical products often include the following content types:

- Feature and benefit statements
- Pricing information and terms of a promotional offer
- Cross-sell and upsell promotions
- Testimonials or quotes from product reviews
- Symbols for product awards or certifications
- System requirements or platform support

The guidelines in this section cover print ads that have the objective of motivating sales or prospect inquiries. Brand and image ads for a company or product are a specialty that cannot be easily captured in a few standard guidelines and so are not covered here.

Effective ads for high-tech products incorporate the principles listed in Figure 10.1.

| Principles |
| --- |
| The ad attracts the target audience |
| The headline is powerful, captures the reader's attention, and draws the reader into the body copy |
| The key message or offer is clear and easy to recognize |
| All copy is easy to read and understandable upon first reading |
| The visuals and copy work together to support the overall message of the ad |
| The call to action is strong and complete |

*Figure 10.1  Principles for effective ads.*

## Online Ads

Banner or text ads on a Web site, in an email newsletter (ezine), or on the results page produced by a search engine are forms of online ads used by technology companies. Web and other online ads can be useful for many marketing activities such as:

- Presenting a special promotion such as an online sale or product of the day
- Announcing new products, services, support programs, and training classes
- Generating registrations for an event or Webcast
- Promoting contests (see Chapter 8 for applicable legal considerations)
- Positioning the company or product brand
- Indicating sponsorship of a Web site's content or tools

In general, the copy in an online ad is brief, clear, and tantalizing because the primary purpose is to motivate the viewer to click on the ad's link. This link typically leads to a designated landing page on the company Web site that presents more information on the product or offer promoted by the ad.

Ad copy can be as brief as just a few words or 1-2 phrases. Web techniques such as scrolling text and animation that displays text blocks in a repeating sequence can give you more room for copy while holding the reader's attention.

## Content Ideas—Online Ads

Consider the following ideas for strengthening the impact of online ads:

**Advertise on the company site.** Use ads on your own Web site to highlight new products, price promotions, breaking news, or new content.

**Target ads.** Create separate ads to focus on the market attracted to different sites. Consider linking each ad to a different landing page on your site as a way to track response rates. Distinct landing pages can be created simply by modifying a Welcome Page with text that is customized to each audience.

**Minimize copy.** Remember, the goal of an online ad is to entice the reader to click through to the target Web site. You do not need to make the complete sale in the ad itself. This guideline applies to both graphical banner ads and text ads that appear in a search engine display, ezine, or a Web site.

**Focus the ad**. Present a single message, product, or promotion and state it clearly so visitors can immediately determine their interest.

**Strengthen the "click here."** Always include a specific, benefit-oriented call to action. *Click here to save!*

**Coordinate the landing page.** Make sure the landing page confirms the visitor has reached the right destination; restates the offer and benefit; presents a clear and compelling call to action; and makes any registration process simple and non-threatening.

## ADVERTORIAL

An advertorial is an *adver*tisement written and designed to resemble the edi*torial* material in a magazine or newspaper. Often written in the form of an article, an advertorial is paid for by the sponsoring company and may be written by the company's staff, a freelance writer, or one of the publication's editors or reporters (policies on who writes advertorials vary with each publication).

Advertorials may be placed on one or more pages in the publication or bound-in as an insert. An advertorial must be labeled as advertising, and most publications require that it use a different type style, layout, or page size to distinguish it from the regular editorial content. While advertorials can cover almost any topic, they usually have content similar to that in articles and white papers (see Chapter 11 for articles; white papers are discussed later in this chapter). In addition, reprints of the advertorial are often used as a sales document, in the same way as a white paper.

Advertorials can present the company's perspective on a market need, technology advance, or industry trend. Products and services are discussed in the context of the advertorial's focus, usually with an emphasis on positioning over detailed description. In most cases, the objective for an advertorial is to generate prospect inquiries by phone or via a Web page created specifically for the advertorial.

## *Content Ideas—Advertorial*

An advertorial can incorporate any of the document elements described in Chapter 5, although the publication in which the advertorial appears may have specific requirements for the content and page layout. Many of the content types described in Chapter 6 are appropriate for advertorials. While advertorials are usually written with a journalistic style, some of the text techniques in Chapter 7 may be appropriate in moderation.

Although an advertorial *per se* typically is not posted to a Web site, you may want to consider the Web tips listed below for brochures.

## BROCHURE

A brochure is typically a multi-page booklet that describes a product, product line, service, or company. Data sheets (discussed later in this chapter) also can serve as brochures, and many companies produce disk-based or Web brochures.

Some high-tech products are so complex they cannot be described adequately in a single brochure. In addition, companies often have "families" of related products that are targeted to different markets, applications, or platforms. In these cases, companies often produce multipart brochures or a literature set, with individual brochures or data sheets for each product, market segment, platform, or application type.

Whether in print or electronic form, a brochure is a critical communication medium because it may be a prospect's only source of information about a product or company. Brochures serve as the cornerstone of most sales efforts, with distribution through any of the following means:

- As part of a mailing, in a seminar, or given to the prospect by a salesperson as a "leave-behind" for a meeting.
- As the incentive for responding to an advertisement, direct-mail or email promotion, or visiting a trade-show booth. This technique has been used successfully by many companies to collect sales leads.
- As a downloadable document from the company Web site.

Print brochures can have a wide variety of formats and levels of production quality. They can be formulaic, as in a set of product brochures that follow a standard format, or highly creative, as in a corporate showcase brochure. The typical length for a brochure is between four and sixteen letter-size pages.

Brochures may involve highly creative and high-cost layouts and production values. Production factors for printed brochures may include full-color printing, extensive use of visuals and white space, foldouts, paper quality, etc. An online or CD-ROM brochure may also include multimedia elements such as audio and video clips, animation, or links to an online product demo.

In contrast, data sheets usually involve simpler, less expensive production, such as two-color printing. A company may also develop a standard template for data sheets that defines the content and layout of text, a product photo, diagrams, certification symbols, and other elements.

### Brochure Types

The following brochure types are commonly produced by technology companies:

**Product overview.** An overview brochure typically presents a complete description of a product or product line. The information may be at a high level to accommodate different audiences and uses. In this case, the overview brochure may be supplemented with detailed information in one or more data sheets. Keeping an overview brochure at a high level can also make it usable for a longer period of time, an important consideration if it involves expensive production.

**Capabilities overview.** A document that describes a company's expertise, services, and resources. A capabilities overview is most often used to market a service company or a service program provided by a product manufacturer. This brochure type also can show "the company behind the product" for high-cost, high-commitment products.

**Market-specific brochure.** Some companies produce different brochures for each market segment. This type of brochure presents the features, benefits, examples, and case studies most relevant to that market. Another type of market-specific brochure are those localized for each country where the product is sold.

**Direct mail.** Brochures are an essential component of direct-mail campaigns, either as a self-mailer or part of a package. The term "self-mailer" describes a brochure with a built-in address area that allows it to be mailed without an envelope. The content, format, and length of a direct-mail brochure will depend on whether its goal is to generate prospect names (sales leads) or to actually sell a product. (See the section on direct-mail packages later in this chapter.)

**Web brochure.** A print brochure may be posted directly on a Web site as a PDF file, preserving its pagination and appearance. Or a Web "brochure" may be created from a series of linked Web pages, with text and visual content selected specifically for Web presentation, navigation, and interactivity.

**Video, demo CD/DVD, or multimedia brochure.** Electronic-media brochures can be especially effective for explaining new technologies and for marketing high-priced, sophisticated products. However, they can be time-consuming, complex, and expensive to develop and produce.

## Content Ideas—Print Brochures

A brochure can accommodate any of the content types, document elements, and text techniques described in Chapters 5 through 7. The ideas given below cover the types of information typically included in a printed brochure for a technology product.

The order of ideas here reflects the most common sequence for presentation of these items in a product brochure. However, you do not need to include every content type listed here in every brochure.

**Overview.** A summary description of the product, its target customers, and key benefits. Usually just a short paragraph; may be only a single sentence.

**Product features and benefits.** This "section" may in fact encompass most of the text in the brochure, as the features and associated benefits are covered extensively in narrative text. It provides a description of the product's features and benefits, as well as options for product configuration or operation. This section also may include a description of accessory products and services offered by your company or other vendors. Benefits may be highlighted separately in a bullet list or the features and benefits may be presented side-by-side in a table.

**Selection guide.** When faced with a product line of multiple models or a product with multiple options, a customer may throw up his hands in frustration and say "Just tell me what to buy." A selection guide helps the customer make the right choice based on relevant factors such as type of user, operating system, capacity needs, local-language version, or other product characteristics. A selection guide presents information in the form of scenarios, tables, or worksheets. An online guide can be particularly useful if it allows the customer to easily view and save multiple comparisons.

**Product operation.** A description of how the product works including architecture or design information, and screen shots or sample output. This section is often given the title "How It Works."

**Product applications.** A discussion of how the product can be implemented to support certain capabilities, operate in certain environments or activities, or solve certain customer problems.

**Customer information.** One or more brief case studies or a list of major or representative customers.

**Supporting evidence.** Brief, positive quotes from current customers, excerpts from product reviews in trade magazines, test results (see Chapter 6 for guidelines), and listings of awards or certifications (in text or with symbols).

**Product specifications.** The technical details about the product's physical and functional characteristics.

**Product bundles.** Companies often package together all the components (called a bundle) a customer needs to implement a complete system. This text describes the included components and presents the advantages of buying and implementing the bundle.

**Service and support programs.** A description of repair, service, and technical support programs; training programs; consulting services for planning or implementation; subscriptions or other programs for minor updates and new versions. This section may also include warranty and guarantee information.

**Company information.** A discussion of the company's expertise, history, and operations; sometimes presented in the form of a letter from a company executive. This section also may include information on relationships with dealers and alliance partners.

**Ordering and pricing information.** Detailed instructions on ordering or buying the product. A list of dealer and sales offices, and information on demonstration tools or evaluation units. Specify product price if the reader is expected or able to buy the product from the brochure; manufacturer's suggested retail price (MSRP) if the customer will buy from a dealer or retailer. If relevant, describe licensing packages for individuals and businesses.

**Visuals.** Photographs, illustrations, or diagrams of the product, its concept, architecture, usage, application, or positioning.

## *Web Tips—Brochures*

Post a print brochure online as a PDF file or create a separate version that takes advantage of Web presentation and content organization techniques.

Adapting a multi-page print brochure for the Web involves several decisions. The first decision is whether to simply post the print brochure as a PDF file for display and printing. This choice has the advantage of a very fast and easy process for creating and posting a PDF file. But a PDF file cannot support dynamic or interactive content; those features require repurposing the brochure text and images into one or more Web pages. When making this choice, determine how you can restructure the content to be more readable and easier to navigate across several Web pages.

Always include a call to action such as *Order this item!* If the action can be completed online, link to an order form or other page. If the action must be completed offline, include all instructions and information necessary for the visitor to take the action.

An online brochure can link to supplementary content such as:

- Other online brochures or catalog pages for related products or accessories to create cross-sell and up-sell opportunities.
- A price/parts list for the product(s) described in the brochure.
- Pages with gift suggestions, a coupon, product inquiry form, or a selection guide to encourage a visitor's further exploration of products and services offered by your business.
- A video clip showing a product demonstration or an audio clip from a presentation.

## CATALOG

A catalog is a book, booklet, or section of a Web site that presents a collection of products sold by a company, distributor, or dealer. Most commonly used for mail-order or online sales, a catalog also can serve as a reference to support sales by dealers or direct-sales staff. Some companies produce their own catalogs, while others participate in catalogs published by distributors or resellers.

A consistent format for the product descriptions in a catalog will help readers find information quickly. For example, a description could present a statement of the product's functionality and applications, follow with an overview of key features and benefits, list the key technical specifications, and end with the part number and price.

## Content Ideas—Catalog

Catalog descriptions present a unique copywriting challenge because they must entice the reader immediately with a limited number of words that are written in a very consistent style. They can incorporate many of the product and company information types described in Chapter 6, as well as many of the document elements described in Chapter 5. The text techniques in Chapter 7 for evocative language, power words, emphasis, and emotion can help you meet this challenge. Also, look at a variety of consumer and business catalogs to identify effective techniques for writing this style of copy.

Figure 10.2 lists the most common elements for a print catalog; many of these elements are also applicable to Web or disk-based catalogs.

---

**Catalog Elements**

---

A table of contents or product index. For a catalog published on the Web, this index can link to separate Web pages for each product.

A welcome letter from a company executive.

Ordering instructions for Web, email, phone, fax, and postal mail orders. Telephone number and hours of operation for the order center.

Printed order form with information on ordering procedures, payment policies, shipping options, and expiration date on prices.

Charts to show options available for each product. Details on product specifications and configurations.

Parts and price lists.

Cross-sell and upsell references to related and accessory products.

Instructions on how to obtain additional product information.

Guarantee or warranty statements.

A list of dealer locations or retail stores if the products in the catalog can be purchased through these outlets.

---

*Figure 10.2  Document elements and content ideas for a catalog.*

## Web Tips—Catalogs

Although you can easily adapt the information from a printed catalog to a Web page, consider taking advantage of the lower cost for

Web documents to add longer text descriptions, more images, video demonstrations, or audio samples.

- Add links to the catalog pages for other models, accessories, and related products to create cross-sell and upsell opportunities or include that information on this page.
- Link to pages with gift suggestions, a coupon, product inquiry form, or a selection guide.
- Always include a call to action such as *Order this item!* with a link that takes the visitor to an online order form or a Web page that presents instructions for taking the action.
- If you sell to an international market, accepting multiple currencies and applying different shipping rates, consider linking to a price/parts list to present that detail.

## COUPON

Given that every consumer enjoys saving money, what better way to encourage sales than with a coupon? Printed or Web coupons can promote product purchases in a retail store, by telephone or postal mail.

### Content Ideas—Coupon

When writing the copy that appears on a coupon, consider the following factors:

- Include a strong call to action and present the offer and its benefits clearly.
- Verify that coupon terms and rules for use comply with all applicable laws and commerce regulations. Clearly state the terms of the coupon as well as limitations, prerequisites, expiration date, and other conditions for redemption.

### Web Tips—Coupon

- If the customer can print an online coupon to use for an offline purchase, include all terms and instructions on the printable document.

- If the coupon is for a product the visitor can purchase online, include a link to the catalog page for that product. Remember, the visitor may not view the product information before seeing the coupon, depending on the navigation paths defined in the site.
- Consider the role of the coupon in encouraging an online sale, and define the navigation path for the sale process accordingly. To do this, include a link to the coupon page from an online catalog page, brochure, order form, or promotional email message.

## DATA SHEET

A data sheet is usually a two-page or four-page document that presents detailed information about a specific product. The focus of the writing is primarily on describing the product, with information on features, benefits, functionality, applications, and specifications. Many companies create a standard format for data sheets to ensure consistency of style, content, and presentation.

Directed primarily to prospects, data sheets also serve as reference material for sales staff and dealers, as an inexpensive handout for trade shows or retail sales, and as a fulfillment piece for an advertising or direct-mail campaign.

### *Content Ideas—Data Sheet*

A data sheet can contain many of the same content types, document elements, and text techniques as a brochure (see the section earlier in this chapter). If a data sheet is the only document that presents the technical specifications for the product, see the guidelines for this content type in Chapter 6. The Web tips listed for brochures also apply to data sheets.

## DIRECT-MAIL PACKAGE

"Junk mail" is the derogatory term often applied to direct postal mail, which in actuality can be one of the most important pieces in the marcom mix for many high-tech products. Direct mail can generate inquiries or directly sell a product, and can be used in a product launch campaign or as an ongoing marketing method (Figure 10.3). The information and ideas discussed in this section for direct mail also apply in large part to email marketing (see next section).

---

**Uses for Direct Mail**

---

Make a sale, where the reply card or a Web link enables the prospect to order the product.

Capture prospect leads, encouraging the recipient to request more information about the product, service, or offer.

Announce the availability of a product and motivate visits to a dealer, retail store, or e-commerce Web site.

Encourage attendance at seminars or other events and visits to a trade-show booth.

Announce new programs or sales incentives to dealers.

Announce and generate orders for product upgrades or cross-sell accessory products and services.

Support advertising, telemarketing, and other sales activities by making multiple contacts with a prospect.

---

*Figure 10.3 Examples of marketing activities that can be supported with direct-mail materials.*

A direct-mail package usually includes a cover letter, a brochure, a "lift note" document with additional information to motivate a response, a reply card or order form, and a reply envelope. Catalogs and CDs/DVDs containing a product demo or multimedia presentation also are often distributed as direct-mail pieces.

A variation on this package is the self-mailer, a brochure with a built-in address area that allows it to be mailed without an envelope. Self-mailers are best suited for information offers or to encourage attendance at an event. Because of postal regulations, this format may not be usable in some countries.

"Whatever your campaign offers the target audience—a free information packet, an instructive Web seminar, a gift for visiting a trade show booth—concentrate on selling the benefits of responding and receiving the offer... selling the product may or may not be achievable (or even advisable) in the space your piece allows—especially if it is a big-ticket item. If you can just get someone interested enough to respond to the offer, you can then leave the real [product] selling to your sales force."[1]

When writing direct-mail copy, repeat the offer statement and key benefits multiple times throughout the package and at least once on each piece. "No matter how interested people are in your product, they won't respond if they're not interested in your offer. Merchandize your offer in all elements of the package."[2] Use an integrated theme for both copy and visuals in all pieces in the package to reinforce the offer or message.

The copy must comply with national and local laws regarding the statement of offer terms and guarantees (see Chapter 8). And, the complete package must comply with postal regulations on mailing size and format, as well as content, appearance, and placement of text that appears on the outside of the envelope.

### Content Ideas—Direct Mail

Direct-mail pieces can use many of the document elements described in Chapter 5 and the text techniques covered in Chapter 7. Many of the content types for product and services information, quotes, comparisons, examples, and offers described in Chapter 6 are also appropriate for direct-mail pieces. In addition, the information below covers specific guidelines for each piece in a direct-mail package.

### Envelope

Use the outside of the envelope (both front and back if postal regulations permit) to present or continue a teaser, show the offer, or present a statement to encourage immediate action: *Limited-Time Offer* or *Act Before December 1 and Enjoy a Special Low Price!*

Any teaser statement on the front of the envelope should encourage the reader to open the package. A teaser can identify the audience: *Attention Network Manager*; state the offer: *Free Demo!*; present a benefit: *Locate any document in 3 seconds or less!*[3]; or announce a product or upgrade: *Introducing the New, Faster Processor.*

Quotes from customers or reviewers can be effective copy for an envelope, if they are brief and specific about the product's quality or benefits. Another content idea is to present a short bullet list of the most important product benefits or features.

### Sales Letter

Most direct marketing experts indicate that long letters (3 to 4 pages) generate a higher response rate than short letters (1 or 2 pages). A long letter is usually necessary to generate purchases, while a short letter can be suitable for generating inquiries.

Consider producing different letters for different prospect groups, customizing the content to the interests and buying factors for each group. Personalize the salutation or use a salutation that describes the person's job function or interest: **Dear Operations Manager** or **Dear Apple Macintosh Enthusiast**.

Place a headline or Johnson Box at the top of the letter to state an offer or key benefit. (A Johnson Box is a block of text placed within a box to catch the reader's attention.) This technique can catch the prospect's attention and encourage further reading. However, using a headline if the letter is individually addressed to the prospect can destroy the sense of personal communication.

Restate the offer, key benefit, and call to action in both the opening and closing paragraphs of the letter. Use the middle paragraphs of the letter to describe product features and additional benefits, and to present supporting evidence about product claims or your company. Also, cover all details about the offer in the body copy, including any guarantee or warranty statements.

The letter should have a "skimmable" format, using short sentences and paragraphs. Use subheads to state key aspects of the offer, key benefits, or messages. Text formatting (e.g., bold, italics) can highlight the words or phrases that emphasize the offer and product benefits, or showcase testimonial quotes.

Include a signature block to support the letter's sense of personal correspondence. A postscript (P.S.) is essential; use it to reinforce the call to action, restate the key message or benefit, or emphasize the value of the promotional offer.

*Note*: Consider the ideas presented in this section when writing any type of sales letter. For example, a cover letter sent with a product brochure to a prospect can advance the sales process by including substantive information and a call to action for the next step.

### Brochure

For selling a product, the brochure in a direct-mail package can be a shorter version of the standalone brochure or data sheet. This version should include the essential information on product features, benefits, and specifications. For an information offer, the brochure can present a brief overview of the product. In any case, state the offer or key benefit in the headline. See the section on brochures earlier in this chapter for additional content ideas.

### Lift Note

A lift note is a brief letter, often printed on a smaller piece of paper, that gives the reader additional motivation for responding to the offer. A lift note can present a variety of information, but the following types are common:

- Provide responses to the typical objections a prospect may have to the product or offer.
- Restate the value of the offer or the key product benefit.
- Present testimonials: *Here's what others have said about our product.*

### Order or Reply Form

An order form or reply card may be included with a direct-mail package, brochure, or advertisement. It provides a convenient way for a reader to request more information, order a product, or register for an event.

These forms typically use only headlines, body copy, and bullet lists as document elements. They can accommodate any of the ideas listed in the "Product Information" and "Offers" sections in Chapter 6.

**Call to action.** Ask for the order by presenting a call to action such as *Call Today!* or *Return This Card Today.*

**Ordering information and instructions.** Present all necessary information and instructions for placing the order by mail, phone, fax, or online. Show the URL for an online order page. For telephone orders, show hours of operation for the call center. Specify payment methods and terms, sales tax rates, delivery options, and shipping and handling costs.

**Customer information.** Include input spaces for all customer information you need to collect for selling the product or delivering the requested information. For example, the customer's name and title; company and department; postal address, mailstop, country, and postal code (allow for international variations); telephone and fax numbers; email address; billing information.

**Customer validation data.** Information required from the customer to process the order such as product number, customer number, or system version.

**Restate the offer.** Summarize the terms of the offer and the key product messages, either in the body copy or as a headline. Some recipients will keep only the order form or reply card, so it should be able to sell on its own.[4] However, include only the key features or benefits; don't overload the form with copy.

**Prospect qualification questions.** For an information offer, qualify prospects by asking them to answer survey questions about purchasing authority, current systems, organization size, and product needs. These questions can help you determine specific interests and which products or promotions would be the best choice to offer to that prospect. However, be careful that you don't ask too many questions or request information the prospect may feel is confidential or inappropriate to disclose early in the sales cycle. An intrusive or complex reply card can discourage response and create a negative perception of your company.

## EMAIL MARKETING

Despite its associations with the unwelcome deluge of spam, email will continue to be an important and effective marketing medium. As a copywriter, your email projects may range from standard replies for routine inquiries, to brief and targeted email messages for a specific campaign, to a lengthy email newsletter (commonly called an "ezine").

Industry practices, technologies, and local laws will continue to evolve for commercial email. See the resources listed at the end of this chapter for books and Web sites that provide relevant information.

## Message Types

The most common email projects for a copywriter can be grouped into two types.

**Promotional campaign.** A single message or a series of related messages to promote a product, event, or offer. For example, the first line in a promotional message might be: *Time is running out— act now to get these special savings on a new purchase of Prime-Widget!* Each message is written specifically to meet the goals of the campaign. Multiple versions of the message may be created to target different recipient groups or to test the response rate for different offers, wording of the offer or call to action, or delivery schedule.

**Standardized communications.** Many business transactions involve the frequent exchange of the same information between the company and its customers or suppliers. It is often possible to write a standard message that can be used for these exchanges, in a format that allows the message to be tailored before it is sent by a sales or customer service representative. Standard messages may also be sent by an automated email tool called an auto-responder. Common types of standard and auto-responder messages include:

- Acknowledgements for an online form or message sent by a customer or Web site visitor
- Order confirmations
- Subscribe/unsubscribe acknowledgments for ezines or information services
- Inquiry fulfillment: *Here's the report on test results you requested*
- Shipment status information

Standard messages also can be triggered on a designated schedule after a transaction has been completed, covering activities such as:

- Follow-up for an inquiry or order. This type of message could include questions such as: *"Did you get what you requested? Did it meet your needs? Do you need anything else?"* Look for cross-sell and up-sell opportunities.
- Use and application tips. An opening line for such a message could be: *Here are a few tips to get the most from your new PrimeWidget.*
- Upgrade and cross-sell promotions: *Here's the latest information about upgrading to PrimeWidget Version 6.0.*
- Renewal reminders. Useful for subscriptions to print or online publications or product download and upgrade services.
- Surveys for feedback on the purchase transaction or a customer service experience.

### Email Messages—Content Ideas

The following techniques are recommended by many email marketing experts as ways to help recipients recognize your legitimate messages and reduce the potential for them to be discarded by a spam filter. More detailed guidelines are presented in the books and Web sites listed in the resources section.

**From/Sender line.** Use the company name as the sender and a legitimate return email address that includes the company domain name.

**Subject line.** To entice the recipient to open the message, make the subject line a clear, specific, and appealing hint of the message content: *PrimeWidget 6.0 Upgrade News.* To avoid the possibility that your message will be viewed as spam, do not use dollar signs and exclamation points, all upper-case words, and suspicious words such as "free," "Hi," and words related to investments, medications, and sexual references.

Also be careful about using the more creative text techniques (described in Chapter 7) when writing email subject lines and the message text. Metaphor, slang, illusion or the latest cultural fad can confuse recipients or cause them to think your message is spam.

Repeat the company or brand name near the beginning of the subject line. Limit subject lines to 3-6 words or no more than 30 characters.

Start the subject line with a verb in the imperative form to encourage action: *Register Today for PrimeWidget World* or *Learn How Wireless PrimeWidget Improves Productivity.*

**Personalization.** Stating the recipient's name in the message subject line may backfire because spammers often use this technique. Recipients also may delete a personalized email without opening it because they instantly recognize the sense of false familiarity as a potentially deceptive sales tactic. However, personalization and customization techniques within the body of the message can give the reader a greater sense of dialogue and engagement.

**Message text.** Limit the message to a single topic and no more than three screens. Readers may delete a long commercial message or file it away for later reading (most likely, to be forgotten). Write short sentences and paragraphs; use formatting and white space to enhance readability of the text. But make sure you present enough information to engage and help the reader understand your offer and call to action.

Direct marketing expert Russell Kern notes, "Keep the message driving to the action desired. Present your offer as early in your message as possible."[7] Presenting an offer early is important not only when the recipient is reading the actual message, but also for attracting attention when the recipient uses a message preview function in an email program.[8]

**Formats.** For both plain-text and HTML format messages, use clear and consistent formats for headlines, subheads, and divider lines to segment the message into smaller chunks that will be easier for readers to understand and keep a sense of place while scrolling through the message.

**Writing Style.** Use a consistent style and tone to increase reader recognition of your messages over time. Depending on the message content and the company's style standards, the email style may be more informal in order to convey a sense of personal correspondence or conversation. Avoid becoming too informal, as this may create a negative impression. Avoid the use of emoticons and email slang and abbreviations (e.g., BTW for "by the way").[9]

**Call to action.** To motivate a response or a click-through to a specific landing page on the associated Web site, the call to action should be more specific than "Click here for more information." Instead, indicate what the visitor will receive or how he will benefit from clicking on the link. For example, *Read the success stories now.*[10] or *Download ATCA white paper to learn how* (to cut development costs).[11] Look at banner ads for ideas on motivational text for the call to action.

Present the call to action with the associated link at the top and the end of the message; also present it again in the middle if the message is lengthy. Use the same link text and URL to avoid confusing readers about what they will reach with a click-through.

**"Housekeeping" information.** Place this text at the end of the message. Examples include: Confirmation of the recipient's opt-in status and instructions for opting-out, a link to the company's privacy policy, the company's physical address, and other information required by law.

## EMAIL NEWSLETTERS (EZINES)

Ezines are a newsletter sent as an email message or posted on a Web site as a (usually) single HTML page. (A print newsletter may also be posted on the Web site as a PDF file.) Like print newsletters, an ezine can be created for varied audiences, product lines, or target markets. They contain a collection of timely, usually short articles. Indeed, all of the content ideas listed in this chapter for print newsletters can be accommodated in an ezine. But ezines differ from print newsletters in several key ways.

**Links.** In an ezine, an article need not appear in full. A common technique is to present the article headline and opening paragraph or synopsis in the originating email, then provide a link to the full article text on the company Web site. It is a way to encourage recipients to read the entire message, something they might not do if they had to scroll through the complete text for each article. In addition, this technique is common for announcing promotions and new products, with the link leading to detailed information or an order form.

Other uses for links include:

- Guiding readers to detailed information on the topics or products covered in the article
- Allowing the reader to send an email to a sales group or to the article's author
- Navigating to an order page from a call to action or promotional offer
- Playing a video or audio clip related to an article

**Easier targeting and customization.** Because of greatly simplified and less costly production than print, it is easier to create multiple versions of an ezine. An ezine can also incorporate personal information about the recipient, drawn automatically from a database or customer relationship management (CRM) system.

**Timeliness.** An ezine can include more up-to-the-minute news or announcements that must be communicated outside of the normal production schedule for a print newsletter.

**Writing guidelines.** Many of the same guidelines for email messages also apply to ezines, especially for brevity and subject line. You may also need to consider different writing techniques depending on whether the ezine is designed in text or HTML format.

For an ezine, include a table of contents at the top of the message (with active links for HTML formats).

## EVENT MATERIALS

A user conference, sales seminar, trade show, and other events usually require numerous promotional and informational materials. Examples include invitations, brochures, and registration forms; presentations, speeches, and handouts; and follow-up materials for event participants. Materials may be in both print and online form.

When developing event materials, you can draw from many of the ideas and tips presented in this book for brochures, white papers, presentations, and email messages. The section "Event Information" in Chapter 6 also provides useful guidelines.

## FORMS

A print or online form gives prospects an easy way to submit an inquiry while providing enough information about their interests or needs to help you return a prompt and targeted response. However, be careful about the number and nature of questions you include on a form. If you ask too many questions or they are too personal, the visitor may not submit the form.

### *Forms for Visitor Interaction*

Direct-response marketers have long understood the value of engaging a prospect in a mail package or advertisement—the more time a prospect spends with the material, the more likely she will place an order.

You can replicate this engagement on a Web site through the interaction it offers to visitors. Creating interaction goes beyond ensuring the ease of a visitor's navigation and exploration. It also means giving visitors opportunities and incentives to enter a dialogue with you, a dialogue that helps build relationships—and sales.

Several types of Web forms can help you initiate and sustain successful interaction with visitors, including:

**Visitor Registration/Survey.** Gathers a range of information about visitor interests, needs, and demographics.

**Product Inquiry.** Helps the visitor send a detailed request for information about a product or service.

**Selection Guide.** Enables the visitor to see specific information about products, or link to specific pages on the site.

### *Content Ideas—Forms*

- Always provide instructions for submitting the form online, via fax, postal mail, or telephone.
- Adapt questions to the interests of visitors and your need for market research. Always include at least one question that allows a free-form, essay-type response.

## *Web Tips—Forms*

- Don't display a form as the first page a visitor sees on a Web site, and don't force visitors to complete a form before granting access to content. Visitors are likely to leave a site because they perceive such an action as unwelcoming and intrusive.
- Display a Send or Submit button at the bottom of the page. If this button appears at the top of the page, the visitor may click on it before completing all entries on the form.
- Present input areas and text labels consistently.
- Size the input areas to give the visitor sufficient space for entering the requested information. For example, allow a minimum of 12 characters for a person's last name.
- Consider responses from international visitors when designing forms. For example, add a field for country, or create a blank, multi-line block for all address information.

Web forms can be scripted to automatically enter any collected information into the appropriate fields. For example, if the visitor has linked to an Order Form from the catalog page for an individual product, the script could fill-in the fields that request information such as product number, name, and price.

Interaction is especially important when visitors complete forms on a Web site. Work with the Web site developer to identify how the form will be processed and what will be displayed after the visitor clicks the "Submit" button. A typical action is to display a screen that presents a message thanking the visitor for submitting the form and indicating when and how the company will respond.

## NEWSLETTER OR MAGAZINE

Newsletters and company-published magazines are news-oriented yet promotional publications sent to customers, employees, dealers, and others interested in your products and company. These publications encourage customer and dealer loyalty by providing ongoing contact and useful information on new products, services, applications, and upgrades.

If your company markets internationally, you may want to create localized editions of the newsletter or magazine for each international market. In addition, some companies produce separate newsletters for salespeople, dealers, and alliance partners.

## Content Ideas—Print Newsletters and Magazines

A newsletter can incorporate many of the document elements, content types, and text techniques described in Chapters 5 through 7. Most newsletters include a mix of the following content:

**Product news.** Announcements of new products and upgrades; in-depth discussion of a particular feature; roundup of user applications; description of current R&D efforts or the history of the product's development; "behind the scenes" articles. For a newsletter targeted to sales representatives and dealers, product news could include pricing updates; policy and procedure changes; description of current or planned promotional campaigns; customer win stories; tips for successful sales strategies and tactics.

**Company news.** Company milestones and successes; mergers and acquisitions; employee achievements; openings of sales offices and support centers; or other company activities.

**Customer profiles and case studies.** Stories about the latest customer wins or unique product applications.

**Feature articles and columns.** Interviews with company staff or industry experts on current issues or strategies; a trends or opinion column from an analyst; a message from the company president or other executive.

**"How to" articles or tips.** Application ideas; technical support tips; Q&A column that addresses the most common user questions.

**Editorial information.** Authors' biographies; an "In This Issue" contents box; "What's Ahead" column; article index; and section for letters to the editor.

**Event calendars and reports.** A calendar and previews of upcoming conferences; user-group meetings; seminars; trade shows; training courses; and other events.

**Reader service information.** Complete contact information for the company; a directory of sales and support offices; URLs for the online version of the newsletter; subscriber and customer service information.

**Writer's guidelines.** A description of the types of articles published in the magazine and instructions for writers on article style, length, format, and submission procedures. Guidelines and an email address or Web URL for submitting a letter to the editor.

### Special Document Elements

**Nameplate.** The nameplate appears on the first page and can include the newsletter name, company or publisher name, date of publication, volume and issue. It also can include a tagline: *The Newsletter for Users of Reflection.*[5]

**Masthead.** The masthead presents publication data for the newsletter. It can include information such as the following:

- Names and affiliations of the publisher, editors, writers, designers, illustrators, photographers, and other contributors
- Publication date, volume and issue numbers, copyright date, and country where printed
- Trademark acknowledgments and information disclaimers (see Chapter 8)
- Contact information for the publication's staff or sponsoring company including postal address, telephone and fax numbers, email address and Web URL

**Order form or reply card.** Give readers a way to request newsletter subscriptions, back issues, or other product literature. To reduce printing and postage expense, you may want to direct readers to specific Web URLs that present additional information about the content in each article.

### Web Tips—Print Newsletter

Post a print newsletter online as a PDF file or create a separate online edition (see the ideas for an ezine earlier in this chapter). An online newsletter can link to supplementary content such as:

- Pages that present more information on any product, people, or organizations mentioned in an article. These links can be embedded in the text or images.

- A glossary page for any words that may be unfamiliar to readers.
- An "In This Issue" list that links to each newsletter article, even if they are placed on the same page. This list gives the visitor a fast way to jump to the topic of interest.

## PACKAGING

The product box or packaging is an important form of marcom for products that are sold in a retail environment. Packaging copy becomes especially important for a low-priced product that could be considered an impulse purchase. In addition, the packaging copy can reinforce the customer's decision to buy the product when the sale is made through mail order or other indirect method. Use a consistent design and images for the product brochures and packaging to help a prospect recognize your product on a crowded retail shelf.

Packaging copy should be strong enough to sell the product on the spot. The information presented on the package must be complete, clear, and include strong statements of features and benefits. Emphasize benefits, but include all feature information that is essential to differentiate the product and to help the buyer make a purchase decision.

Use all surfaces of the package for copy, including the top, sides, and bottom. Place the product name and key message on each of these surfaces. Test the draft copy, images, and layout on a prototype that is placed in an actual selling environment to ensure the desired messages will attract the wandering eye of a prospect.

### Content Ideas—Packaging

Packaging can include many of the document elements and text techniques described in Chapters 5 and 7. The content types described in the "Product Information" and "Comparisons" section in Chapter 6 are also appropriate. In addition, packaging may include the following items:

- Quotes from product reviews or testimonials from users.
- Callouts or a text box to highlight rebates or other promotional offers, premiums that are included in the package, or other sales incentives.
- Summary statement of what the product does and the target user on the package front.
- Service and support program information.
- List or description of package contents. Platform information or description of compatibility with other products. Identification of localized versions.
- URL for a page on the company Web site that provides detailed product information or a promotional offer.

## PROPOSAL

A proposal is a document that details a company's bid for a project or product sale. Typically a proposal includes comprehensive information on the proposed project or product, its applicability to the customer's requirements, and the capabilities of the proposing company. It also may include copies of the sales materials described in this chapter.

A proposal may be created in response to a Request for Proposal (RFP) or in a competitive bid situation. It is often developed near the end of the sales cycle, when the customer will make a specific selection from the proposals submitted by several vendors.

Because proposals can vary so widely in content and format, they are described only briefly and no content ideas are presented here. See the Resources section for useful references that focus on proposals.

## SALES LETTER

A sales letter typically accompanies a brochure or other marketing material in an inquiry fulfillment package. This package is sent in response to a prospect's request for additional information or as a follow-up for visitors to a Web site, seminar, or trade show booth.

A common mistake is to treat a sales letter as a simple cover sheet: "Enclosed is the material you requested. Please contact us if we can be a further service." This approach misses an important opportunity for promoting the product, reinforcing the company brand, and moving the prospect to the next step in the buying process.

At a minimum, a sales letter should outline the key benefits or marketing messages for the product or service, present a call to action, and provide complete contact information. Write bullet points that guide the prospect in looking at each document enclosed in the package. Describe how the prospect will benefit from reading the material, viewing an enclosed disk, or visiting an associated Web site.

The length of a sales letter will vary depending on its objective and what it accompanies. As a cover sheet for materials, a sales letter is typically one or two pages. A longer, direct mail-style letter may be appropriate if the purpose of the package is to motivate an immediate purchase. (See the section on direct mail earlier in this chapter for additional ideas on this type of sales letter.)

### Content Ideas—Sales Letter

Many readers will believe that only the brochure or other pieces in the mailing provide substantial information, so they will give the letter only a cursory look. The opener must be strong to compel the reader to continue through the letter. Use the opener to make an offer, provide news, or ask a question.

Use a Postscript message (P.S.) or a Johnson Box to emphasize the key message or call to action again at the end of the letter.

If the letter is personalized, don't repeat the person's name more than once in the body copy. Otherwise, your attempt at sincerity will seem fake to the reader.

Don't create a "one letter fits all" that promotes too many products or contains information for both prospects and dealers. Instead, write separate letters that provide targeted information for each product and prospect group.

Always provide contact information for a specific Web page, sales representative, or dealer. Don't make the reader call the general corporate number or search through a Web site to obtain this information. Also, don't assume that a reader will keep all the materials in the package; place contact information on each document.

## WHITE PAPER

A white paper is an educational, essay-style document that presents an analysis or in-depth explanation of a product, technology, market trend, or issue. A white paper is intended to provide useful background information and supporting evidence that prospects can use when considering a product or comparing technologies. According to a survey of IT professionals conducted by the publication site Bitpipe, 79% of respondents said they are likely to consult white papers and case studies before making critical buying decisions.[6]

White papers typically address business or technical issues related to a product, a new technology, or a company strategy. A white paper also can be an advocacy piece that presents a company's viewpoint on industry standards, trends, and directions.

White papers are most often produced for highly complex, expensive products that have a significant impact on a customer's operations or business. They are useful in the early and intermediate stages of a sales cycle, when a prospect needs a comprehensive understanding of technologies, applications, and strategies in order to narrow a list of candidate products for further consideration.

Naming an author for the white paper can add credibility if that person is a recognized industry expert. (The paper may actually be ghostwritten by a professional writer.) In some cases, the white paper may be written by and attributed to an industry analyst, but sponsored by a company under an exclusive-use agreement.

The content of the white paper should emphasize the topic under discussion, not promotional information for the product. However, you can include information about how the product and company address the issues or problems you describe in the paper discussion.

Promotional information typically appears at the end of the white paper and has a "soft-sell" approach compared to other forms of marketing materials. Taking a "hard sell" approach to product and company information may detract from the more detached impression you are trying to achieve with a white paper. However, this doesn't mean the paper should read like a dry research document. Instead, the headlines, writing style, and tone of the paper can be creative and engaging to capture and hold the reader's interest.

### Audiences for White Papers

Although customers and prospects are the usual audiences for white papers, these documents can also educate salespeople and dealers, technical support staff, journalists, and analysts. It may be appropriate to segment the audiences for a particular white paper according to industry or job type (e.g., technical staff vs. business executives).

Depending on the subject matter, you may want to develop multiple, audience-specific versions of a white paper. One version could present technical detail for an engineering or expert audience. Another version could present the business case for an executive audience. If the content is not sufficient to justify separate papers, target individual sections of the document to different readers. Then encourage readers to "pass-along" the white paper to their managers and colleagues.

### Production and Distribution

The typical length for a white paper is eight to sixteen letter-size pages, although some journalists say they are more likely to read shorter, tightly focused papers of four to six pages. If the document exceeds 20 pages, look for a way to restructure the content into two or more separate papers, or consider printing the white paper as a short book.

Many white papers are printed with black ink, on plain paper, with a simple design and layout. Careful use of color, as a design element or in visuals, can enhance the appeal of a white paper. But if the design makes the white paper resemble a brochure, some readers may discard it as "just another slick piece of marketing fluff." On the Web, a white paper is typically posted as a PDF file for download.

White papers are distributed through any of the following means:

- As part of a mailing, in a seminar, or given to the prospect by a salesperson as a "leave-behind" for a meeting.
- As the incentive for responding to an advertisement, direct-mail or email promotion, or visiting a trade-show booth. This technique has been used successfully by many companies to collect sales leads.
- As a downloadable document from the company Web site. To capture sales leads, the company may require visitors to complete a registration form before they can access the file.

## *White Paper Types*

The following are the most common types of white papers:

**Technology Briefing.** Explains the underlying technology incorporated into a product.

**Business Case.** Describes the factors that justify a product purchase from managerial, financial, and operational perspectives. This type of white paper is especially important for large and complex products that require a significant investment of money, time, personnel, and other resources to implement and maintain. It is also important for unproven products and technologies that may bring a significant change to a customer's strategy or activity over a period of months or years.

**Competitive Analysis.** Discusses the strengths and weaknesses of alternatives in comparison to your product or technology. While this type of white paper can be a very strong tool for positioning a product, the content must be developed carefully. In most cases, it is safer to reference alternatives by generic descriptors instead of specific product or company names. See the section "Comparisons" in Chapter 6 and "Comparative Advertising" in Chapter 8 for additional guidelines on presenting information about competitors.

**Industry Trend Overview.** Analyzes current market, operational, or technology trends. This type of white paper may be commissioned from an external market research or analyst firm, with full authorship and copyright retained by that firm. In this case, your company may be listed as the paper's sponsor.

**Application Digest.** Describes potential applications for a product or technology in a typical customer environment or for different customer types.

**Planning Guide.** Presents guidelines for implementing a new technology or preparing for future industry changes.

**Strategy Review.** Describes strategies planned by your company or that are recommended to customers for implementing a product or technology.

**Issues or Standards Analysis.** Describes the nature of an industry issue or proposed standard, and offers the company's viewpoint or recommendations for a customer's response.

**Survey, test, or research report.** As an alternative to writing your own white paper, you may want to purchase reprint rights for a report produced by a market research firm, industry analyst, or testing lab.

### Content Ideas—White Paper

A white paper can include many of the content types and document elements described in Chapters 5 and 6. The Web tips presented for brochures earlier in this chapter also apply to white papers that are posted online.

White papers often incorporate the following items:

**Reference elements.** A table of contents; executive overview at the beginning and a summary of key points or conclusions at the end of the paper; glossary of terms, standards information, research and literature citations, and a bibliography. Addresses for relevant Web sites, such as for standards bodies and publications as well as for your company.

**Decision tools.** Diagrams, illustrations, decision trees, flow charts, and product application photos; checklists and worksheets for making a decision or comparing products, technologies, configurations, or other factors that differentiate your product or service from the competition.

## RESOURCES

The recommended books and other resources listed below provide additional information on the topics discussed in this chapter. For an updated list and other materials related to this book, visit **writinghightech.com.**

### Books

Donna Baier Stein and Floyd Kemske: *Write on Target: The Direct Marketer's Copywriting Handbook.* NTC Business Books, 1997. A very good resource for the specialty of direct-mail copywriting.

Robert W. Bly: *The Online Copywriter's Handbook: Everything You Need to Know to Write Electronic Copy That Sells.* McGraw Hill, 2003. Although geared for more hard-sell, small business Web sites, provides useful guidelines and examples.

Robert Johnson-Sheehan and Sam Dragga: *Writing Proposals.* Longman, 2001. Designed as a college textbook, but a comprehensive guide to writing proposals, with examples for high-tech.

Barbara K. Kaye and Norman J. Medoff: *Just a Click Away.* Allyn and Bacon, 2001. A complete guide to online advertising.

Russell M. Kern: *S.U.R.E.-Fire Direct Response Marketing.* McGraw-Hill, 2001. A good general book for direct mail, both print and online.

Jim Sterne and Anthony Priore: *Email Marketing: Using Email to Reach Your Target Audience and Build Customer Relationships.* Wiley, 2000. A bit dated, but presents a good overview of all issues involved in email marketing.

### Web Sites

*Target Marketing* (**targeting.com**). The Web site for Web marketing author and consultant Jim Sterne; contains an archive of useful articles.

*WordBiz* (**wordbiz.com**). Covers ezine publications and email campaigns.

*Bitpipe* (**bitpipe.com**). An outlet for publicizing white papers available from your company. Also contains useful articles and surveys about writing and promoting these documents.

The following sites provide articles, reports, and tips relating to sales materials, both offline and online:

Advertising Age Magazine (**advertisingage.com**)

Ad Week Magazine (**adweek.com**)

MarketingProfs.com (**marketingprofs.com**)

ClickZ (**clickz.com**)
Marketing Sherpa (**marketingsherpa.com**)
Web Digest for Marketers (**wdfm.com**)
BtoB Online Magazine (**btobonline.com**)
Technology Marketing Magazine (**technologymarketing.com**)

## REFERENCES

[1] Douglas Smith: "8 Ways to Make Your Direct Marketing Copy Work Harder." Article, not dated. **marketingprofs.com**

[2] Howard J. Sewell: CompuServe message, 1994

[3] Direct mail package, Phoenix Technologies Ltd.

[4] Susan K. Jones: *Creative Strategy in Direct Marketing*. NTC Business Books, 1991

[5] Newsletter, Walker, Richer & Quinn, Inc.

[6] "How the industry obtains, values and uses vendor literature," Executive Survey of IT Professionals, Bitpipe Inc., 2000. **bitpipe.com**

[7] Russell M. Kern: *S.U.R.E.-Fire Direct Response Marketing*, McGraw-Hill, 2001

[8] Debbie Weil: "AIDA Plus the Five Ws", October 17, 2001. **clikz.com**.

[9] Nick Usborne: *Net Words: Creating High-Impact Online Copy*. McGraw Hill, 2002.

[10] Sun Microsystems banner ad on **commweb.com**, July 29, 2004

[11] Intel banner ad on **commweb.com**, July 29, 2004

# 11

# PRESS MATERIALS

## REACHING JOURNALISTS AND ANALYSTS

Press materials are directed to journalists and industry analysts with the primary objective of encouraging them to write about a product or company, or publish a contributed article. Some of these materials, especially press releases, are developed for a specific marketing activity or event such as a new product introduction. Other materials, especially backgrounders, are developed to be enduring documents that a journalist can save for future reference or access in a "Media Center" on the company Web site.

### ARTICLE

An article is an essay, analysis, case study, or editorial written by a company employee, consultant, or freelance writer. To maximize the PR value of articles, most are contributed to external publications such as an industry magazine, newspaper, or professional journal. (The general business press rarely accepts articles written by outside resources.) An article also can be published internally on the company Web site or in a printed company newsletter.

Articles are often planned as part of a new marketing effort, such as a product launch. They are also an effective form of ongoing publicity because articles typically cover topics with long-term information value.

Articles can be developed to create awareness, provide education, or promote the desired positioning for a product or a company. Articles also are an effective medium to build support for a technical strategy or issue. After publication, article reprints can be used as part of the sales collateral for a product.

Articles are usually not written as a speculative project. Instead, they are commissioned by the publication, based on the topic ideas suggested in a press kit (see section later in this chapter) or in a "pitch" letter, outline, or synopsis that proposes the article to an editor. Publications may also want to reprint articles written for a company magazine or Web site, either "as is" or as the concept for an article written by a reporter. Syndicators of Web content may also be interested in feature articles from your company for posting on industry, dealer, or market-specific Web sites.

Some articles have very specialized content, suitable only for a particular publication. Other articles may be of interest to multiple, noncompeting publications. To address the different audiences of multiple publications efficiently, develop a base article or outline that can be tailored to each publication. For example, if you are writing a "How to Select a . . ." article, it could be tailored easily for different vertical market publications by incorporating relevant examples, quotes, or decision factors. However, verify each editor's policy on multiple submissions and prior publication before submitting an article to multiple publications.

## Article Types

This section focuses on feature articles that are submitted by a company to a trade publication or professional journal. News articles are not described here because they are typically written by the publication's reporters and editors.

For an article, choose one of the types listed below based on the planned topic, your objective for writing an article instead of another document, and the publication's standards.

**Product selection guide.** Covers "How to select a… " (fill in the blank with the product type). This article gives information to help prospects in evaluating potential solutions to a problem, in particular, your product against its competition. A product selection guide also can set the purchasing agenda in a prospect's mind.

**Technology primer.** Explains the concepts, architecture, or applications of a product's underlying technology. A primer is a good educational resource for describing new types of technology, to introduce a technology to new markets, or to discuss product uses that may not be obvious to users.

**Research findings or analysis.** Reports the methodology and results of a technology research project, an attitudes or perceptions survey, or a market research effort. This article type usually includes a large amount of statistics, data, and other supporting evidence for the research results or conclusions.

**Case study.** Describes a customer's problem or need and how the product provided a solution. This article type serves as an important reference for your product or company. (See the section on case studies later in this chapter.)

**Trend analysis.** Discusses current or future trends in an industry, market, or technology. This article type is especially effective for positioning your company as knowledgeable about its industry or market.

**Processes or practices description.** Covers procedures, processes, or best practices that can help a user obtain the most benefit from the product.

**Editorial or opinion piece.** States your company's position on a current issue or controversy. This article type is often used to correct a misperception or advocate a certain viewpoint.

**Profile or interview.** A profile presents a biography of a person or an overview of a company. An interview reports the information gathered in a question-and-answer session with a company official, industry expert, customer, or user panel.

**Conference paper.** The published version of a paper presented at a professional conference by an employee or customer of your company.

## Planning the Article

Develop an article plan after you determine the article type, topic, and target publication. Planning an article involves the general guidelines presented in Chapter 1 as well as rules and procedures specific to each trade magazine, journal, or in-house publication. Also consider the guidelines below when planning an article.

**Matching the publication's needs.** Most editors publish an information sheet about audience interests and expectations for the article's type, length, writing style, and content. In addition, look at several issues of the publication to understand the focus, organization, and tone of articles.

**Meeting submission requirements.** Confirm the editor's due dates for an outline and the full article. In addition, confirm the editor's expectations for number of words in the article and the use of sidebars, callouts, and other document elements. Verify the procedure for submitting the article to the editor, including file formats for text and visuals. If you or a colleague will receive a byline on the article, check the publication's policy for including a job title, company name, email address, and other contact information.

**Handling product mentions.** Ask the editor about the number of times and in what manner your company or product can be named in the article. Most trade publications are very strict about this limit and editors are savvy to subtle forms of product promotion that you may place in the article.

## Seeing an Article in Print

When you submit an article, realize that the publication may not print it in full or without modification. Editors may make changes to the article based on their perceptions of readers' knowledge and interests, or to make your text conform to the publication's writing style or limitations on article length.

In addition to the article text you may also want to submit other materials to make the editor's job easier. Include a list of supplemental materials, photos, customer and internal contacts, or other resources you can provide to the editor. Always include or suggest visuals that can be used with the article. Photos, illustrations, diagrams, screen shots, code examples, and flowcharts are possible images that can accompany your text. In some cases the publication will use these visuals directly; in other cases, the publication will adapt the visuals to a standard style or use other images.

Include a complete caption with all photos, diagrams, and illustrations that you submit to help ensure the accuracy of names, model numbers, and other product information. A caption also can support the messages presented in the article text.

## Content Ideas—Articles

One way to learn how to write good feature articles is to read widely and find examples to emulate for writing style and content organization. A number of good books are also available that cover writing techniques for non-fiction articles, essays, and the like; see the Resources section at the end of this chapter.

The purpose for writing an article should guide all of your decisions as you develop the article content, including choices for the elements listed in Figure 11.1.

| Article Element | Decision Factors |
| --- | --- |
| Openers and closers | How the article will capture the reader's attention and sustain interest until the end |
| Headlines, subheads, and captions | How these elements can reinforce key messages or guide the reader through the story |
| Bullet lists, pull quotes and sidebars | How these elements can be used to present: |
| | Quotes from customers, company experts, or industry analysts that support or enhance the article's message |
| | Anecdotes, examples, or case studies that illustrate problems and solutions |
| | Statistics and evidence that support the results presented in the article |
| | Technical details about a product, event, or other topic |
| | Contact information |
| | Resource lists |

*Figure 11.1. Guidelines for choosing document elements for an article.*

The text techniques described in Chapter 7 may help you transform raw material into an interesting, polished article. An article can accommodate many of the content types described in Chapter 5 and the document elements covered in Chapter 6, however most articles contain additional document elements.

**Nut graph.** The first element unique to articles is the "nut graph" (taken from the phrase, "in a nutshell"), a succinct paragraph that summarizes the direction of the article and provides a compelling reason for continued reading. Following the nut graph are the strongest points-of-fact or supporting evidence, presented in one or more paragraphs.

**Author information.** A sentence or paragraph of author information including names, titles, company affiliations, and email address. This information is typically placed at the end of the article.

**Deck.** A deck, also called a slug, usually summarizes the article content or major topic, especially if the headline does not do so directly. It can be a phrase, a sentence, or a short paragraph that appears beneath the headline or in a pull-quote box. A deck should be written to draw the reader's interest in the piece and be coordinated with the headline and overline (if any) to present a cohesive message that guides the reader into the article.

## Web Tips—Articles

Online articles can link to supplementary content, such as:
- Pages that present more information on any product, people, or organizations mentioned in the article. These links can be embedded in the text or in images such as a product photograph.
- A glossary page or a pop-up definition window for any words that may be unfamiliar to readers.
- Video or audio clips related to the article's topic.
- A profile page or an email form the reader can use to send a message to the article author(s).

Embedded links to your company's Web site may not be permitted when you submit an article to an online publication or a print publication that posts the article to its own Web site. Ask the editor about the number and nature of links that can be embedded in the article.

Verify that all links work and the target pages will remain available for at least a year after article publication.

## BACKGROUNDER

A backgrounder is a document that provides in-depth information on a company, technology, or product. Most high-tech companies produce two types of backgrounders—one for each product or product line and one for the company as a whole.

A backgrounder gives detailed, context information to a journalist, supplementing a press release that may present only the basic facts about the product. Depending on their content, white papers also may be used as product backgrounders (see Chapter 10).

While backgrounders are used primarily as press materials, they may also be appropriate to include in the sales collateral for a product or company. However, backgrounders usually have an information purpose that should be reflected in the writing style, organization, and content.

### *Content Ideas—Product Backgrounder*

A product backgrounder describes the design and function of a product or its underlying technology. It can accommodate any of the content types described in the "Product Information" section in Chapter 6. Most product backgrounders include a mix of the following information:

**Architecture.** A discussion of the product's architecture or design, configurations or applications. Diagrams to show product functionality, architecture, data flow, operational processes, configuration, or other concepts. A description of the relationship to other products in the product line or to products and technologies from other companies.

**Product details.** A description of the product's physical characteristics, components, options, and any accessory products. An overview of the product's development history if it is important for understanding the current market position. Purchasing information, including pricing, distribution channels, and availability dates.

**Future plans.** A discussion of future plans or strategies for product development or marketing.

**For more information.** Information on contacts for editors (usually a public relations person) and for readers who want more information about the product (usually the toll-free telephone number for a sales center and a Web URL).

## Content Ideas—Corporate Backgrounder

A corporate backgrounder presents an overview of the company's capabilities, structure, and operation. It can accommodate any of the content types described in the "Company Information" section in Chapter 6. On the Web, a corporate backgrounder may appear as an "About XYZ Company" page.

Most corporate backgrounders include a mix of the following information:

**Corporate description.** A company description, including mission, history, strategies, domestic and international operations, and information on parent, subsidiary, and affiliated companies. Biographies of company executives and a list of directors or key investors (e.g., venture capital firms).

**Market position.** Information on the company's key markets and position in each. May include a list of major customers and information on distribution channels and alliances. Quotes from analysts, customers, and others may be cited in a print document or appear in the sidebar on a Web page. An analysis of competitors by product line or by market.

**Product information.** An overview of products developed and marketed by the company; involvement with industry groups and standards bodies. Key technologies, development and manufacturing capabilities, and support operations. For service companies, a capabilities statement typically describes the services offered and special expertise or experience of employees.

**Industry recognition.** Information on the award of patents, licenses, or certifications by testing laboratories, standards bodies, government agencies, or other institutions. This information also can describe compliance with regulations, standards, or military specifications. A description of quality processes and customer support programs.

**Contacts.** Information on contacts for editors (usually a public relations person) and for readers who want more information about the company (usually the toll-free telephone number for a sales center and a Web URL).

### Web Tips—Backgrounders

When posted online, backgrounders can link to supplementary content, such as:

- Pages that present more information on any products, people, or organizations mentioned in the backgrounder. These links can be embedded in the text or images.
- A glossary page for any words that may be unfamiliar to readers.
- A "What's New" page to encourage journalists and other site visitors to view the latest company news.

## BIOGRAPHY

A biography or profile presents information about a person, such as a company executive. These documents are useful for supporting messages about company leadership, providing insights to journalists and investors, and promoting the executives as conference speakers.

### Content Ideas and Web Tips—Biography

- Provide basic personal data: Name, title, age; city of residence; summary of professional experience, especially with your company; education.
- Describe any specialized knowledge, experience, or services offered by this person.
- List memberships or leadership positions in relevant standards bodies, industry associations, or professional groups; link to their Web sites if appropriate.

- List any books, articles, or other published works; link to pages that present more information or the works themselves.
- Calendar of recent or upcoming presentations. Post slides, audio, and video files from previous speeches or presentations. Link to a seminar description page or the site for an external conference or other event.
- Link to an email form the visitor can use to send a message to the person profiled.

## CASE STUDY

> *Anytime you get a chance, tell a story.*
> —*James Carville*

A case study (also called a "success story," "testimonial," or a "customer profile") describes how a particular customer uses a product, the problem it solved, and the benefits obtained. A case study may be included in a brochure or produced as a separate document that is part of the sales collateral for a product. The typical length for a printed case study is two to four pages.

Many trade publications make extensive use of case studies, either as full-length feature articles or as brief fillers. When a case study will appear as an article in a trade magazine, you may want to name the customer as the author. In addition, customer quotes from a case study are often excerpted in advertisements, presentations, press releases, and other promotional material.

A case study may also be produced as a video, showing the customer interview, presentation, or demonstration. The principles for content and procedures covered in this section are applicable to all case studies, whether in print, video, or multimedia form.

Customer case studies are among the most powerful marketing tools for a high-tech product or service. They build credibility for a product by providing user references and helping prospects better understand how the product or service relates to real-world problems and circumstances. Although prospects are the usual audiences for case studies, these documents can also educate salespeople and dealers, technical support staff, journalists, and analysts.

Case studies can also provide positive, no-cost publicity for customers, giving them an incentive for participation. Customers who agree to a case study may also cooperate on other marketing activities such as presenting at conferences, giving interviews to journalists and analysts, and talking to prospects (reference calls).

A "win story" is a variation of the case study that focuses on the sales strategy, partnerships, and other factors involved in winning a contract award or major purchase. This document is typically produced for internal use by salespeople and perhaps dealers or partners as a sales education piece.

Most case studies follow a common structure, describing the customer's challenge, the solution provided by your company, and the results achieved from that solution. Developing an effective case study involves showing the "hows and whys" of the customer's situation, product choice, and outcome of the implementation.

A case study should emphasize the benefits and results achieved by the customer, both quantitative (such as financial data or productivity statistics) and qualitative (such as operational improvements). To get this information, ask probing, open-ended questions when you interview the customer. You may want to start the interview with a list of standard questions, but be sure to explore other topics that add to the interest of the case study as they arise in the conversation.

## *Recruiting Good Candidates*

Given how difficult it can be to get any customer to talk, it's tempting to say "yes" to any case study candidate a sales representative or dealer wants to promote. But a little bit of effort to qualify the candidate will help to smooth the process of working with the candidate and obtaining a good story.

The questions below will help you qualify candidates for case studies.

**Story appeal.** Do you know enough about the nature of the story to be confident it will be a story you will want to tell? For example, does the story offer the potential to discuss an interesting problem, solution, or application? Is the company in a particular industry, country, or market you want to target? Will the story make a statement about your competitiveness?

**Timing.** Is the story ready to tell? Do you want to tell the story of winning a customer's business or wait until you can report the results the customer achieved after implementing your product or service? It is possible to do both: use a press release to announce the customer win, then write the case study later, when the customer has implemented the product successfully.

**Participation agreement.** Have any agreements been made with the customer for telling the story? Many high-tech vendors request that customers agree to a case study as a condition of receiving a beta version or early shipment of a commercial product.

**Customer preparation.** Has the customer been briefed about the process for developing the case study? A briefing should include information on how the case study will be used by your company, how much time and effort the interview (and photography or filming, if applicable) will require, telephone and site logistics, and how the material will be submitted to the customer for review and approval before publication. Develop a standard letter or information sheet to simplify this process.

**Contacts.** Are you talking to the right person within the customer organization? You may need to talk with multiple people in order to get the right information about the business challenges, the reasons behind the selection of your product and company, and the results achieved. In addition, you want to talk with at least one person who is at the right management level, with authority to speak for the organization.

**PR involvement.** Do you need to involve or get approval from a company public relations person before starting the interviews or publishing the case study? Do you need to arrange access to employees and facilities for photography or filming?

## *Handling Reviews and Approvals*

Certainly, an accurate and well-written case study is essential for gaining customer approval. But your follow-through during the review process will determine whether, and how quickly, the customer will approve the case study. A good follow-through process reflects the guidelines below.

**Internal reviews first.** Always complete any internal reviews before sending the first draft to the customer. This step usually means limiting the number of internal reviewers, giving them a very short deadline, and using an approach of "If I don't hear from you I will assume it's OK." Customers should never be asked to go through the approval process more than once because of late comments or follow-up questions from your internal reviewers.

**Fast turnaround for the draft.** Deliver the first draft soon after the customer has given an interview. If it takes more than two weeks to get the review materials into a customer's hand, your contact is likely to have forgotten about it. Delays on your side also can send the message that the case study isn't urgent, which can lead the customer to give the review a low priority.

**Send a complete package.** Along with the draft text, send any photos, diagrams, or other illustrations that will accompany the case study. Ask the reviewers to check captions, callouts, names, and legends. For a video or multimedia story, include the first cut of the video and all text, pop-ups, and other material that will be included on the same tape, disk, or Web page.

**Use an approval form.** For all case studies, give the customer a standard approval form with a checklist covering all requested uses for the information (e.g., posting on your company's public Web site, submitting to trade magazines, using excerpted quotes or results in an advertisement). The list should allow the customer to check the specific approved uses for the case study information; grant releases for all photography, video, and other multimedia elements; and specify any other conditions. Always include a signature line for a customer representative, and don't publish the case study until you have received the signed approval form.

**Follow-up for approval.** If your customer contact is slow about responding with comments or approval, be polite but persistent in your follow-up messages. Ask the customer's PR person or your company sales rep for assistance in expediting the process.

**Send a thank-you.** Send the final case study, thank-you notes, and perhaps a nominal gift such as a company T-shirt to everyone involved. Include the URL for a posted version or printed copies of the published case study. (In one case, this thoughtfulness led a customer to contact me later for a follow-up story after a major expansion of the solution.)

**Celebrate!** As a final activity, promote the case study internally. Send copies to the sales and marketing staff with a cover memo thanking the internal people involved, giving the URL for the case study on the company's internal or external Web sites, and describing any press coverage. Giving salespeople a useful story will encourage them to help you with future case studies.

## Content Ideas—Case Studies

A case study can include many of the content types described in the "Applications" and "Customer Information" sections in Chapter 6. As standalone documents, case studies are typically written as a free-form article or in a standard structure that includes these sections:

**Customer overview.** Brief overview of the customer's business or profile of an individual.

**Problem statement.** Customer's problem, need, or application that motivated the search for your product. A description of any previous solution or way of addressing the need, if applicable. Reasons for choosing this solution; alternative solutions considered and why they were rejected.

**Solution.** A description of the solution provided by your company, including a list of products and services and a description of the implementation (e.g., environment, geographic scope, project phases). If the solution was a consulting engagement, describe the services provided, the project scope, methodologies, and personnel (it may be appropriate only to use titles or descriptors such as "project team" instead of naming individuals).

**Results.** Quantitative and qualitative results and benefits the customer gained from the solution; new capabilities; user feedback; a discussion of how the new solution integrated with the legacy environment. To increase the credibility of the results, encourage the customer to be as specific and detailed as possible—without disclosing confidential information, of course.

**Why XYZ Company?** Customer's perception of your company as a vendor.

In addition, a case study can include any mix of the following elements:

**Visuals.** The customer's logo; "before-and-after" diagrams, photos, or video of the customer's processes, environment, product use, or results. Verify that all diagrams clearly show the implementation of your company's products.

**Strategies and selection criteria.** A description of the customer's evaluation or decision process. If the case study will be used only for sales training, discuss successful sales strategies and if appropriate, the revenue associated with the sale and the names of the account team. Include background information on the customer's industry or trends that influenced the customer's need or purchase decision.

**Future plans.** A discussion of future plans for use of the product or expansion of the solution; how the solution will help the customer meet or prepare for future needs.

**Partners.** Information about and quotes from dealers and partners involved in developing or delivering the solution. Look at other players in the story: Are their messages, interests, activities, and contributions covered with sufficient detail and with the correct emphasis or positioning?

**Additional services.** A discussion of training and support services utilized by the customer to assure a successful implementation.

**Contacts.** Names of contacts at your company and, if appropriate, in the customer's organization. Anytime a customer's name appears in a case study, interested readers will try to contact that customer directly. Depending on the circumstances and the customer's willingness to field these inquiries, you may want to indicate that all reference calls and interview requests be made through a contact at your company instead of being sent directly to the customer.

### Web Tips—Case Studies

- Link to the Web site of the customer and any dealer or partner mentioned in the story.
- Link to detailed information about the products used by the customer.
- List case studies that are related by industry or application.

## FACT SHEET

A fact sheet is a single page of key information about a product, event, or company. Fact sheets help reporters quickly find the most commonly requested information. They are a standard component of press kits and may accompany individual press releases.

### Content Ideas—Company Fact Sheet

A company fact sheet can include any of the content types described in the "Company Information" section in Chapter 6. Most include additional content such as the following:

**Company overview.** A brief company description including mission, date founded, and names of founders or a statement about the company's origins or history. A list of company executives. A brief overview of products and services offered by the company. Number of employees.

**Key financial data.** A statement of revenue and other key financial data for the most recent fiscal year or year-to-date. Stock ticker symbol and exchange name for public companies. List of key investors (e.g., venture capital firms) for private companies.

**Marketing and production.** A list of markets or customers and a brief statement about marketing and sales strategies and distribution channels. A description of sales, manufacturing, laboratory, or other significant facilities or resources.

## Content Ideas—Product Fact Sheet

A product fact sheet can include any of the content types described in the "Product Information" section in Chapter 6. Most include the following content:

**Product details.** Hardware components; software incorporated into or supported by the product. Key features and benefits; key specifications. System requirements and platforms supported; localized versions available.

**Market information.** Suggested retail price, distribution channels, and availability dates. Typical product applications. Awards, reviewer comments, and customer testimonials.

## Web Tips—Fact Sheet

Online fact sheets can link to supplementary content, such as:

- Pages that present more information on the company or product
- A glossary page for any words that may be unfamiliar to readers
- A "What's New" page to encourage journalists and other site visitors to view the latest news about the product or company

## PRESS KIT

A press kit is a collection of press releases, fact sheets, backgrounders, photos, diagrams, and other material that gives a reporter or analyst complete information about a product, service, event, or company. It is not a media kit, which is an information package that publications use to market their advertising space.

A press kit is distributed to journalists and analysts during press tours, at a press conference or trade show, or in a mailing. Because editors are often deluged with printed press kits, more creative packaging can help yours stand out in the pile. For example, one client of mine used a child's lunch pail, custom-printed with the text and images from the theme for a product launch. Work with a designer to brainstorm ideas that will work for these special PR occasions.

Some companies provide their press kits on a CD/DVD, as file attachments in an email message, or in the "News" area of the corporate Web site. These methods reduce printing costs and make information access faster and simpler for journalists. Verify the file formats used by each of your target publications to ensure that editors can actually use the electronic files. Regardless of whether the documents are in print or electronic form, always remember to include the name, telephone number, and email address of a contact person on all press materials.

## Content Ideas—Press Kit

You do not need to include all of the pieces described here in every press kit you distribute. Instead, choose the documents that are the most relevant to each editor, and include a list of other documents that are available.

Label each page of every document with the company name, the document title or headline, date, a contact phone number, and "Page x of y." Provide complete captions for all photos, diagrams, and illustrations included in the kit. A credit line naming the photographer or illustrator may also be appropriate.

For any press kit, consider including the following documents:

**Basic press documents.** Press releases, backgrounders, fact sheets, Q&A documents, and brochures or data sheets related to the announcement. A glossary of terms unique to your company or industry. Biographies of company executives and key technologists; copies of their speeches or presentations if the release is related to an event.

**Customer stories.** Case studies, a list of endorsement quotes from customers and analysts, or a list of customer references who have agreed to be contacted for interviews.

**Company financial information.** Annual reports and securities documents.

**Visuals.** A disk or CD-ROM with relevant photos, screen shots, company logo, diagrams, presentation slides, or video clips; a demo CD/DVD or an instruction sheet for a Web-based demo; instructions for accessing a video news release (VNR).

**Related articles.** Reprints of articles already published about your product or company. Always show the name of the publication and the date or issue number in which the article appeared and the direct URL if the article is available on a Web site. Also, develop a list of topic ideas for feature articles or interviews related to your product, industry, or company. The goal of this document is to encourage an editor to write or commission an article based on one of your suggested topics.

**Resources.** A list of additional materials, photos, evaluation units, suggested review criteria, or contacts that are available to editors. Business cards for the company and agency PR contacts. A file card with the URL for the company's Web Media Center.

### *Web Tips—Press Kit*

A "Press Center" on the company Web site can function as an online press kit, presenting all of the documents listed here. Most Web press centers also provide links to an archive of press releases, telephone and email contact information for PR staff, an investor relations section, and an email alert service that allows reporters to receive new information as it is released.

### PRESS RELEASE

A press release is a document that attempts to generate publicity by announcing current news about a company, product, service, or event. A press release is usually developed as a printed piece, distributed via email, postal mail, fax, or news wire service and posted on the company's Web site. A video news release is distributed for broadcast on television news programs.

The subject of a press release must be genuinely newsworthy in order to catch an editor's attention. Many events and activities can justify a press release, including:

**Product information.** Announcement of new products, options, add-ons, or upgrades; new applications or platforms for an existing product; price changes (especially if the price is reduced).

**Achievements and milestones.** Publicity for product awards, reaching a high level of product sales, or achieving a high market ranking.

**Company information.** Announcement of new customer contracts; new partnerships and joint ventures; acquisitions and divestitures; organizational changes including appointments or departures of key executives; new facilities; expansion into new market areas. Public companies also use press releases to announce earnings and other financial information as required by securities regulators. (These investor relations materials are beyond the scope of this book.)

**Event information.** Notice of product demonstrations, special exhibits, or presentations at trade shows; reports on user-group meetings; announcement of event sponsorships by your company.

Some companies produce two press releases when announcing a new product. One release is targeted for technical publications and emphasizes the technical features, benefits, and differentiators for the product. A second release is targeted to general business or vertical-market publications and emphasizes the strategic advantages of the product.

Press releases follow a standard format that incorporates the elements listed below for both print and Web versions.

**Release date.** The date when the information in the press release can be published. Stated either as *For Immediate Release* or as an embargo date *Hold Until:* (date and time). The release date may or may not be the same as the date of the actual announcement or event.

**Editorial contacts.** Always list the person from your company an editor can contact for more information. List a contact person from each company involved if the release covers a joint announcement with a customer, alliance partner, or other company. List the contact at your public relations agency if appropriate and in-country contacts for releases that are distributed internationally. For each contact person, give the full name; office, cellular, and fax phone numbers (if appropriate); and email address. As an alternative, some companies direct all reporter inquiries to a general "media contact" telephone number and email address.

**Headline.** The headline should be a summary of the most essential news in the release. Keep it brief; no more than ten words and using a format that answers the question "what happened?".[1] Use a subhead to present a key product feature or benefit, a list of partner names, or a point of supporting evidence. For example:

Headline: *Motorola Expands Bluetooth® Portfolio With New Wireless Headset*

Subhead: *Motorola Wireless Headset HS820 with Bluetooth® wireless technology Empowers Consumers with Stylish Hands-Free Connections and Affordability*[2]

**Dateline.** The date and place of the announcement: *Bellevue, WA May 1, 2004 —*. In most cases, the place will be the city where your company headquarters is located. Alternatively, the place may be a trade show or press conference if the announcement is being made there. The date on the dateline may or may not be the same as the release date when the press release is issued.

**Opener.** Use the opening sentence to present the key news or story, and the second sentence to describe the benefits to readers or the target market. Another technique is to use the 5Ws of journalism (Who, What, When, Where, and Why) in the opening sentence. Get to the point immediately; avoid prepositional and participial phrases as the lead in the opening sentence.[3] For a product announcement, consider using a box at the top of the release to highlight key information such as full product name, version number, ship date, MSRP, platform, and target market(s).

**Body.** Follow the standards of news writing when writing the body copy for the release. Present an overview of the whole story and the most important facts in the first paragraph, then use the remaining paragraphs for supporting information. Write the body copy so an editor can end the story after any paragraph without losing important information. Include the title and affiliation for any persons quoted in the release (see the section "Citing Sources" in Chapter 6). Use trademark symbols where appropriate in the text and include trademark acknowledgments at the end of the release. Include the URL for the page on your company Web site where an editor can find more information.

**Customer contact.** Include information on how a reader can contact your company in the body of the release. This may be a different person than the editorial contacts listed on the release.

**Company boilerplate.** A press release usually ends with a paragraph of general information about the company, including the ticker symbol and exchange if the company's stock is publicly traded. Press releases that announce contract awards, financial information, and future directions for company activity or product development may require additional boilerplate text to meet securities regulations. Contact the investor relations officer for your company to obtain guidance.

**Formatting Elements.** The standard format for press releases includes double-spaced text, printed single-side, at least a one-inch margin on all sides, and notations that indicate the continuation (*-more-*) and end of the release (*- 30 -*, *###*, *- end -*).

## Media Alert

A special form of a press release is the *media alert*. This public relations document does just what its name implies: It alerts journalists to an upcoming event or Webcast they are invited to attend. For high-tech companies, media alerts are often used to announce press conferences, an online meeting with a technical expert or company executive, or special demonstrations at trade shows.

A media alert is typically a single-page document that provides only the essential information about the event:

- All facts related to the event: date and time, location, type of activity, a description of what will be announced or demonstrated at the event, names of key participants.
- Description of facilities or services that will be available to attending journalists, such as the opportunity for individual interviews with customers or company executives.
- Instructions on how to register for the event (if necessary) and any technical prerequisites necessary for participating in a conference call or Webcast.

## Web Tips—Press Releases

Press releases on a Web site are a convenient way to inform visitors about new developments in your company or organization. An online archive of previous releases, backgrounders, and other documents also provides a useful resource for journalists.

These tips will help you adapt a press release for the Web:

- Link to pages that present more information on any product, people, or organizations mentioned in the press release. These links can be embedded in the text or images.
- Link to a glossary page for any words that may be unfamiliar and to a FAQ page as a convenience for visitors.
- Create a "Media Contacts" page listing the name, telephone number(s), and email address (create an email link) for each public relations representative for your organization, grouping the contacts by department, location, or subject expertise. Instead of listing specific editorial contacts in a press release, link to the general "Media Center" email address in order to avoid the problem of outdated contact information, especially for archived releases.
- Include a photograph, illustration, or audio or video clip related to the subject.

## Q&A DOCUMENT

A question-and-answer (Q&A) or frequently asked questions (FAQ) document does just what its name implies: It presents answers to the questions most commonly asked about a product or company. This document helps journalists understand user interests, obtain information in an easy-to-understand format, and save time when writing a story.

FAQ documents typically appear only on a Web site. Although a well-structured Web site can help visitors find targeted information quickly, sometimes they need a higher level perspective or guidance on where to start. This type of information can be provided by a FAQ document.

FAQ is an Internet-specific acronym that may have no meaning for your visitors. You may want to use other phrases such as

"About XYZ Organization," or "About This Site" in the banner and headline for this page. Choose a focus for the FAQ: your company, products, services, or the Web site. If your FAQ list is small, you can cover all of these topics in one document, but group related questions together and identify each group with a subhead. Check the content regularly to ensure that it remains current and to add or delete questions based on the inquiries you receive from visitors.

### Content Ideas—Q&A Document

The easiest way to come up with content for a Q&A document is to think of the questions you would ask if you were an outsider reading the press information for the first time. These techniques can also be effective:

- Include information that is not presented in other materials in the press kit because it is very detailed or is secondary to the announcement.
- Include a question for every key message in the announcement. Place questions into categories if the document is lengthy or certain questions are relevant only to particular markets, publications, or readers.
- Use a bold or italic font style to distinguish question text from answer text.
- If the text is brief, consider using a two-column table, with questions in one column and answers in the other, with one Q&A pair per row.

### Web Tips—FAQ

- Don't try to answer every possible question. Present an email link to encourage the reader to contact you with complex or unique questions.
- Keep your answers short. Link to other pages on your site where the visitor can find detailed information about the product or topic.

## REVIEWER GUIDE

A reviewer guide provides instructions and background information that will help a journalist or analyst evaluate a product or Web site.

### Content Ideas—Reviewer Guide

- Brief product description; bullet points for key features/benefits, applications, and competitive differentiators
- Instructions for installation, configuration, and set-up; provide a set of product documentation if available
- System requirements and technical specifications
- Information on how to get technical support for the evaluation unit
- Customer ordering information such as prices, sales channels, availability date

## RESOURCES

The recommended books and other resources listed below provide additional information on the topics discussed in this chapter. For an updated list, visit **writinghightech.com**.

### Books

William E. Blundell: *The Art and Craft of Feature Writing.* Plume, 1988. A bit dated, but filled with ideas and techniques for telling a good story and working effectively with different elements of an article. Written by former reporter for *The Wall Street Journal.*

Theodore A. Rees Cheney: *Writing Creative Nonfiction: Fiction Techniques for Crafting Great Nonfiction.* Ten Speed Press, 2001. Full of techniques for writing feature articles for general-interest publications, but also useful for corporate magazines.

Norm Goldstein, editor: *The Associated Press Stylebook and Briefing on Media Law.* Perseus, 2002. A standard reference for writing style used by many journalists and corporate writers.

Dennis L. Wilcox and Patrick Jackson: *Public Relations Writing and Media Techniques.* Longman, 2000. A college textbook, but a useful guide for writing public relations materials.

## *Web Sites*

The Poynter Institute (**poynter.org**). A site for journalists, contains numerous resources for writing articles and understanding the needs and interests of the press.

Public Relations Society of America (**prsa.org**). Members receive publications that cover a wide range of PR issues, including writing techniques.

## REFERENCES

[1] Ann Wylie, "Anatomy of a Press Release," *PRSA Tactics,* September, 2003

[2] Press release, Motorola, Inc., June 4, 2004

[3] Dennis L. Wilcox and Lawrence W. Nolte: *Public Relations Writing and Media Techniques.* Harper Collins, 1990

# 12

## ALLIANCE MATERIALS

### REACHING DEALERS AND PARTNERS

For every product there is a salesperson; probably a distributor, dealer, or retail store; and perhaps a solution integrator or other marketing partner. All of these salespeople need information that will help them sell your product successfully. And in many cases, you will need materials that convince these sales partners of the value and opportunities in the product and market. You must sell *to* alliance partners as well as sell *through* them.

This chapter describes the types of marketing materials commonly used to attract, educate, and motivate dealers, distributors, retailers, and alliance partners.

### APPLICATION GUIDE

> *"Just tell me what to buy."*
> —*line from an ad campaign for Subaru automobiles*

The more complex the product, the more an application guide can help a sales force explain it and prospects understand it. This type of guide is especially valuable for products that truly involve an "application sell," where a salesperson shows how different aspects of the product can solve a prospect's unique problem.

An application guide is typically a booklet, worksheet, or software tool that presents information about potential product uses, often categorized according to customer type, industry, job function, or subject interest. It is a directory or handbook for choosing among products, models, or configurations within a product line to meet a specific need. This guide also can suggest applications for a product that may not be obvious from an initial assessment of the product's features.

Application guides can be organized by product, by market or industry, or by application type. Some companies produce application guides for use only by the sales staff or dealers, while others develop guides that are also suitable for distribution to potential buyers.

Readers should be able to understand the organization of the guide quickly and easily find information that is relevant to their need or situation. This means presenting similar information or content types consistently in the guide and clearly identifying optional or configuration-specific items.

### Content Ideas—Application Guide

An application guide can accommodate many of the document elements and content types described in Chapters 5 and 6. In addition, an application guide may include the following material.

**Guidance material.** A table of contents and indexes by product name, model or part number; cross-references to options or accessory products. A glossary of product, technical, or industry terminology.

**Visuals.** Charts, checklists, or worksheets to show the match between products and applications or problems/needs. Design or configuration diagrams.

**Application guidelines.** Recommendations for planning the configuration and use of the product for each application. A list of product-selection criteria. A situation analysis worksheet.

### Web Tips—Application Guide

A Web site can support an interactive application guide, helping the reader through multiple scenarios with configuration tools and worksheets. Work with your Web development team to determine the most effective—and feasible—way to present an application guide online.

## DEMO OR MULTIMEDIA PRESENTATION DISK

A demonstration (demo) disk, delivered on a CD or DVD, is a software-based presentation that shows a product's capabilities, applications, and benefits. It can be a fulfillment piece for inquiries generated by advertising, direct-mail campaigns, or publicity.

Demo disks can be included in press kits, run on a salesperson's notebook computer for use in a group presentation, or be content posted for download from a Web site. They can be used for speaker support at speeches and presentations. Disks also can present an electronic "brochure" (in the form of a multimedia presentation) for a product or service.

When distributed by postal mail or at a trade show, a disk usually accompanies a package of materials, either in print or in additional files on the disk, that provide more detailed information on the product and company.

### *Types of Demo and Presentation Disks*

**Hardware demonstration.** A disk with a multimedia program is often the only practical medium for presenting demonstrations of hardware products. This is especially true in the case where an evaluation unit is too expensive or impractical to offer to every prospect, or when it would be difficult to set up a live demonstration. Video and multimedia techniques can show live operation in a lab or customer setting, or provide a simulation that incorporates product images or video clips of the hardware unit's operation.

**Sales force education and support.** The large amount of information that can be stored on a disk can help salespeople and dealers understand an extensive product line that has constant changes, additions, and deletions. If a demo program is included on the disk, it can help to ensure the consistency of demos among salespeople.

**Demonstration kiosks.** When kiosks are placed in a trade show or retail environment, the demo software can incorporate a tracking capability that measures the number of people who access the demo and what they do with it. An interactive survey can be included with the demo to ask questions and record responses from users.

## Content Ideas—Demo and Presentation Disks

The content of a demo or presentation disk will vary depending on whether it is in a "brochure" or "working model" form. Where possible, follow these guidelines:

- State the system requirements and instructions for running the demo on the disk label.
- Use a title screen to present the primary marketing message, instructions for running the demo, and a list of any special keys that control the program.
- Use a closing screen to present a call to action or contact information, or to restate the key marketing message. Program the demo to always show this screen before terminating, regardless of the point where the viewer exits the demo.
- Present an overview of the product before you present detailed feature information. This introduction section should be brief, as prospects will be anxious to get into the "meat" of the demo quickly.
- Make sure the prospect will be able to distinguish between the text in your demo messages and any text that appears in the product demonstrated.
- Organize the demo around a presentation of features or applications, or show a typical user session for the product. However, verify that the on-screen copy presents benefits as well as feature information.
- Show the same examples and messages in the printed materials that accompany the demo disk.
- Include product literature or a purchase discount coupon that a user can print from the disk.

### Content Ideas—Materials in the Disk Package

Many demo disks are accompanied by a brochure and other printed material, such as:

- A cover letter to encourage viewing of the demo program, state the key marketing messages, and provide a call to action and contact information.
- Product brochure or data sheet for the main product as well as accessory products.
- Instruction booklet for a "test drive" or "working model" demo.
- Samples of printed output if the demo or working model does not offer a printing capability.
- Specially designed mailing envelope or box for the demo disk and its accompanying materials.
- Order form and information on pricing and options if the objective of the demo is to motivate an immediate product purchase.

## PARTNERS PROGRAM COLLATERAL

If your company sells extensively through dealers, marketing partners, or third-party developers, you may develop a complete set of marcom materials targeted to this group. A partners program brochure is the most common of these materials. It describes the benefits of working with your company, the market opportunities addressed by your products, and the programs, services, and support offered to partners. Many of the ideas presented in this section also apply to programs that serve third-party developers.

### Content Ideas—Partners Program Collateral

Any partners program collateral can incorporate many of the content types described in Chapter 6 for sales, services, and company information. More specifically, materials targeted to partners usually describe the benefits of becoming a partner such as:

- Marketing programs, materials, sales and technical support, sales lead programs, and other services and resources offered to partners.
- Sales incentives, discounted prices, financing options, and cooperative advertising funds.
- Conferences and special events, training and certification offerings.

In addition, partner materials may cover:

- Descriptions of the partnership levels.
- Information programs and resources that require payment of an additional fee.
- Requirements of candidates and procedures for acceptance into the partners program.
- Guidelines for using the company and partner program brands, with logo and other files available for download.

### Web Content for Resellers and Partners

Many companies maintain a Web site dedicated to the interests of resellers. All of the materials described in this section can be posted to or adapted for a Web site. In addition, Web content can take advantage of other capabilities, such as:

- Dealer locator and links.
- Collection of information about prospective customers (lead gathering) through online registration, surveys, and contests promoted to site visitors.
- Downloads area and sales/technical support newsgroups or bulletin board area.
- An email newsletter for promotions and information on new products, tailored to resellers and partners.

## POINT-OF-SALE MATERIAL

If your product is sold in retail stores, you may write copy for small brochures, flyers, signs, or other pieces displayed in the area where a customer actually purchases the product. Called point-of-sale (POS) or point-of-purchase materials, they may appear on shelves, kiosks, aisle ends, and cash-register counters.

The primary objective of these materials is to catch the attention of a browsing shopper and encourage him to read the product's package for more information or make an impulse purchase. POS materials can announce special offers such as a sale price, competitive upgrades, or purchase incentives. They also can support promotional activity by a retailer such as a special price when the customer purchases a product bundle.

### Content Ideas—POS Materials

POS materials typically focus on product information (see Chapter 6). They can use many of the text techniques described in Chapter 7. However, because you may be working with a small size, limit the amount of text and choose words that convey the point with clarity, conciseness, and impact. Your message must attract attention at a glance, so limit each piece to one high-impact message.

The following types of information are presented most frequently in POS materials:

- Highlights of product features or a new version
- Information on special prices or sales incentive offers
- Quotes from product reviews or customer testimonials
- Comparisons of product models
- Cross-sell of accessories, supplies, or related products
- Guarantee or warranty statements

## SALES GUIDE OR KIT

No matter how highly you think of a product, salespeople or dealers may not share your enthusiasm at first. You need to sell them on the idea of selling the product, especially if they have many other products competing for their time, mind share, or shelf space. A sales guide supports this education and motivation process for a specific product, a product line, or all products sold by your company.

A sales guide is a notebook, CD/DVD, or package of Web content or printed materials that helps a salesperson learn about a product and how to sell it. The guide should contain material that is specifically targeted to the sales staff, not a rehash of customer material.

### Content Ideas—Sales Guide

A sales guide can incorporate many of the content types, document elements, and text techniques described in Chapters 5 through 7. This guide can also be posted on the company Web site as a PDF file or as HTML content with links to the listed information and tools.

**Dealer program information.** Description of the dealer program for the product. Policies, training, incentives, and support services provided by your company. Plans for advertising, publicity, seminars, and trade-show activity by your company to support the dealer's efforts.

**Market information.** Needs, trends, opportunities, buying factors, and other characteristics of each target market. Guidelines for qualifying prospects and determining the potential success and value of a sales opportunity.

**Product information.** Product overview, including key features and benefits as well as platforms and options. Product catalogs or a complete set of product literature, press clippings, and case studies. Company information such as a capabilities overview, annual report, or corporate backgrounder.

**Sales strategies.** Description of the typical sales process and techniques for effective selling; key selling points for the product and advice on how to overcome prospect objections.

**Competitive position.** Information on strengths and weaknesses of competitive vendors and products; ideas for selling against the competition.

**Sales tools.** A description of or links to the sales tools your company will offer to dealers. Examples include:

- Presentation slides with speaker notes, product demonstration guidelines or a demo script, an application guide, configuration worksheets, and proposal template.
- Electronic files and reproducible master prints for ads, brochures, sales letters, Web content, banner ads, email messages, and other print or online materials that can be customized with the dealer's name and contact information.

- Copies of sales bulletins or newsletters. Produced on a monthly or quarterly basis, these documents reinforce the salesperson's interest in your product, provide information on new product capabilities or applications, and offer selling tips.
- Price lists showing dealer pricing and suggested retail prices.
- Ordering information and forms for products, sales collateral, and other dealer materials or services.

**Company contacts.** Resources and contacts for selling assistance and additional information; include telephone numbers, email addresses, and Web URLs for your company's dealer program.

## SALES PRESENTATION

Sales presentation materials are typically computer slides or a multimedia demo that a salesperson can use in a face-to-face meeting with a prospect or in a standup presentation for a group.

A presentation can be made to sell a product (Figure 12.1), describe the capabilities of your company, offer viewpoints on industry trends or issues, or provide a tutorial about a technology or application.

| Sales Presentation Section |
| --- |
| Overview or agenda for the presentation |
| Customer needs, current situation, or trends |
| Description of the product or solution, with features and benefits |
| Possible applications (if relevant) |
| Case studies, test results, or other supporting evidence for the stated benefits and features |
| Implementation plans; service and support |
| Future directions for the product or solution |
| Strengths of your company as a vendor |
| Restatement of proposed solution, its key benefit, and how it meets customer needs |
| Call to action; can be an open-ended question to start the discussion when the presentation is made in a group meeting |

*Figure 12.1 A standard structure for a sales presentation.*

Preparing a presentation usually involves creating two sets of materials: the slides and a script or set of speaker's notes.

## Content Ideas—Presentation

While they can accommodate any subject matter, presentation slides are more effective for engaging audience members when they incorporate the following guidelines:

- Present only one major topic or message per slide.
- Use phrases; complete sentences are not necessary.
- Convey substantive information in all text, including titles. Use phrases that convey action, benefits, or news such as *Performance more than doubles*, not Performance Improvements.
- Use callouts to highlight key information on a chart or graphic.
- Format text into bullet points; minimize the line length and number of bullets on each slide. For most slide formats, this means a maximum of seven words per line and seven lines per slide.
- Use a subtitle to expand a message, especially for a slide that has a graphic as the major element.
- Use abbreviations and acronyms only when they are known by the audience, explained by the speaker, or defined on handout material.

Some presentations are developed to run independently, with a recorded narration. Videos, demo disks, and audio files stored on a Web page also need narration scripts. The guidelines below will help you write narration that is engaging, understandable, and effective for delivering its message.

## Content Ideas—Narration

**Writing style.** Use short sentences and active voice. Choose the shortest and simplest words that will convey your meaning; avoid words that have multiple syllables or are difficult to pronounce. Use a style and tone that is somewhere between the formality of written text and the informality of conversational speech. As with all text, avoid colloquialisms and local references if they might be misunderstood or misinterpreted by listeners.

**Acronyms.** List the component words of acronyms, then state the acronym. For example: *"…connects universal serial bus devices, also known as USB devices, to the PC… "* If the presentation is lengthy, you may want to restate the component words later in the script.

**Pronunciation.** Provide a pronunciation guide for names and terms that may be unfamiliar to the narrator. Place the pronunciation in brackets next to the term and use bold or italic type to show which syllable(s) should receive emphasis.

**Practice.** Read the narration aloud to verify correct and complete use of all punctuation. Use an ellipsis (…) to indicate a pause within a sentence or between phrases.

## SPEECH

A speech is a spoken presentation made by a company representative. It may be accompanied by visual aids such as slides, video, or a demonstration, but it is primarily read from a text written in advance. A speech can be made on almost any topic, but it typically provides information or a viewpoint on industry trends and issues.

In addition to the promotional value of the actual speech presentation, copies of the speech can be distributed as handouts, included in a press kit, posted on the Web, or adapted for a magazine article.

Writing a speech involves the special challenge of matching the text to the speaker's personality and speaking skills. Work with the speaker to identify her speech patterns, preferred expressions, and delivery style.

It is absolutely essential that you read a draft speech aloud yourself. Better yet, ask the speaker to practice delivering the speech. In this rehearsal, verify that the speaker can read the text easily, without stumbles, running out of breath, or misplaced pauses. Based on this practice delivery, you can work with the speaker to revise the structure, specific words, or pacing cues of the speech.

In addition to the speech text itself, you may want to prepare two other documents for each speech. The first is a biographical paragraph the event host can read when introducing the speaker. The second is a list of anticipated questions (and their answers) to guide the speaker if a question period will follow the speech.

## *Content Ideas—Speech*

A speech can accommodate many of the content types covered in Chapter 6 and the text techniques in Chapter 7. In addition, consider these items for every speech:

- The speech title should clearly convey the topic or viewpoint discussed in the speech.
- A single theme or message should be carried through the entire speech. The end of the speech should summarize the messages or tie back into the theme, and give the audience a signal that the speaker is drawing to a close.
- Use short, declarative sentences and repeat nouns instead of using pronouns.

Any use of humor, imagery, and anecdotes must be appropriate to the topic, as well as understandable and acceptable to the audience.

## VIDEO, AUDIO, AND ANIMATION PROJECTS

The multimedia elements of audio, video, and animation can be an important part of Web content, multimedia presentations, and Webcasts. In addition, a video can be a project itself. You may receive an assignment to write a script for a video or for audio narration of a demo disk or presentation.

As a copywriter, you will need to understand how to use these elements effectively across different marcom projects. Yet when writing for multimedia projects, Horton advises writers to "overcome your bias for words. ... Do not let your proficiency and familiarity with words lead you to use them when a picture or sound effect would better tell the story."[1]

*Caution:* Verify that your company has the rights or a license to use any multimedia element produced by someone else. For example, you cannot include a clip from a favorite music recording without obtaining permission or a license. (See Chapter 8 for a detailed discussion of rights and licensing.)

**Audio.** An audio file or clip can appear on a Web page or in an HTML-formatted email, provide the narration for a promotional disk or trade-show demo system, or be part of a multimedia presentation delivered by a speaker. On a Web site, audio can be an engaging way to deliver a welcome message, sales offer, or call to action. Customer testimonials, speeches, seminars, and press briefings are other content types that may be suitable for presentation as audio elements. Always capture audio clips from a high-quality recording and consider providing a written transcript for users who may have trouble downloading or listening to the audio file.

**Video.** A video clip can show a product demonstration, a speech or event (live or via Webcast), or customer testimonials. The guidelines for audio also apply to video clips posted to a Web site. A sales or news video can promote a product or company. Videos are commonly used to:

- Introduce a new product or upgrade by providing information and a demonstration.
- Show customer case studies.
- Present capabilities information about the company.
- Record a speech, presentation, user-group meeting, or other event.

All or portions of a video can be distributed on tape, CD/DVD, or posted for download from a Web site.

Videoconference broadcasts or streaming video on a Web site (Webcasts) are used by some high-tech companies to announce new products or discuss financial results. A video recording of the broadcast may be made at that time for later distribution; Webcasts can be available on the site indefinitely. Broadcasts also may be used for live demonstrations of products that are conducted at a remote site but viewed at a conference, trade show, or on a Web site.

From a copywriter's perspective, a broadcast may combine aspects of a sales presentation, speech, and demo script. Supporting materials are often available to members of the audience, such as an agenda, copies of presentation slides, Q&A sheets, press kits, or product materials.

**Animation.** Use animation techniques to simulate an action, process, or activity. For example, an animated graph can show changes in data over time; a product demonstration can be simulated by creating an animation from several sequential images.

## Content Ideas—Video

Writing video scripts is a unique and specific form of marketing writing; see the Resources section for recommended books. The following are general guidelines for using copy in a video:

- The opener and closer of the video should work together in terms of both messages and visuals.
- Present a call to action and show contact information at the end of the video.
- Place a marketing message on the video packaging. This may be in the form of a teaser to encourage viewing.
- For any text that appears on-screen, keep it brief and use phrases instead of complete sentences.
- Use caption text to identify people interviewed for the video; show name, job title, company or organization.
- If the video includes a product demonstration, make a statement at the beginning about what will be covered in the demonstration.

## Content Ideas—Audio Narration

For a video or multimedia presentation, you may need to write a script for audio narration. Keep in mind these pointers:

- Read the script aloud to verify pacing, emphasis, clarity of message, and appropriate pauses. If possible, read the script while reviewing the actual video or multimedia sequence to verify correct timing.
- Show the pronunciation of technical terms, acronyms, and product names if the narrator is not familiar with those words. Place the pronunciation in parentheses immediately after the appropriate term.

- Use underline or bold format to highlight key words for the narrator to emphasize when reading the script.
- If the narrator will be reading the script while viewing the video or multimedia sequence, include cues about what is displayed at each major transition.

## RESOURCES

The recommended books and other resources listed below provide additional information on the topics discussed in this chapter. For an updated list and other materials related to this book, visit **writinghightech.com**.

### *Books*

Anthony Friedmann: *Writing for Visual Media*. Focal Press, 2001. A textbook on writing video scripts; includes a CD with additional material and example clips.

Catherine Kitcho: *High-Tech Product Launch*. Pele Publications, 1999. Provides an in-depth discussion of product launch activities and strategies.

Michael E. McGrath: *Product Strategy for High Technology Companies*. McGraw-Hill, 2000. A good general book on marketing for high-tech products.

William Van Nostran: *The Media Writer's Guide: Writing for Business and Educational Programming*. Focal Press, 1999. Covers writing techniques for multimedia projects.

### *Web Sites*

CRN Magazine, formerly *Computer Reseller News* (**crn.com**)

*VAR Business* Magazine, (**varbusiness.com**)

You may also get ideas for alliance materials and Web content by looking at the major technology company Web sites such as Microsoft (**microsoft.com**) and IBM (**ibm.com**).

## REFERENCES

[1] William Horton: "New Media Literacy," *Technical Communication,* Fourth Quarter 1993

# APPENDIX A
# COPYWRITING CHECKLIST

This checklist will give you a quick reference for reviewing your marcom documents. You may want to create a similar checklist of your own, with questions and items that are specific to your projects and company standards.

## Overall Document

Has the right document type been selected, based on the message, objective, purpose, and audience? Does this document fit well with other pieces in the set?

Does the document follow the guidelines and strategies established by the marcom plan, creative platform, and document plan?

Is the amount, type, tone, style, and structure of the copy appropriate? Is the copy grammatically correct and does it follow the principles of good writing? Do the text and visuals comply with brand standards?

Are the key messages presented clearly? Do the words, visuals, and multimedia elements support each other in delivering the intended messages? Can the reader recognize the unique selling proposition for the product or service?

Does the information flow logically from one section or paragraph to the next? Is the copy easy to read and understand?

Is all important information included? Is the amount of detail appropriate? Does the document contain extraneous information that could be eliminated?

Could the reader be misled by any statement in the copy? Have all quotes, statistics, and other reference information been verified?

Does the document contain the correct document number, revision number, publication or release date?

Is the contact information complete and correct?

## Document Elements

Are the different document elements being used effectively? Could the clarity and impact of the text be improved by using other document elements?

Will the headlines capture the reader's interest? Do the headlines and subheads present all of the key messages or selling points for the skimming reader? Do the subheads guide the reader through the piece? Is there a good match between a headline and the body copy that follows? Do the other document elements reinforce key messages or features and benefits?

Is the opener strong and engaging? Does it identify the target audience? Do the opening sentences or paragraphs deliver key messages or information quickly and effectively?

Does the closer fit well with the rest of the document? Does it bring the topic or discussion to a graceful conclusion?

Is the call to action compelling and stated clearly? Does it include all information needed by the reader to take the next step?

## Content Types

Does the document contain the correct content types given its objective and purpose? Is the information presented for each content type complete and appropriate?

Are feature and benefit statements presented clearly? Are comparisons presented fairly and backed by verifiable evidence?

Are you taking advantage of opportunities to make a cross-sell or upsell?

Are statistics, test results, and numerical information presented fairly and accurately?

Are quotes presented accurately and the source cited correctly? Are paraphrases a fair representation of the original quote or source material?

## Text Techniques

Are text techniques used appropriately given the writing style, tone, content, and audience for the document?

If using any form of imagery, do the text and visuals work together to support the image? Will readers understand the imagery? Does the use of imagery enhance the message or will it distract or confuse the reader?

If using humor, is it appropriate to the content and audience for the document?

Does the text contain any of the mistakes described in Chapter 7?

## Legal and Ethical Considerations

Does the text comply with all legal and regulatory requirements? Has the document been reviewed by the company attorney?

Are all claims about product features and performance based on actual capabilities and verifiable evidence? Are offer terms, warranties, and guarantees presented clearly and completely?

Does the use of text and images produced by external resources comply with the terms of the usage rights purchased? Have the proper releases and licenses been obtained?

Does any information violate the privacy rights of an individual or company? Does the text reveal any confidential information?

Are trademark symbols used correctly on product names in the text and do trademark acknowledgements appear at the end of the document? Is a copyright notice included? Are disclaimer statements and other legal boilerplate presented correctly?

Does the project raise any of the ethical concerns described in Chapter 8?

## International Marketing

Do the text and images reflect the cultural considerations of the target market(s)? Have all text and visuals been reviewed by in-country reviewers, whether translated or not?

Is the market-specific information accurate and appropriate?

Have you considered the guidelines for style, tone, and writing techniques described in Chapter 9?

## Web Content and Email

For Web content, do the text, visuals, and other elements comply with the creative platform, standards, access device, or content management system requirements for the site?

Is the content well organized and presented clearly and consistently, both within pages and across the site as a whole? Can visitors easily find the information they want? Is a mechanism in place to ensure that information is kept up-to-date?

Do the links clearly guide visitor navigation through online transactions? Are the links appropriate and do they work? Can a visitor communicate with you at any point in the site through a form or email link?

Does the site content address the interests and concerns of international visitors? Does the site include information such as international purchasing options, country-specific information, or local language text?

Does a strong and clear call to action appear on all pages that lead to an online sale?

## Web Content and Email *(continued)*

Is the style and tone of text, images, and multimedia elements congruent and consistent on all pages? Is microcontent clear and consistent?

Do site content and email messages comply with laws and regulations for electronic commerce? Do email campaigns comply with anti-spam laws?

# APPENDIX B
# GLOSSARY

**Acronym** An abbreviation of a term that is comprised of multiple words. An acronym is usually formed by combining a single letter from each word in sequence. An initialism is a form of acronym that contains only the first letter from each component word.

**Advertorial** An *adver*tisement that is written and designed to resemble the edi*torial* content in a magazine or newspaper. Often written in the form of an article, an advertorial is developed and paid for by the sponsoring company. Advertorials may be placed on one or more pages in the publication, or bound in as an insert. Most publications require that an advertorial be labeled explicitly as advertising and use a different type style or layout to distinguish it from the editorial content.

**Advertisement** A paid message from a company that appears in a print, online, or broadcast medium. Advertising can generate inquiries about a product or build a company's image in the market (called brand advertising). In the case of products that have a low price or involve low risk in making a purchase decision, advertising can generate an immediate order by the customer (called direct-response advertising).

**AIDA** Attention, Interest, Desire, Action. A traditional marketing concept for the decision-making process followed by a buyer when considering a product purchase.

**Application Guide** A booklet, worksheet, or online interactive form that presents information about potential product applications, often categorized according to customer type or problem.

An application guide helps in choosing the best product to meet a particular customer need.

**Article** An essay, report, or other material contributed to a trade publication or professional journal under the byline of a person who is not on the editorial staff. Sometimes articles are ghost-written for a company executive or customer.

**Backgrounder** An essay-style document that provides detailed information about a product, technology, or company. Often included in press kits.

**Banner Ad** A small, graphical advertisement that appears on a Web page or within an email message.

**Blurb** Comic-strip-style balloon text that appears to be coming from the mouth of a person depicted in a photo or illustration. Also a slang term for boilerplate text.

**Body Copy** The main text of any marcom document.

**Boilerplate** A standard paragraph or section of text that describes a company or product; is used in many marketing and PR materials.

**Brand** A name, logo, or other identifying "mark" that represents a product or company. A broader definition encompasses how a product or company is represented through all communications, customer service, and business activity.

**Brochure** A multi-page booklet that describes a product, service, or company.

**BRC** Business Reply Card; see Reply Card.

**Bundle** Two or more products sold as a set, often for a special price.

**Business-to-Business** Describes the marketing of products sold primarily to businesses. Contrast with business-to-consumer, which describes marketing to individual consumers. This distinction is made because of the different marketing strategies, tactics, issues, and techniques involved.

**Bylined Article** An article or other material contributed to a trade publication under the byline of a person who is not on the editorial staff. Also used sometimes as a label for articles that are ghost-written for a company executive or customer.

**C-Level** A broad term to describe executive-level job titles such as chief executive officer (CEO), chief information officer (CIO), etc.

**Call to Action** A sentence or phrase, usually appearing at the end of a marketing piece or in a button on a Web page, that motivates the reader to buy the product, contact a dealer, request more information, or take another action in the sales process.

**Callout** A line of text that points to a detail in a diagram, illustration, or photograph.

**Campaign** A series of planned marketing activities that can include multiple forms of communication and contact with prospects or customers. Campaigns can be organized around activities such as a product launch or to encourage attendance at an event.

**Capabilities Overview** A document that describes a company's expertise, services, resources, and experience. Usually in the form of a brochure, a capabilities overview typically markets a company's services. This document also can show "the company behind the product" for high-cost, high-commitment products.

**Case Study** An article that describes how a particular customer uses a product. Sometimes called a profile, application note, or success story.

**Catalog** A booklet or set of Web content that presents a collection of products offered for sale by the manufacturer, a dealer, through a retail store, or on a Web site.

**Collateral** A general term for any type of (usually) printed marketing material such as brochures, data sheets, catalogs, and newsletters.

**CMS** Content Management System. A software and database system for storing text, visual, and multimedia elements that can be used in multiple documents or Web pages.

**CPM** Cost per thousand. The unit of measurement typically used for buying names on direct mail and email lists, as well as exposures for print, broadcast, and Web banner ads.

**Creative Platform** A document that describes the strategy, messages, and guidelines for the visual and written elements of a piece. A creative platform also may include a description of acceptable style and word usage. Sometimes called a creative brief or copy plan (if describing the copy only).

**CRM** Customer Relationship Management. A combination of software systems, databases, and processes for tracking customer purchases and related sales activities.

**Cross-Sell** Promoting an accessory or related product as part of the sale of a base product.

**Cutline** See Overline.

**Data Sheet** Usually a single sheet (with one or two pages) that presents detailed information about a specific product, service, option, or application. A data sheet often supplements a higher-level product or product line brochure and can have many of the same attributes, uses, and distribution methods.

**Dateline** The location and date attributed to a press release. The release may actually be sent to journalists before the date (often with an embargo on publication) and from a different location, as when releases are sent via email or a distribution service.

**Dealer** A company that sells a manufacturer's product. A dealer may be a consultant, a systems-integration company, or a retail store. Some high-tech companies sell their products only through dealers, while others use a combination of dealers and a direct sales force.

**Deck** A phrase or sentence that describes the premise of an article or provides a clarifying explanation of the headline. Also called a slug.

**Direct Mailer** A brochure or package that is mailed to a prospect for the purpose of generating inquiries or to directly sell a product. Direct mailers can be used in a product launch campaign or as a key ongoing marketing method. A direct mail package usually includes a cover letter, a brochure, a lift note, a reply card or order form, and an envelope. A variation on this package is the self-mailer, a brochure with a built-in address area that allows it to be mailed without an envelope.

**Editorial Copy** The articles, news reports, columns, and other non-advertising material in a magazine or newspaper.

**Emoticons** Symbols to express emotion in online text, created using English keyboard characters. For example, the emoticon :>) expresses a smile or happiness.

**End Cap** A display at the end of an aisle in a retail store, designed to draw attention to a featured product. The display may be placed on shelves or in a standalone unit.

**Ezine** An electronic newsletter, usually distributed in an email message and posted on a Web site.

**Fact Sheet** A single page of key information about a product, event, or company that is usually distributed in a press kit. Fact sheets help reporters find the most commonly requested data quickly.

**FAQ** Frequently Asked Questions document. Typically a Web page of questions and answers commonly asked about a product, company, or topic. See also Q&A Sheet.

**FCS** First Commercial Sale. Usually the date when a product is available for sale or shipment to a customer. May be different than the date of product announcement.

**Feedback Device** A reply card, survey, comment form, or other print or online document that enables a reader to provide advice, suggestions, or market research data to the product's developer or manufacturer. Sometimes called an action device, response device, or bounceback.

**Formatting Device** Changes in type size or style, use of a different color, use of punctuation, or changes in copy layout that are made to highlight key messages in the text.

**FTC** Federal Trade Commission. A U.S. government agency that regulates many commercial activities, including advertising.

**FUD** Fear, Uncertainty and Doubt. A marketing tactic for positioning a product or company in a more favorable position than competitors.

**Fulfillment Piece** A brochure, white paper, article reprint, or other marcom document that is sent in response to a reader's request for more information about a product.

**Initialism** See Acronym.

**Insert** A separate page or brochure that is inserted into a trade publication. It may be bound into the publication (the most common method is called "tip-in"), inserted loose, or placed with the publication in an envelope or wrapper.

**Interstitial** A pop-up window that appears when a visitor enters or leaves a Web page. Often used to display a banner ad, promote a special offer, encourage site registration, or promote another message or activity related to the content of the page or the visitor's activity.

**Involvement Device** A checklist, quiz, worksheet, or other element that prompts a reader to pause and "become involved" with the document.

**Johnson Box** An introductory paragraph at the top of a sales letter that describes the offer or provides a teaser to entice the reader into the body of the letter. Usually appears in an indented, boxed format.

**Launch** The date and activity associated with the first public announcement of a product. This date may be far in advance of the date when the product will actually be ready for shipment to a customer (see FCS). Also called a go-to-market date.

**Lead** A person who has expressed an interest in a product. Contact information for a lead can be collected through a trade show, Web site, direct mail response, or other mechanism. Companies typically track leads in a database and pass them to salespeople or dealers for follow-up contact.

**Leave-Behind** Marketing materials that are left with the prospect by a salesperson after a meeting.

**Lift Note** A brief letter included in a direct mail package to convince recipients who need additional motivation before buying the product. A lift note attempts to overcome a recipient's objections to the offer that is presented in the direct mail package.

**Logotype** The graphical image of a company name, usually printed in a specified color and typeface. The logotype may be separate from the company's logo symbol, or may itself serve as the logo.

**Marketing Mix** The combination of marketing activities (such as sales materials and dealer programs) and publicity activities (such as press tours and article placement) that will be used to promote a product or service. Also called the promotion mix.

**Masthead** A box that lists contact information for a periodical's publishing and editorial staff. Contrast with nameplate, which is the title area of the publication.

**Media Kit** A package of information that a publication uses to sell advertising space. A media kit typically includes data about the publication's circulation, target readership, advertising rates, production services, and mechanical specifications. Compare to Press Kit.

**MSRP** Manufacturer's Suggested Retail Price. The price at which the manufacturer offers a product directly to customers and which it recommends to dealers. However, manufacturers cannot specify or control the price at which a dealer will sell the product, so a customer may find that different sources offer the product at different prices.

**Multimedia** An electronic form of marketing communication that combines audio, image, text, and video elements. This content may be posted on the Web site or distributed on a CD/DVD.

**Newsletter** A news-oriented publication that is targeted to a limited, often highly-specific group of employees, customers, or other readers. Internal newsletters are also called house organs.

**Nut Graph** A succinct paragraph that summarizes the premise of an article and provides a compelling reason for continued reading. Taken from the phrase, "in a nutshell."

**OEM** An Original Equipment Manufacturer is a company that buys a generic product, then customizes or labels it for sale under its own brand name.

**Offer** The specific combination of buying terms for a product or service, including price, payment options, delivery terms, time limitations, and purchase incentives.

**Overline** A line of text that appears over a main headline to serve as a lead-in. An overline is one way to present a secondary idea in a headline (the other way is to use a deck to state the secondary idea after the main headline). Sometimes called an eyebrow or cutline.

**Package Insert** Catalogs, brochures, or other marketing materials that are placed in product packaging. These materials typically promote add-on or cross-sell products, or service plans.

**PDA** Personal Digital Assistant. A hand-held computer. Some models offer capabilities for wireless email and Web access, making PDAs a target device for wireless marketing.

**PDF** Portable Document Format, a file format for preserving the layout and pagination of a printed document when it is transferred in electronic form. One of the formats typically offered for documents that a visitor can download from a Web site for printing offline.

**Pitch Letter** A letter written to an editor proposing an article idea or other coverage opportunity for a product or company. A pitch letter often includes an outline or synopsis of the proposed article and information on the author's expertise.

**POS** Point-of-Sale materials are brochures, flyers, signs, or other pieces for display in the area where a customer actually purchases the product. POS materials are used extensively in retail stores for display on shelves, kiosks, aisle ends, or near cash registers. Also called point-of-purchase materials.

**Positioning** The market perception of a product, service, or company; often a statement of the perception that the company wants to achieve.

**Press Kit** A collection of press releases, fact sheets, backgrounders, photos, diagrams, and other materials that give a reporter or analyst complete information about a product, service, event or company. A press kit is usually packaged in a presentation folder. Contrast to Media Kit.

**Press Release** A document that is intended to generate publicity by announcing current news about a company, product, service, or event. Usually developed as a printed piece, but also may be produced as a video. Also called a news release.

**Press Tour** A set of individual interviews with publication editors and industry analysts, held in their offices (hence "tour"). Usually involves a company executive, product manager, or technical expert, with coordination and participation by a public relations specialist.

**Profile** An article that describes a person or company. Profiles are often produced in a question-and-answer format.

**Publicity** Materials and activities designed to generate favorable news coverage about a product, service, event, or company. Publicity is considered to be just one element of a public relations program.

**Pull Quote** A statement or quotation that appears in a boxed area within the body of a brochure or article. A pull quote is a technique for emphasizing a very positive quotation or key message, especially for readers who only skim the text.

**Q&A Sheet** A document that presents answers to the questions most commonly asked about a product or company to help journalists understand user interests. Typically written in a format that presents the question, then the answer, with a very conversational style.

**Qualifying Questions** Multiple-choice questions on a reply card, online form, or other feedback device that collect information about a prospect's interest level, budget, decision-making authority, environment, and purchasing plans for a product or service.

**Reply Card** A card that is included in an ad, brochure, or direct mail package to encourage the reader to order a product or request more information. Most companies use a postal permit that allows prospects to mail the reply card postage-free. Also called a BRC (Business Reply Card).

**Repurposing** The process of adapting text and visuals in a print document into Web content. May require adaptation into multiple forms to meet the constraints of different Web access devices. This adaptation effort typically involves restructuring the text into shorter sentences and sections, reorganizing the flow of ideas, and altering images for improved appearance on a Web page.

**Reseller** A company that resells a manufacturer's product, often as part of a package with other products to offer the customer a complete solution. In this case, the company is often called a Value-Added Reseller. This term is often synonymous with dealer or retailer.

**RFP** Request for Proposal. A questionnaire or specifications document issued by a customer who wants to receive bids for a product or service. Typically, multiple vendors respond to an RFP with detailed proposals.

**Sales Guide**  A book, kit, or other package of information that helps a salesperson understand and sell a product.

**Self-Mailer**  A brochure designed with an address area that allows it to be mailed without an envelope. A self-mailer is commonly used for direct mail.

**Shelf Life**  For promotional material, the amount of time it should remain useful and accurate before requiring update or replacement.

**Shelf Talker**  A small card or sign designed for placement on the shelf where the product is displayed in a retail store. A shelf talker often includes excerpts from positive product reviews, or sales-motivating words such as "New," "Special Price," or "Limited-Time Offer." Also called a flagger.

**SME**  Subject Matter Expert. A company employee, analyst, or other person who has knowledge about a particular product, technology, or topic. SMEs act as information sources for interviews and research when developing marcom material.

**Stock Image**  A photograph or other visual selected from a library of images that can be used for multiple marcom projects. These images are typically not commissioned by the company and reflect more generic imagery than a visual that portrays a specific product or facility.

**System Integrator**  A company that creates a solution for a particular customer by implementing and integrating multiple products, usually from different vendors.

**Tag Line**  A single line of copy that presents a key product or company message. Also called a slogan. A tag line is usually placed at the end of an advertisement or printed underneath the company logo.

**TCO**  Total Cost of Ownership. A measure of product value that considers all costs across the life cycle, such as initial capital investment, upgrade or expansion costs, maintenance, integration services, etc.

**Teaser**  Most commonly a phrase that appears on the outside of a direct mail envelope to entice the recipient to open the package. Sometimes called corner copy. A teaser also can be advertising that provides limited information at the beginning of a multistage advertising campaign to entice the reader to watch for follow-on ads.

**Testimonial** A quote, case study, or other information from a customer that endorses a product, service, or company.

**Trade Publication** A magazine or newspaper that is targeted to a specialized industry or market.

**Upsell** Promoting a bigger, higher-function, or more expensive model when the customer is considering a product purchase.

**URL** A Uniform Resource Locator is an address that specifies the exact location of a Web site or individual Web page.

**USP** The Unique Selling Proposition is intended to define the key differentiating factor for a product. This factor may become the key marketing message.

**Vertical Market** An industry or other market segment with customers that have similar characteristics or with similar needs for a class of products. Many high-tech companies develop product lines or positioning strategies that are based on the needs of selected vertical markets.

**Webcast** An audio or video broadcast transmitted live or stored for playback on a Web site.

**White Paper** An essay-style document that provides in-depth explanation of a product, technology, issue, trend, or application. A white paper also can present a company's viewpoint on industry strategies and directions.

**WIIFM** What's In It For Me? A shorthand reminder to present a benefit or address a customer need when writing text.

# INDEX

# ABOUT THE AUTHOR
# JANICE M. KING

Janice King is an award-winning freelance copywriter who serves leading high-tech companies throughout North America such as Cisco Systems, Hewlett-Packard, Sprint, SBC/Ameritech, Texas Instruments, and Philips Medical Systems. Typical projects include white papers, case studies, magazine articles, product brochures, press backgrounders, and trade show materials.

Janice established WriteSpark Press to bring her insight and techniques for copywriting to wider audiences. A planned series of books, resource guides, and companion Web sites will help writers and marketers in a variety of businesses as well as non-profit organizations.

You can also bring Janice's expertise to your company! Learn how Janice's insights and expert writing skills can enhance your marcom projects by visiting **writespark.com** or contacting Janice at: **info@writespark.com**.

**Visit the companion Web site for this book**
**writinghightech.com**

# WHAT READERS SAY . . .

*Copywriting That Sells High Tech* contains content from Janice King's first book, *Writing High-Tech Copy That Sells*. Here are some of the comments from reviewers and readers of that first book.

> *"For anyone doing high-tech marketing,
> this is a solid reference book."*
> WRITING CONCEPTS

> *"It's an excellent resource for anyone who's ever been asked
> to produce promotional materials for a technical product."*
> INDEPENDENT PERSPECTIVE

> *"Janice King's book is meant to be read
> and then kept close by for easy reference while you
> write your marcom project."*
> TECHNICAL COMMUNICATION

> *"This one text could easily replace half a dozen others
> on a writer's bookshelf."*
> MARKETING COMMUNICATIONS FORUM

> *"An indispensable book for those seeking to advance
> their knowledge and skill in this growing aspect
> of professional communications."*
> TECHNICAL COMMUNICATION QUARTERLY

> *"What makes this book particularly appealing to me
> is that it's not just some dry textbook.
> It's a clear guide for anyone who writes
> marketing or press materials in high-tech."*

*"This is the first book I've seen that really aligns itself specifically with the sort of work we're doing, whether its direct mail, press releases, data sheets, white papers, or online publications."*

*I can tell it's going to be an invaluable resource for our marcom department. Thanks for writing it! "*

*"The book was well received by my fellow students, who found it a really good read and also very entertaining."*

*"I love this book! It's so pertinent."*

*"The book looks, reads, and is wonderful. Well done!"*